Dizzy and the Gas House Gang

Dizzy and the Gas House Gang

The 1934 St. Louis Cardinals and Depression-Era Baseball

by
DOUG FELDMANN

McFarland & Company, Inc., Publishers
Jefferson, North Carolina, and London

Library of Congress Cataloguing-in-Publication Data

Feldmann, Doug, 1970–
    Dizzy and the Gas House Gang : the 1934 St. Louis
Cardinals and Depression-era baseball / by Doug Feldmann.
        p.   cm.
    Includes index.

        ISBN 978-0-7864-0858-0
        softcover : 50# alkaline paper ∞

    1. St. Louis Cardinals (Baseball team) — History.
    2. Dean, Dizzy, 1911–   . I. Title.
    GV875.S3F45   2000
    796.357'64'0977866 — dc21   99-59367

British Library Cataloguing-in-Publication data are available

Manufactured in the United States of America

*McFarland & Company, Inc., Publishers
    Box 611, Jefferson, North Carolina 28640
    www.mcfarlandpub.com*

To
Mom and Dad

Acknowledgments

I have many people to thank for helping in the research for this book. From the friendly folks in the coffee shops of southern Mississippi to the research assistants at the many libraries, the long journey of putting this work together brought with it the benefit of new friendships.

I visited a multitude of libraries, all of which permitted me to spend countless hours in their microform rooms. Their collections of newspaper accounts of the 1934 baseball season allowed me to truly bring to life the culture of baseball during America's most troubled times. Though the historical inquiry for this book was long and painstaking, it was also a joy. It was indeed a pleasure to relive each day of the 1934 campaign—the greatest of all National League seasons. The beat writers from the newspapers—including J. Roy Stockton of the *St. Louis Post-Dispatch*, Martin Haley of the *St. Louis Globe-Democrat* (who also served as the Cardinals' official scorer at Sportsman's Park), and Sid Keener of the *St. Louis Star-Times*, among others from St. Louis and around the country—gave rich, colorful descriptions of the games. I have quoted their comments in many places, attempting to describe the game as it was known to them in 1934.

I hope you enjoy our trip as we return to an epoch of pure baseball.

Doug Feldmann

Contents

Prologue

While this book focuses on the magical baseball season of 1934 in St. Louis, it is my intention for it to reach further—both chronologically and allegorically. When the stock market crashed in October 1929, its profound impact on society reached all aspects of American life. Baseball, at that point entrenching itself as the true American game, was affected directly and indirectly by the events before, during, and after Black Thursday. Many minor league teams folded, most major league teams found themselves in severe debt, and everybody involved with the game—from owners to players to fans—found themselves exercising the utmost creativity in an attempt to maximize enjoyment of the game when work and food were in short supply.

After the United States toiled through four years of a struggling economy, President Franklin Delano Roosevelt in 1933 offered the nation a "New Deal"; not increased handouts, but labor opportunities that would better the nation while simultaneously providing an income for heads of households. In the same spirit were born innovations in baseball, such as the "farm system" of Branch Rickey, the baseball mastermind of many an idea. In his tenure with the Cardinals, Rickey knew that his organization did not have the money to buy big-name stars from other clubs, as was the case in New York. Instead, he decided to "grow his own" (a phrase that would later be attributed, patriotically, to domestic food during wartime). Rickey's plan was to identify players who would be trained, internally, in the Cardinal philosophy of baseball.

With slow, painful steps, society—and baseball—saw progress as rebuilding efforts began to take root. The wheels of industry, which had virtually ground to a halt, creaked to life again. By the mid–1930s, people actually discovered a little spending money in their pockets, and they returned to the major league ballparks as cash-paying customers. Kenesaw Mountain Landis, who became baseball's czar after the alleged throwing of the 1919 World Series by the Chicago White Sox, summarized the hope of the country on November 13, 1933: "Steel, factories, railroads, newspapers, agriculture, baseball—we rode down together, and we'll ride back together." Thus, from the time the market crashed to the advent of World War II, baseball represented a perfect microcosm of American resurgence.

In a sport that is itself unique in its history, nuances, and nostalgia, St. Louis Cardinals baseball is also one of a kind. The Cardinals are part of a city like no other ballclub. Growing up in Chicago, I've been told on numerous occasions that the Cubs have the greatest metropolitan following in the sport. That may be true, as the North Side is flooded with Cubbies hats, T-shirts, and other items. In terms of encompassing an entire region, however, the Cardinals are unparalleled. This status was recognized by St. Louis being named as the "Best Baseball City" by *Baseball America* magazine in 1998. Mark McGwire, the game's most feared home run slugger, gave up family roots in California—and millions of dollars—to sign a long-term contract with the Cardinals. Upon his arrival in July of 1997, McGwire was overwhelmed by the support of St. Louisans for their "Redbirds."

For many years, the Cardinals were the westernmost and southernmost major league team, and evidence of their fan base was seen in a great radius. Through the late 1930s, '40s, '50s, and into the '60s, a game broadcast on the powerful KMOX station in St. Louis reached the deepest corners of the country. A barber shop in Mississippi, a restaurant in Memphis, a gas station in Joplin—all had attentive ears lurking on the premises, taking in the words of Harry Caray and Jack Buck over the airwaves. An entire section of the country hung on every swing of Stan Musial and every fastball of Bob Gibson.

Expansion in the late sixties brought major league franchises to Kansas City, Houston, and Atlanta, but a strong contingent of Cardinal fans remained in the South and West. KMOX—and St. Louis itself—remained at the core of baseball life in the Heartland. As a child in the seventies, some of my boldest memories are those of visiting relatives in southern Illinois, where Cardinal loyalty runs deep. As we made the drive south on Interstate 55 from Chicago, we could notice the baseball landscape gradually changing. The "gray" area between Bloomington and Springfield, Illinois, possesses a mixture of Cubs and

Cardinals fans; once beyond Springfield, however, we knew that we were in enemy territory. When our car pulled up in the driveway of my uncle's farm, my cousins could be seen peeking around the corner of the garage. Donning bright red Cardinals T-shirts, they were preparing to pounce on the blue-clad invaders wearing Cubs regalia. The passion runs very strong on both sides; if one attends a Cardinals-Cubs game at Busch Stadium or Wrigley Field, an equal throng of Chicago and St. Louis supporters will be found at each venue.

Across the generations, I am far removed from the blue-collar heroes that treaded the basepaths of Sportsman's Park. However, one such hero from which I am not far removed is my father, John, who while playing at St. Louis University in the spring of 1947 walked down the street to Sportsman's for a tryout with the St. Louis Browns. As he describes for me his childhood memory of Johnny Mize hammering a home run over the right field pavilion, I can only close my eyes and wonder. In the future, a young person I talk to may only wonder as I describe the night of May 16, 1998, when I saw McGwire hit his 545-foot blast off of Livan Hernandez of the Florida Marlins. Games come and go—for that matter, even ballparks come and go—but the stories live forever.

From these stories come legends, and the legend of the Gas House Gang is one that should never be forgotten.

PART ONE

The Era

*"When you get to the end of your rope,
tie a knot and hang on."*

—Franklin Delano Roosevelt

The Golden Age

The hot July sun of 1932 was beating down mercilessly on Griggs-ville Park. A ball game was in progress, with the locals battling the Coalers from Valley City. The field was so full of dust that a thick cloud formed each time a batter slammed a ball to the turf. Cigar smoke wafted throughout the stands, and everyone's nostrils absorbed the aroma of peanuts roasting in the vendor's box. Nearby, a man was writing notes feverishly onto a little pad, and noticed a younger fellow peering over his shoulder—curious to know the nature of the man's script.

"What gives?" asked the man with the notes.

"Oh, nothing, mister. Just fixin' to see whatcha got down there," the young man answered.

"I'm a scout for the St. Louis Cardinals."

"Yeah, you never know when the next Chick Hafey will pop up 'round here," squawked the young fellow, in half-belief of what the man had just told him. After chuckling to himself, he leaned back on the last row of the bleachers. A minute later, however, he squinted his eyes in serious thought, hunched forward once again, and questioned the man.

"If you are a Cardinals scout, as you say you are, what would the Cardinals be scoutin' for? What kinda player?"

The man turned around, gave a quick convincing nod, and responded.

"Tough guys," he said. "I don't care if they can field or not. I want strong-armed, strong-legged men who can hit and run and throw. Guys like—well, like Pepper Martin."

This was often the scene before the encroachment of television and multi-year/no-cut contracts into professional sports. This is still the scene in some places, like Beckemeyer, Illinois, where communities with less than a thousand residents are still curious to know the status of the local ballclub for the coming summer. During the Golden Age, baseball was the focus of athletic life in most of America. Basketball and football were merely passive activities in the colder months to stay in shape, as experts in all towns gathered around the warmth of the "Hot Stove League" to discuss how the next baseball season would shape up after the snow melted. Despite the great masses that continued to flock to the industrialized cities in the 1920s and 1930s, the United States was still very much an agrarian nation. Small towns took simple, honest pride in the success of their labors on the farms, in the mills and mines, and on their baseball fields—and little else mattered. A week's worth of hard work was met with a church service on Sunday, and often a local doubleheader at the nearby ballfield. A resident of southern Illinois recently noted to the author, "If a person doesn't fish, hunt, or play ball, he doesn't quite fit in around here."

When Babe Ruth of the New York Yankees received $20,000 from owner Colonel Ruppert in the early 1930s, the exorbitant sum was seen as preposterous; how could a ballplayer make more than the President of the United States? Ruth's reasoning would become famous: "Because I had a better year than he did." Money changed the meaning of the game, and the game changed the meaning of money into the 1950s and '60s—with television coverage becoming a third conspirator. Baseball was not a lucrative profession for young men at this time, and boys often had difficulty convincing family members that a career in baseball held more promise than an opportunity to go to college.

Even college graduates were turning up in professional baseball— something rarely seen in years before the depression-laden 1930s. In June of 1934, writer W.H. James noted the trend. "In the last few months they have been breaking into the big leagues, probably on the theory that it's better to be a well-fed ballplayer than a hungry bond salesman."

So, Griggsville and Valley City continued their Sunday battle-recreation. The entertainment they provided, for both themselves and their fellow townspeople, was indeed an excursion from the harsh reality of life. The Dust Bowl was beginning to form across the Midwest, and rain hadn't been seen for weeks. Thousands of wanderers began heading west on Old Route 66, later made famous by John Steinbeck's novel *The Grapes of Wrath*, in search of any type of meager existence. The ground, dry and cracked, looked as bleak as the economic outlook of the nation. Yet, throughout all of this was born the player of baseball's Golden Age. Not from the big cities or colleges, but from Hutchinson, Kansas, and Carthage, Missouri, and Aviston, Illinois. These players were cherished possessions of the towns from whence they came. Such was the case of the Cardinals' great Pepper Martin, who the folks back home in Temple, Oklahoma, said "was so fast that he spent his boyhood chasing down rabbits." And such was the case of Griggsville's left fielder, anonymous outside the reaches of his little town, who caught a Valley City flyball for the third out and trudged off the field. In his floppy, dirty uniform, that Golden Age player wiped his mouth with the back of his sleeve, and gave a starry-eyed smile to his proud, cheering girlfriend in the fourth row.

2

Crash and Recovery in Society and Baseball, 1929–1933

The modern interstate system has rendered it obsolete, but there was a time when Old U.S. Route 66 was the heart of a nation on the move. Upon its completion in the mid–1920s, one could finally travel from Chicago to Los Angeles on one stretch of road. It was vibrant and alive, and along the way, it was full of everything that made America great. Imposing cities, rich farmland, deep coal fields, picturesque bridges, unique diners, ma-and-pa stores, and friendly people—they all made appearances as the great path wound and wound. Today's sightseers can trace its weed-grown skeleton along the bullying four-lane expressways. On Interstate 55 through Illinois, The Mother Road (as 66 is called by those who still love her) serves as a frontage road in most parts. Following the map carefully, one can still pull into the Ariston Restaurant in Litchfield, or the old A&W in Edwardsville for "good eats" in either place.

Through Missouri, Interstate 44 becomes its parallel, creeping down through the Ozarks as the land becomes somewhat hilly. About twenty miles past Springfield, it veers due west towards the town of Miller on Missouri Route 96. Along this road the Mickey Owen Baseball School sits, still training young men for the game as it did when it started in 1959. Founded by the major league catcher that bears its name, the school is pretty much all that speaks of the town of Miller. Dust is exchanged between Route 96 and the baseball school by means of passing trucks and active cleats.

Mickey Owen, the founder of the school and rocket-armed catcher for the Cardinals and Dodgers during the late '30s and early '40s, recalled another period of time when the dust flew. "I grew up in Nixa, Missouri [a few miles south of Springfield], where I played ball with Bobby Doerr everyday. But one day, when I was about 17 or 18, we couldn't play. We looked and saw a storm cloud coming, and we thought it was going to rain, so we packed up and started home. It wasn't rain, though. It was dirt."

It was the early 1930s, and the nation, still reeling from the stock market crash of 1929, was now faced with an ecological disaster as well. Fleeing like refugees from a war, agrarian citizens packed what they could and headed west—west to, what they heard, were fruited plains and amber waves of grain. Labor was needed, they heard, to pick the bounty of grapes, peaches, and apples growing wild in the orchards of California. The "Breadbasket of the World" seemed to be drying up, and the land was no longer arable. Route 66 had changed from an exciting, inspiring road of adventure and progress to a last-chance escape hatch. The grapes were indeed the wrath of the Steinbeck-created Joad family as well as thousands of others. From Missouri through Oklahoma, Texas, and beyond, jalopies stuffed to the brim waddled along, slower and slower, until coming to a screeching halt. Out of gas, a flat tire, out of food, or no blankets for the children when the temperature dropped at night. Calamities of any kind occurred regularly.

In the midst of the hopelessness, thousands of men roamed the countryside, looking for work. Unfortunately, married men who deserted their families—out of shame or simple compromise of their responsibilities—joined the single men on the road. Some found work, and earned wages or simply a bite to eat; some did not, and took the food anyway. There were other young men who hitchhiked their way south, through Memphis, Huntsville, Birmingham, Biloxi, and beyond. In the month of March, there were jobs to be had in professional baseball, they heard. Some of these jobs could pay $50 a month or more, and the teams were getting ready to leave Florida and head north for the summer, they heard. At most of the teams' practice sites, a man could just walk up and request a tryout, they heard.

Showing up malnourished and in rags for clothes, many of the hopefuls could not stand up in the batter's box. Would-be pitchers did not have the strength to make the sixty feet and six inch throw to home plate.

As they found, baseball was not an endless font of prosperity. On the white-collar side of the game, nearly all of the major league teams experienced a yearly financial loss after 1929. Only the New York Yankees and the New York Giants finished in the black consistently. The St. Louis Browns averaged only 1,500 fans per game from 1930 to 1932, as they and other teams did whatever was necessary to trim costs and attract customers. Unknown to many, Browns officials even considered a move to the West Coast, set to take place in the mid- to late-1930s. The idea was gaining further strength with club officials, as financial losses from the Depression began to pile up. The plan, however, was aborted with the coming of World War II. Even Joe Cronin, the star shortstop of the Washington Senators, was sold off by Senators owner Clark Griffith—who also happened to be his father-in-law. Teams held wild promotions and giveaways to bring more fans into the park. More than half the minor league teams operating in 1929 folded by 1931. Nonetheless, *The Sporting News* called baseball "The National Tonic," one of the very resources that would pull the country out of all its problems.

Attendance for all of major league baseball was a troubling 8.1 million in 1932, but subsequently lowered to a staggering 6.3 million the following year. Between 1929 and 1933, overall salaries in professional baseball had dropped a full 25 percent. As baseball entered the 1930s, it seemed as if St. Louis was big enough for only one team, as the Cardinals drew 508,000 in 1930, but the Browns a measly 152,000.

Fans, however, did not want to hear about financial problems that the clubs were having. They had enough of their own, and they went to the ballpark to escape these problems. In fact, many would pay a nickel for a hot dog at the game, and it would be their only meal of the day. And though suffering from poor attendance, St. Louis did indeed continue to have two teams in town, as the Browns maintained a group of loyal followers despite their inept play. The Browns won only one pennant during their stay in St. Louis (1944), and most of their players—such as shortstop Johnny Berardino, who went on to star in the soap opera *General Hospital*—had to find work in other professions.

It was the Cardinals who ruled the roost in St. Louis. The team's identity was its role as the underdog—a microcosm of a nation down on its luck from the Great Depression. To some they represented the exploited working man, while teams like the Giants and the Yankees represented more of the "corporate" culture. As one of the many colorful team owners in the early part of the century, "Singing Sam" Breadon brought his own style to the Cardinals. In the 1920s, one of his employees was a former light-hitting, poor fielding catcher named Branch Rickey. In just over three seasons, Rickey compiled a batting average of .239 and discovered that his career as a player would not amount to much. Therefore, he took interest in the management and development of players. Breadon recognized a shrewd, hard-working, honest man in Rickey, and made him the Cardinals field manager in 1919. Rickey believed in the Puritan work ethic, frugality, and temperance. While in college in Ohio, Rickey's mother sent him one dollar a month to help with his expenses; every month, he sent the dollar back. Within a few short years, he was already being regarded as the smartest man in baseball; his legend was cemented by bringing Jackie Robinson to the Brooklyn Dodgers in 1947.

Rickey's love of baseball was complete and unconditional, unusual in those days for a man with so much formal education. "Man may penetrate the outer reaches of the universe," he once said, "but for me, the ultimate human experience is to witness the flawless execution of the hit-and-run."

Between 1919 and 1925, however, Rickey was unable to win a championship as a field manager with the Cardinals, and the job was turned over to Rogers Hornsby, the star player of the team and perhaps the greatest right-handed hitter the game has ever seen. Breadon, however, kept Rickey on as the "general manager," a newly-found term for the handler on baseball personnel in the organization. With their dirty uniforms, low-paying contracts, and blue-collar personna, nobody gave the Cardinals a chance in their World Series appearances in the late '20s and early '30s. Fans in St. Louis were familiar with Ruth, as the Yankees regularly visited Sportsman's Park to play the Browns. Greater interest was taken, however, when the Cardinals matched up against New York in postseason play. In 1926, a baserunning blunder by Ruth ended the series as the Cardinals won, four games to three. In 1928, however, the Yankees returned with a vengeance. They swept the Birds in four straight, winning by a combined score of 27–10 as Ruth displayed his awesome power with three home runs and a .625 average in the series.

The Cardinals fared well in the National League, but usually seemed to be overmatched by clubs from the junior circuit. A lull in Yankee dominance occurred between the years 1929–1931, as Connie Mack's Philadelphia A's averaged 104 wins per year during the stretch. In 1930, the Cardinals won the National League pennant again with eight starting players hitting over .300, and a National League–record 1,004 runs scored (which still stands); in fact, every team in the National League had a batting average over .300 with the exception of Cincinnati and Boston. St. Louis won the flag by going 21–4 in September, a torrid stretch that culminated in a rookie pitcher named Dizzy Dean getting his first major league victory on the season's final day. As expected, the A's beat the Cardinals in the 1930 World Series, four games to two.

Despite the prolific pounding of the baseball that occurred during the regular season, pitching by the Cardinals and the A's during the 1930 World Series was stellar. Star Philadelphia thrower Lefty Grove had mustered a 28–5 record during the year, and the A's also had the talented George Earnshaw at their disposal. During the six games of the 1930 World Series, the Cardinals batted .197 (35 for 178) and the A's .200 (38 for 190). Grove was beaten by the Cardinals in Game 4 at St. Louis, but Lefty managed victories in two other games in the series, as did Earnshaw.

With the league so starved for pitching, it was a surprise to many that the Cardinals didn't make Dean, the flashy newcomer, a member of the squad for the 1931 season. He had shown promise in the minor leagues, but Rickey and manager Gabby Street wanted him to get more innings before permanently coming to St. Louis. While some of the Cardinals were not fond of Dizzy's cockiness, others knew that he could help the team. News of Dean's return to the minors shocked pitcher Jim Lindsey. "That," he asserted, "is the first time a ballclub lost thirty games in one day."

The pitching staff was still strong, however, with Bill Hallahan and youngster Paul Derringer leading the way. The Cardinals would lose Derringer to the Reds two years later in an important trade, but he honed his skills while throwing in Sportsman's Park. Along with Burleigh Grimes, St. Louis had enough pitching to give their potent offense many chances to win games. Hallahan led the league in strikeouts with 159 (as well as walks with 112), and had 19 wins and four saves. Derringer (18–8) and Grimes (17–9) also had strong records, as the staff also produced a league-high 17 shutouts.

The Cardinals returned a strong outfit for the 1931 season, and the offensive output was evenly distributed. First baseman "Sunny Jim" Bottomley batted a lofty .348, which was only a point lower than league leader and teammate, outfielder Chick Hafey. Hafey not only outdistanced Bottomley by less than a percentage point, but New York's formidable Bill Terry as well. Frankie Frisch, a tough second baseman acquired from the Giants for the great Rogers Hornsby, led the NL with 28 stolen bases, and struck out only 13 times in 563 plate appearances. At shortstop, Sparky Adams led the circuit with 46 doubles, and outfielder George Watkins pounded out 13 triples as part of a .477 slugging percentage. The Cardinals were solid on defense, were the fastest team in the league, and had a deep pitching staff. Regardless, they were heavy underdogs in their World Series rematch with the A's, winners of 107 games during the 1931 regular season in the American League.

With three future Hall of Famers in the lineup and two on the pitching staff, the A's had obscured the output of the "Murderer's Row" Yankees of the late 1920s. The batting attack was relentless, as stars Al Simmons (.390), Mickey Cochrane (.349), Mule Haas (.323), and Jimmie Foxx (.293, 30 home runs) feasted on opposing pitchers. Max Bishop rivaled Frisch as the best defensive second baseman in the game, and Dib Williams was his able complement at shortstop. On the mound, the incomparable Grove (31–4, 2.05 ERA) was said to be so fast, noted one sportswriter, that he could "throw a lamb chop past a wolf." Other beneficiaries of the A's mighty offensive production in 1931 were Earnshaw (21–7), Rube Walberg (20–12), and Lee Roy Mahaffey (15–4). Mack was managing his greatest club since 1914, going for their third straight World Series victory and their second in a row over the Cardinals.

What the series turned out to be, however, was Pepper Martin's personal stage, as he dominated catcher Cochrane's feared throwing arm on the basepaths.

With the series tied at two games apiece, Martin moved his play into high gear. In Game 5, he got three hits and drove in four runs in a 5–1 St. Louis victory. Grove evened matters again in the sixth game, with an 8–1 Philadelphia triumph. In the series finale, Martin, still hitting the ball hard on nearly every at bat and tearing up the bases, also flashed defensive heroics. He sealed the championship by snaring a blazing line drive off the bat of Max Bishop in the ninth inning with two out, two men on base, and the Cardinals leading 4–2. For the series, Martin batted .500 (a then–record 12 hits in 24 at bats), with four doubles, a home run, and five RBIs. His career batting average in World Series play of .418 remains a record—testimony of his penchant for delivering in the clutch.

Without a lot of fanfare, the Cardinals acquired portly slugger Hack Wilson from the Cubs after the 1931 season in exchange for

Burleigh Grimes. Grimes, who would return to St. Louis in 1933, was making $20,000, and Rickey wanted to free up salary money for other players that he deemed priorities to keep. As it would turn out, Wilson would never take a hack in a Cardinal uniform, as Rickey shipped him to the Dodgers in 1932 for $45,000 cash.

After a three-year hiatus, the Yankees returned to the World Series in 1932. In 1932, New York still had much of its "Murderer's Row" intact from their great teams of the 1920s. Despite still being the shadow of Ruth, Lou Gehrig had already firmly established himself a superstar in his own right, belting 34 home runs with 151 RBIs and a .349 average during the 1932 season. Tony "Poosh 'em Up" Lazzeri was still a strong contributor at second base (.300, 113 RBIs), Bill Dickey (.310) was still gunning down baserunners from his catcher's position, and the speedy Ben Chapman (15 triples, 38 stolen bases) was patrolling centerfield.

And of course there was Ruth, who while having his last great season (.341–41–137), was beginning to show signs of wear at age 37. His weight, which he had under control since his behavioral problems during the 1926 season, was beginning to creep up once again. While still generating great power from his left-handed swing, he was now a liability in the outfield, and could hardly get around the bases as a runner. Nonetheless, he was a walking legend, and when the Chicago Cubs met the Yankees in the 1932 World Series, he placed himself in the center of perhaps the greatest controversy in the history of the game.

Despite leading the Cubs to the pennant, Hornsby—who had arrived from New York in 1930—was fired by club officers on August 2, and the manager's job was given to first baseman Charlie Grimm. It was reported that Hornsby had been released when it was discovered he was borrowing money from other players to pay off gambling debts. He would resurface the following year as player-manager of the Browns, as the recent death of Browns owner Phil Ball had sent the organization into a tailspin and made it ripe for radical change.

The Cubbies nudged the Pirates for the National League flag by four games, and met New York for the World Championship. The Yankees easily won the first two games of the series at home, 12–6 and 5–2, and the two clubs hopped on the train for Chicago. Cubs fans had not seen a World Series victory since 1908 (nor since) and were not friendly to the visitors from the Bronx. Ruth was booed loudly from the moment he trotted onto the grass at Wrigley Field.

In the first inning of Game 3, Ruth stepped to the plate against

Cubs pitcher Charlie Root. Ruth crushed the first pitch over the rightfield wall for a three-run homer, and the fans were enraged further. As he circled the bases, he waved gleefully to his tormentors in the stands and the Cubs dugout. The "boos" grew louder when he tipped his cap before disappearing down the dugout steps.

He returned to the plate in the third, and the fans' rage surfaced again. The Babe took two pitched balls, then cheers replaced the anger when Root whistled two strikes by the slugger. At this point, Ruth gestured with two fingers in a vague direction—some say towards the Cubs dugout, whose occupants were still riding him—or the outfield bleachers, as others claim. In any event, the next pitch landed off the centerfield scoreboard, the longest home run seen in Wrigley to that date.

Most of the Cubs players swore that Ruth never pointed to the bleachers. Billy Herman, the Chicago second baseman, was one of the individuals harassing Ruth from the dugout. He knew for sure, he stated, that Ruth was pointing at the Cubs bench, not the bleachers. He further noted that since the dugout was the direction of the Ruth's fingers, it was quite a ways from centerfield, the direction of the home run—thus nullifying any prediction on Ruth's part. Until his dying day, Root affirms that he would have knocked Ruth down with the next pitch had he known he was pointing to the bleachers.

Franklin Delano Roosevelt, who a month later would be elected president of the United States for the first time, witnessed the event from his box seat. When Ruth trotted back towards the Yankee dugout after the bomb, Roosevelt sent out hearty laughter at the Babe's entertainment. Ironically, it would be Ruth's last home run in World Series play.

By the early 1930s, radio broadcasts of major league games had yet to be heard on a wide scale. The World Series had been on the airwaves since 1922, but because money was scarce, most owners (including Breadon) were afraid to broadcast home games, fearing that attendance would suffer. As more and more clubs relented, however, it was discovered that entire families listening to games at home created entire families of fans; thus, a new source of cash-paying customers at the ballpark was now available, rather than the typical "single man" that had usually attended ballgames to that point. Wives, mothers, sisters, and little brothers became fans of baseball and knowledgeable about the sport, and became interested in going to see a game in person themselves.

An interesting cat-and-mouse game occurred between Breadon

and his friend, Tom Convey, as the latter attempted to pirate the broadcasts of Cardinal games after Breadon had blacked them out in 1934.
Convey would sit on the roof of the YMCA across from centerfield at
Sportsman's Park in St. Louis, use binoculars, and send the games over
the ham airwaves. Breadon threatened him with a lawsuit, and Convey
backed off.

3

Grand and Dodier

In modern-day St. Louis, visitors find much of the city's activity near the banks of the Mississippi River, with the Arch, Busch Stadium, and other attractions marking the area. In the 1930s, however, there was excitement to be found further west. "Grand old Grand" Avenue was the major north-south thoroughfare, possessing the ornate Fox Theater, St. Louis University, and the home of the Cardinals until 1966, Sportsman's Park. Sitting on the corner of Grand and Dodier Street, Sportsman's was truly a neighborhood ballpark, the essence of which in contemporary times is seen only at the intersection of Addison and Clark streets in Chicago.

Perhaps the most interesting aspect of Sportsman's Park was its ownership. The less-successful team of the city, the Browns of the American League, were the landlords and the Cardinals were the tenants. The Cardinals had their offices at 3623 Dodier, while the Browns did business at 2911 North Grand. Despite the two teams sharing the location for many years, however, baseball was played at the site long before either franchise made its arrival. With the conception of the National League in 1876, the league granted the city of St. Louis a team known as, ironically, the Browns—unrelated to its future namesake. The franchise folded within two years, and the park at Grand and Dodier was used for local exhibition games and little else. These exhibitions, in an effort to keep baseball alive in the city, were the products of future founder of *The Sporting News*, Al Spink. On February 16, 1880, the Sportsman's Park and Club Association was formed to procure future improvements to the playing grounds.

The Browns returned to the location in 1882 to join the new league called the American Association of Base Ball Clubs, with the first game being played at the site on May 5. Under the financial guidance of local beer guru Chris Von der Ahe, the club enjoyed considerable monetary success and municipal support. Sportsman's Park, previously possessing only wooden bleachers, received a major face-lift with a roofed grandstand and improved seating quality. Von der Ahe was also an avid fan of horse racing, and soon he had thoroughbreds marching on the Sportsman's Park turf. In addition, Von der Ahe had arc lights installed for nighttime horse racing, and this has led some historians to believe that the first major league baseball game played at night may have actually occurred here in the 1890s. The stadium was the site for the Browns' claim to their first league championship in 1886, with a defeat of the Chicago White Stockings and their legendary player, Cap Anson.

Six fires in a ten-year period—from 1888 to 1898—caused a perpetual re-building of the park, and forced Von der Ahe to relinquish his share of team ownership by the turn of the century. The final blaze in 1898 occurred during a game with the Cubs, with one spectator being killed and several others injured.

Under new leadership, the National League club known as the "Cardinals" inhabited the city, playing at a crosstown field at Vandeventer Park called Union Grounds, located at the intersection of Vandeventer and Natural Bridge Road. The team's name emerged as a result of a female fan being astounded by the bright red caps and socks of the players. The remark was within earshot of local sportswriter Willie McHale, who made the suggestion for the team name in his column the following day. The Browns continued to function as an American League team in Sportsman's Park, and were finally joined by the Cardinals at the location in 1920. (When the Cardinals left Union Grounds in 1920, it left behind the last all-wooden stadium in the major leagues.) To accompany the dual-team occupancy, significant architectural changes were undertaken. In 1925, Browns owner Phil Ball, at a cost of $500,000, authorized the double-decking of the grandstand down the first and third base lines, as well as the construction of a roof on the right field pavilion. The only previous change to the final version of the park occurred in 1909, when bleachers and an additional grandstand were installed. The capacity of Sportsman's went from 8,000 to 18,000 after the 1909 improvements, and up to 30,000 after the renovations in 1925.

Marketing renovation occurred during this period as well. The idea of allowing women a day of free admission to the ballpark came to St. Louis in 1917. The concept of a "Ladies' Day" had originated with the

Brooklyn organization before the turn of the century, and club owners soon saw it as an opportunity for increased food, beverage, and cigarette sales at the ballpark. In recent years, pressure from women's rights groups have caused most clubs to drop the practice, although many still offer discounts on certain occasions.

A feature of Sportsman's Park different from other parks in the league was the screen in front of the right field pavilion. The screen, extending towards center field from the foul pole and 156 feet in length, was not present when Ruth hit his then-record 60 home runs in 1927. Four balls that the Bambino drilled into the stands in St. Louis that year would have been mere doubles in later seasons. The Babe's most memorable day in St. Louis, however, came on October 6, 1926. In the fourth game of the World Series against the Cardinals, Ruth swatted three home runs for the Yankees. It was the third-inning blast off of Flint Rhem, however, that was the most powerful. The ball cleared the roof of the right field pavilion, took one hop off Grand Avenue, and smashed the show window of the Wells Chevrolet dealership across the street. Two years to the game—contest number four of the 1928 World Series—the Babe had another three-homer day in Sportsman's Park, including his locally-famous "second chance" shot off of Cardinals pitcher Willie Sherdel. Sherdel thought he had caught Ruth looking on strike three, but home plate umpire Cy Pfirman ruled he had quick-pitched, thus nullifying the strike. The Babe proceeded to launch a missile into the center field stands on the next pitch.

Upon deciding that home runs were coming too cheaply for hitters in right field, officials decided in 1930 to construct the barrier in front of the bleachers in that section of the park—perhaps mostly because the Cardinals were fearing another World Series visit from Ruth. This move did not suit the fate of A's slugger Foxx, who in 1932 not only smacked 58 home runs, but also crushed 12 shots against the screen in Sportsman's Park against the Browns. Hence, Foxx would have then broken Ruth's record of 60 home runs in season if the screen had not been installed.

In 1955, at the request of Cardinals manager Eddie Stanky, the screen in front of the right field stands at Sportsman's Park was removed. Stanky's reasoning was that, in light of the Cardinals' predominantly left-handed hitting lineup, they would be able to generate more home runs without it. In 1956, new general manager Frank Lane returned the screen. Lane contended that weak hitters should not enjoy the luxury of "short porch" home runs.

In addition to his feats in the World Series, A's pitcher Lefty Grove also provided at least one other memorable moment in Sportsman's Park during regular season play. While blazing through the American League hitters in 1931 en route to his 31–4 record, he brought a 16-game winning streak into Sportsman's Park on August 23rd. A win against the Browns that day would have given Grove the record for consecutive victories, a mark held jointly by Walter Johnson and "Smokey" Joe Wood. Grove and Browns' starter Dick Coffman—a mediocre pitcher at best—locked horns in a scoreless duel until late in the game. Then, reserve A's outfielder Jimmy Moore could not locate a routine fly ball, which dropped in fair territory and allowed the Browns' Fred Schulte to score the game's only run, thus ending Grove's streak. Lefty then proceeded to rampage through the A's clubhouse after the game, throwing chairs, breaking lockers, and cursing out the A's players—especially Simmons, the regular left fielder who wanted to sit out the day's game to rest. Grove attacked him, feeling Simmons—not Moore—was responsible for his streak being ended.

As with most ballparks of baseball's Golden Age, advertisements adorned much of the area behind the outfield at Sportsman's Park. Among the most evident of these was the famous billboard for Griesedieck's Beer, which for decades stared back at players and fans from the right field wall. Other frequent suitors included Kellogg's, Sayman's Soap, Buick, Martin Washington Coffee and Teas, and Lennox Hotels, among many others. The Griesedieck brewers became one of the chief sponsors of Cardinals' radio broadcasts in the 1940s, with Harry Caray and Gabby Street in the announcers' booth. In addition, the *Globe-Democrat* would honor the "star" from the previous game on the right field wall. Former Cardinals catcher Joe Garagiola once noted that it seemed the name "Musial" was permanently etched in that spot.

Despite its romantic qualities, however, Sportsman's Park at times seemed to lag behind other stadiums in most amenities. Many players complained about the poor quality of the grass and infield dirt, resulting from it being the only major league park on which two teams called home (thus it being in perpetual use). Furthermore, Sportsman's was among the dwindling number of parks in the 1930s that continued to operate without a modern public address system. In lieu of an advanced electronic system, Sportsman's fans were privy to the megaphone antics of various announcers who blared out lineup changes manually up until 1936. It was not uncommon for the announcer to sprint around the outfield walls with the megaphone in a futile attempt to inform the entire crowd. Often, play had resumed before he had encircled the entire field. The trend of using a more modern public address system was simultaneously being embraced by even the most traditional organizations in the league. In 1934, the Cubs allowed to have an improved system installed in Chicago's Wrigley Field. Initially, Cubs manager Charlie Grimm was opposed to the idea, fearing that music records played over the system would disrupt pregame practice. Finally, in 1937, St. Louis saw the appearance of George Carson and his efficient electronic microphone, which boomed a voice from the heavens never heard before by the patrons in Sportsman's Park.

Babe Ruth's teammate, Yankees center fielder Earle Combs, suffered a devastating blow at Sportsman's on July 24, 1934. On a typical 1934 day of searing St. Louis summer heat, the light-headed and fatigued Combs crashed into the concrete wall in left field in pursuit of a fly ball. Fracturing his knee, shoulder, and skull on the play, Combs' life hung from a thread for several days, but he ultimately recovered. Unfortunately, the injury prematurely ended his magnificent career.

The oppressive heat that caused Combs' injury was viewed as an unavoidable aspect of baseball. As the game entered the mid 1930s, it seemed that the hot, oppressive daytime would remain the only hours during which ballgames would be played. On February 8, 1934, *The Sporting News* wrote, "It seems that night baseball is definitely on its way out. The mourners probably will be few. It was a noble experiment, but, like so many others, it didn't live up to the expectations of its supporters." Until this time, baseball after sunset had been witnessed only in the minor leagues. Other teams, such as some in the Negro Leagues, would haul portable light stands with them on the road and play as many as three games in a day.

Two major league clubs met under the lights for the first time on March 22, 1931, as the Chicago White Sox and New York Giants played an exhibition game at Buffs Stadium in Houston. Owners of the two clubs, and others, were awaiting a great return on the event; unfortunately, less than a thousands fans showed up. Mosquitoes were in plentiful supply in the swampy area of the stadium, and many of the spectators and players spent most of the night shooing them away.

With owners desperate to boost gate receipts, night baseball was finally introduced into the major league regular season on May 24, 1935, in Cincinnati. Lee MacPhail, the innovative general manager of the Reds, got league approval to pursue the idea. MacPhail arranged the gala event so that President Roosevelt, from the White House, would throw the switch that would illuminate Crosley Field. The Reds beat the Phillies, 2–1, and afterwards the debate about the merit of night baseball was again cast into the open. Breadon, in changing his attitude about the idea, had become among the most vocal supporters of the concept for the previous few years. He predicted that it would "make everyday a Sunday," in terms of attendance. However, he had little recourse since the Browns were the owners of Sportsman's Park. Night baseball finally came to St. Louis on May 24, 1940, when the Browns lost to the Cleveland Indians 3–2, before a crowd of almost 26,000. In addition, the game marked the first major league home run off the bat of Bob Feller. A couple of weeks later, on June 4th, the Cardinals would make their nocturnal debut at Sportsman's Park with a 10–1 loss to the Brooklyn Dodgers. Despite the increasing occurrence of playing after dark, the concept still seemed strange and unnatural to many. Consequently, the Cardinals raised many eyebrows ten years later in 1950 when the club asked the league to have its opening game at night. Notwithstanding the protests of their guests, the Pittsburgh Pirates, the Redbirds responded with a 4–2 victory in front of 20,871 happy spectators.

Converts were quickly made of nearly everyone, as between May 1939 and May 1941 nine other major league clubs made their debuts under the lights. The other holdouts—namely, the Yankees, Boston Red Sox, Detroit Tigers, and the Boston Braves—played their first night games shortly after World War II. And of course, the Cubs did not begin play after dark until August 8, 1988 (memorable as 8-8-88), only to have that contest rained out and completed the next day.

The modern Busch Stadium, which today stands proudly in downtown St. Louis in the shadow of the Gateway Arch, is not the first ballpark in the city to hold that name. Upon the sale of Sportsman's Park by Bill Veeck to August A. Busch, Jr., on April 9, 1953, the latter changed the name to his own, and held it until its demolition in 1966. After the sale, however, part of Veeck's family continued to live in an apartment that was underneath the stadium. Immediately after purchasing the park, Busch pumped $1.5 million into a renovation project for Sportsman's, improving the box seating area and upgrading both dugouts and clubhouses. He also had the on-field flag pole removed which for years stood at the base of the centerfield wall. Initially, Busch toyed with the idea of calling the structure Budweiser Stadium, but National League officials pressured him to choose another name. Interestingly, several stadiums of today—including Coors Field in Denver and Miller Park in Milwaukee—bear the names of beer.

The final game at Sportsman's Park (known by then as Busch Stadium), May 8, 1966. (From the collections of the St. Louis Mercantile Library at the University of Missouri–St. Louis.)

When Busch purchased the Cardinals, it had been seven years since they had won a pennant; it would be eleven more years until they won another. In fact, ground had been broken for the new Busch Stadium in downtown St. Louis before the Cardinals secured their first National League championship under the Busch family. That year, 1964, also included a World Series victory over the Yankees with the Cardinals being directed by manager Johnny Keane. This series proved to be the first showcase of Bob Gibson and Lou Brock, who would lead the Cardinals to other championships in the new ballpark only a few years later.

Jerry Gibson, who was the Cardinals' last bat boy in Sportsman's Park, was bittersweet about the move to the new stadium. Despite the charm of Sportsman's, he mentioned of its clubhouses, "No matter how hard I worked, they never seemed to get clean."

The end of one of baseball's historic stadiums came at 3:15 P.M. on May 8, 1966, when the Cardinals suffered a 10–5 defeat at the hands of the San Francisco Giants. Shortly after the game, a helicopter hovered over second base as home plate was unearthed and loaded into its cargo bin for transport to the shining new downtown stadium. Within a short time, the structure that contained nearly all of St. Louis' baseball history was razed.

Today, urban blight has wrought its effect on the neighborhood near the intersection of Grand and Dodier. A boys' club now stands at the location, and a baseball field is still there—with home plate still at the corner of Dodier and Spring streets, as it was in 1934.

PART TWO

The Team

"Luck is the residue of design"
—Branch Rickey

4

Frankie the Flash and Some Arkansas Lightning

Despite a World Series victory in 1926, Hornsby found that he was living in disfavor of the St. Louis management. The problem came to a head before the start of the 1927 season. In November of 1926, he asked Breadon for a then-unprecedented sum of $50,000 for each of the following three years, carrying double duty as player-manager. Breadon, already disenchanted with Hornsby because of his gambling habits, offered a one-year deal at this figure, which Hornsby refused. Many in St. Louis thought that Rickey and Breadon would not have courage to deal Hornsby, whose popularity was at an all-time high with Cardinal fans. Rickey proved, nonetheless, that no player was above what he believed to be the best interests of the team. In looking for another second baseman, Frankie Frisch was the player that Rickey had wanted all along; and now he had an opportunity to get him.

Frisch was the hub for the great New York Giants teams of the 1920s under manager John McGraw, who seemed to easily dominate the league in the early part of the decade. McGraw knew that Frisch had leadership skills, and he soon made him captain after Frisch came to the Giants from Fordham University. Winners of four straight National League pennants from 1921 to 1924, the Giants were nearly unbeatable as Frisch was developing into the top keystoner in the game. By 1926, however, he and McGraw began to have personal differences. Ironically (as with the case with Hornsby and the Cardinals' brass), it was in St. Louis late in the 1926 season when things boiled over between the two. Frisch botched a defensive play on a double steal by the Cardinals, and McGraw verbally assaulted him in front of the team. Afterwards, Frisch vowed that he would never play for the Giants again, and demanded to be traded. He finished out the season with New York, but did receive his wish over the winter. On December 20th, he and Jimmy Ring were sent to the Cardinals for Hornsby, a player McGraw had wanted for seven years. Because of the legendary status of "The Rajah," the trade for Frisch initially created more anger within the St. Louis baseball community than any transaction in history. Despite the pressure, Frisch responded strongly during the 1927 season, batting .337 with 11 triples and a league-leading 48 stolen bases.

Rickey, however, didn't feel quite comfortable at that point in giving the manager's job to Frisch. He knew that Frisch would make a great leader someday, but for the meantime hired Bob O'Farrell for the job. O'Farrell lasted one year, in which he led the Cardinals to a second-place finish with a 92–61 record in 1927, only a game-and-a-half behind the pennant-winning Pirates. He was replaced with Bill McKechnie, who took the Cardinals back to the top the following year but was replaced by Billy Southworth in 1929. Breadon and Rickey thought they had found a permanent solution in Street, but he fought alcohol problems, inconsistent decision-making, and poor discipline en route to his demise. A short time later, Street would join Harry Caray in the Cardinals' radio booth.

Frisch was a renaissance man. He displayed a knowledge of fine wines, Italian music, and even maintained an impressive private garden. He was intelligent, articulate, and polished, yet possessed a raging competitive fire that consumed his baseball opponents. A chemistry major at Fordham, he also excelled at football in college, being named as a halfback to Walter Camp's All-American team in 1918. It took Frisch many hours to convince his parents that life as a professional baseball player would be honorable, let alone financially rewarding. Going straight to the Giants from the Fordham campus, Frisch never played a single game in the minor leagues. And despite the greatness of Hornsby, the acquisition of Frisch by Breadon signaled a new era in Cardinals history.

After seven years with the Cardinals, Frisch was 35 years old in 1934 when he was about to begin his first full season in directing the team. At first, the players had a difficult time adjusting to Frisch. He began his tenure by enforcing many more rules than did Street, and

The heavy hitters of the Gas House Gang (left to right): Rip Collins, Joe Medwick, Pepper Martin, and Frankie Frisch. (From the collections of the St. Louis Mercantile Library at the University of Missouri–St. Louis.)

Cardinals were not fond of the strictness exercised by the new leader. Before long, however, Frisch and the players began to meet in the middle; he loosened his grip, and the players ultimately developed more respect for him.

"It isn't original with me," Frisch responded, when asked what his managerial style would be. "The secret of success lies in knowing your men—and when to take out your pitcher." At the end of the 1933 season, during which Frisch steered the club to an 82–71 final record (36–26 under his helm), he nonetheless stated, "This is the worst ball club I've ever played on." Ironically, that club would not differ greatly from the immortal team that would take the field a year later. When spring training for the 1934 season arrived, he had renewed optimism. Frisch was a catalyst for the Cardinals that Street could not be—both on the field and from the dugout. Not only did he preach hustle, but also practiced it, extracting every drop of fight and energy in his body. "Frisch is the strictest manager in either league," wrote Harold Parrott of the *Brooklyn Eagle* during the 1934 season. "He makes the Redbirds check in by eleven, insists they eat at regular hours, and he does a bit of snooping.

Yet, the Cardinals all swear by him." Because of the work ethic he exemplified, the Cardinals broke camp in April 1934 as the most well-conditioned and eager team to come north.

There was never a doubt that Frisch was from the "Old School." He decried his contemporaries as lazy players whose attention was not focused on the fundamentals of the sport. When a player wanted to rest an injury by sitting out a game, his response often was, "What's this damned game coming to?" He emulated McGraw's hard-nosed tactics in many ways, and exceeded them in others. One witness claimed, beyond any doubt, that Frisch's clubhouse tongue-lashing of players made McGraw look like "a Sunday-school teacher scolding the class clown." And, because the ire of McGraw was locally famous, New York sportswriters, in particular, were expecting great things from Frisch as a manager. Meanwhile, St. Louis journalists generally waited to judge his merit. Despite good signs in the spring, the jury appeared to remain out in St. Louis on whether Frisch could mold the '34 club into a winner, pitting itself against the competitive National League.

As Frisch took the helm, the Cardinals' roster was evolving into a defining model of baseball and America in the face of crisis during the 1930s. Knotty-muscled individuals with tobacco juice drooling and uniforms stained, each game they played was an all-out war to the finish. Baseball was not a way of life for these men; it was life. Their persistence to survive was one of many such examples of human will during the nation's most difficult days.

They were the sons of sharecroppers from Arkansas; sons of Hungarian immigrants from New Jersey; sons of cattle ranchers from Oklahoma. Although few, they were also college graduates; in fact, the Cardinals of the 1930s had baseball's only Phi Beta Kappa scholar in utility infielder Burgess Whitehead. The Cardinals were as diverse as the struggling nation, and, like America, strained to produce a communal *esprit de corps* that would help it emerge from its darkest days. The St. Louis ball club, not unlike the United States at the time, was willing to do whatever was necessary to emerge victorious. They would not only hit, run, pitch, and field, but also scratch, claw, kick, and growl until the final out was made. St. Louis was not a favorite destination for visiting teams in the 1930s. The scorching heat and the aggressiveness of the home club typically made for an unpleasant visit.

In the morning edition of the *New York Telegraph* on October 9, 1934, a peculiar cartoon appeared. Sportswriter Dan Daniel described some rough-looking ballplayers with their cleats slung over their shoulders, crossing the railroad tracks to the "nice" part of town to play the "nice" team. The rough team, depicted as the Cardinals, was labeled as "The Gas House Gang," coming from the tough gas house district of town. Little did Mr. Daniel know at the time that the moniker would be forever linked with the most hard-nosed team in the history of American sports.

Strangely enough, the most notable person in this collection was an itinerant sharecropper. His background was so inexact, in fact, that it greatly added to his mystique. It was ultimately resolved that, despite the various dates and places he gave to different reporters, Jay Hanna Dean was born on January 16, 1910, in Lucas, Arkansas. He would ultimately change his name to Jerome Herman Dean in memory of a childhood friend who had died. In the long run, however, he would simply become known as "Dizzy," nomenclature describing both his wavering personality and his fastball's effect on hitters.

The son of migrant workers, Dean grew up in impoverished surroundings, starting to pick cotton with his father at age four. Years later, he would say that by the age of ten he was doing the work of a man, picking four to five hundred pounds of cotton a day. As a result of his family's transient lifestyle, he was never afforded much formal education—nor were his brothers, Elmer and Paul. He would ultimately get to the fourth grade ("However, I didn't do too well in the third grade either," Dean noted). He would always show up to school on Fridays, the day ballgames were played; school rules required players to be in school the day of a contest. Aside from skipping rocks, fishing, and general wandering, the only boyhood interest that developed for Diz was baseball. He soon honed his craft, and with Paul at shortstop and Elmer in the outfield, the 12-year-old arm of Jay Dean began to throw bullets past the local high school players. Town folks called the boy a "wonder—a lightnin' bolt for a right arm." Playing baseball meant everything to the Dean boys. The brothers would sometimes sneak away from work in the fields to play ball, only to encounter a whipping from their father when they got home.

While Paul is not quite as famous as Dizzy, oldest brother Elmer is completely obscure. Elmer had mild mental retardation, but was nonetheless a competent ball player. He worked in the minor leagues as a peanut vendor, and later would be invited to St. Louis in the same capacity, although he did not accept the position. From the stands he would cry, "Get your goobers [peanuts] from me, and I'll tell ya how I taught my brother Dizzy Dean how to pitch." Elmer's shortcomings, however, were often a source of concern to the family. One time, Dizzy, Paul, and their father were riding along in the family car, and Elmer was following along in a pickup truck. They came to a railroad track, and Paul sped through, narrowly missing a crossing train. Elmer, being stuck on the other side, got separated from them and never reached the common destination. When he didn't show up for days, then weeks, then months, friends of the family became worried. "Elmer? Nah, he'll be all right. He'll turn up someday," said "Pa" Dean when asked about his son's whereabouts. As it turned out, they would not see Elmer again for nearly four years.

When Dizzy was 16, he lied about his age and enlisted in the army. It was in the service that he received his first new pair of shoes, and also received regular meals for the first time in his life. In fact, he would later say that the only reason he joined was so he could "eat and pitch on a regular basis." When Dean started playing with the army team, he soon showed off his magical arm. Despite his pitching prowess, however, he did not make a very good soldier. He was frequently late, out of uniform, and did not complete assignments. It was also in the army where he got his immortal nickname, as his peers found it correlative to his actions.

A short time later, Dizzy learned of a job opportunity with the San Antonio Public Utilities Company. The Dean family scraped up enough to legally buy him a discharge from the army, and Dizzy began to pitch for the company's baseball team. Soon after, Cardinals scout Don Curtis discovered him, and signed Dean to his first professional contract. He was sent to Houston of the Texas League for the 1930 season.

After a brief stay at Houston, he was reassigned to the St. Joseph (MO) Saints of the Western League, which was considered a lesser-quality class "A" league than that of the Texas League. In his first taste of professional baseball Dean pitched well, finishing with a record of 17–8 and a 3.69 ERA, with 134 strikeouts in 217 innings. Then, on that last day of the 1930 major league season, he was called up to pitch his first game with the Cardinals. St. Louis mayor Victor Miller was in attendance at the game, sitting near the field in a box seat. Curious about the new pitcher, he called Cardinals manager Street over for some information. "Mr. Mayor," Street warned him, "I think he's going to be a great pitcher, but I'm afraid we'll never know from one minute to the next what he's going to do." The result was a complete game three-hitter against the Pittsburgh Pirates. In earning a 3–1 victory, he struck out five batters in front of a mere 6,000 fans at Sportsman's Park. The performance, coupled with Dean's own immense self-confidence, seemed to assure Dizzy—at least in his own mind—a roster spot on the parent club for the 1931 season.

Nonetheless, the decision of Cardinal management was that Dizzy did not have enough extended experience at a higher level of competition. Much to his chagrin (he responded to Rickey, the Cardinals general manager, "Don't you want to win the pennant *this* year?"), he was assigned to Houston for the 1931 season. Taking out his frustrations on the hitters of the Texas League, he fired his way to a 26–10 record, a 1.57 ERA, and only allowing 210 hits in 304 innings pitched, with 303 strikeouts. This was reason enough for St. Louis to make him a permanent member of their staff for 1932.

Dizzy had his sights set on the destruction of the entire National League when he arrived in Bradenton, Florida, for the Cardinals 1932 spring training session. Calling himself "The Great Dean," he offered his autograph to anyone who would take it. Trying to keep him happy, the club gave him a spending allowance for his entertainment. When that money ran out, he began charging things to the ballclub's account, saying, "Just put it on Mr. Breadon's tab." Often, he would eat four or five meals a day, buy girls milkshakes at the drugstore, and purchase endless cigarettes and candy on credit with no true means to pay for them. A couple of times, he went as far as to sign Rickey's name on some bad checks. He also offered the citizens of Bradenton the chance to "feel the arm of a real big-league pitcher, like m'self, for free."

Such practices began to wear the patience of Street and several players as well. Street suspended him for three days in an effort to calm his actions. Diz apologized, and headed north with the ballclub to St. Louis. In order to exploit his skyrocketing popularity, the Cardinals' plan was to have him pitch almost exclusively on Sunday during the first half of the 1932 season, in an effort to draw a large crowd on a non-working day. As noted previously, night baseball had yet to make its appearance in the big leagues, and owners counted on large weekend attendance figures to offset the paltry showings during the workweek.

As the 1932 season unfolded, Dean began to show unusual poise for a rookie pitcher; in fact, he acted like no other pitcher before his time. He would make comments to hitters as they approached the plate, give them funny looks as he went into his windup, and then laugh out loud after he struck them out. Despite his general good humor, he could get extremely angry on the mound as well. His biggest pet peeve was the batter who incessantly dug his back foot in the batters' box before being ready to hit. When the hitter would do this, Dean would walk halfway to home plate, disgustedly put his hands on his hips, and nod his head until the hitter was finished. "Just keep on diggin'," he would instruct the batter, "'cause that's where they're gonna bury you." And on the next pitch, the batter would find a quick one coming at his head. Dean called his fastball his "fogger," and when it whizzed up towards the plate, the hitter was lucky to see it. Diz also insisted on calling his own pitches. "I think pitchers are a better judge of what to throw than catchers," he claimed. "The pitcher's throwing it, ain't he?"

The trademark Dean cockiness only grew with the passing of time. Before a game in the 1935 season, he walked in front of the Boston Braves' dugout (a dugout which included Babe Ruth, who was in the final year of his career), and offered a proposition. "Boys, ya know somethin'? If a pitcher's good enough, all he needs is a fast one—no curves, no nuthin' else to do the job." And he proceeded to throw fastballs—and only fastballs—at the Braves all day long, en route to a 5–3 complete game victory. He had the fogger working that day, and several of the game's greatest hitters from the era said that his fastball was, without question, the most powerful in baseball. Catcher Al Lopez of the Brooklyn Dodgers simply noted when facing Dean, "That ball came up there so fast it jumped like a jackrabbit when it crossed the plate."

In a career cut short by injuries, Dizzy Dean would only pitch in six full big league seasons (1932–1937). However, nobody made a bigger impact in such a brief tenure. "It is reported that Dizzy Dean signed a contract calling for a salary of $12,000," Sid Keener of the *St. Louis Star-Times* reported on November 6, 1933. "That's a lot of scratch, but he's worth every penny of it."

The Muscular Duck

Joe Medwick is the last winner of the National League Triple Crown, a feat he accomplished in 1937. Nonetheless, he remains a figure from the Gas House Gang relatively obscured by the immortality of Dean, the managerial longevity of Leo Durocher, and the charisma of Pepper Martin. Like Dean, Medwick made few friends on the Cardinals—or in baseball for that matter. Part of this attitude, however, was what made the Gas House Gang Cardinals great; the attitude was also shared by Martin, Durocher, Dean, Frisch, and others on the team. Their raucous style of play made them winners. In Medwick's case, however, the fact that he carried it over into off-the-field skirmishes may have tarnished his reputation, particularly with sportswriters. While in the minor leagues, he was dubbed "The Duck" by a female fan who likened his gait to that of a mallard. A local newspaperman made the name stick, and Joe was ornery with the media ever since. Thus, it is Medwick that is often the misunderstood personality in the mix of colorful figures on the Cardinals' roster of the 1930s. Furthermore, it is believed by many that Medwick's brash personality delayed his entry into the Hall of Fame, which was granted in 1968—seven years before his death.

Very much the product of a blue-collar background, Medwick was born the son of Hungarian immigrants on April 4, 1911, in Carteret, New Jersey. Although standing only five-foot-ten, his sinewy build proved quite imposing to opposing pitchers. Signed by Cardinals scout Charlie Kelchner, Joe's first year of professional ball resulted in a .419 batting average at Scottsdale, Pennsylvania, of the Middle Atlantic League, the loop's top batting figure for 1930. The following year, he joined Dean at Houston of the Texas League. He hit .305 and .354 in his two years there, plus .349 in a 26-game September call-up with the Cardinals in 1932. After this short display in the majors, he was already being hailed as baseball's next great hitter.

Medwick soon became known as a player who could knock out the opposition equally with a three-run homer or a right hook. He, as well as a few other Cardinal players, also made it a common practice to show up at the opponent's batting cage during pregame, and verbally (and sometimes physically) assault the enemy's best hitters. He was truly representative of the Cardinals' rough style of baseball. Interestingly, the fights in which the Cardinals found themselves—with Medwick often in the middle of them—were not unique to the opposing team. Cardinals pitcher Tex Carleton discovered this during pregame batting practice one day. The bell rang, indicating that Medwick's turn in the cage was over. When Carleton—who was described by Whitehead as "the team's toughest player"—yanked on Ducky's arm to remove him, Joe shrugged him off, and motioned to the batting practice pitcher for some more throws. When Tex tugged again, Medwick dropped his bat, turned, and dropped Carleton into the netting with a bruising fist. Tex should have stayed down, for his counter-attack met with the same fate. BOOM—down he went again, and finally Cardinal players intervened. Shortstop Durocher saw what happened, and turned to yell to Frisch. "Hey Frankie, you'd better find another starting pitcher for the game today, because right now we don't have one."

The fact that this incident took place during the formative stages of the 1934 season (May 15) cemented the Cardinals' reputation throughout the National League as an ultra-surly bunch, who would "out-holler, out-race, out-smart, out-throw, out-fight anybody, any place, any time," according to one eyewitness. Carleton continued to have problems with other teammates as well, particularly Dean. The antipathy with Diz began when the two were teammates in the minor leagues, through Tex's tenure in St. Louis, and even after he was dealt to the Cubs in 1935 (the season in which he was an integral factor in Chicago's torrid September stretch drive to the pennant). In one game in 1936, the two traded insults from the dugouts and the pitching mound at Wrigley Field, ultimately leading to a bench-clearing brawl. During his years with the Cardinals, Carleton felt (along with many other pitchers on the team) that management showed too much favoritism towards Diz.

Medwick, in terms of decisions, knockouts, and TKOs, was the undisputed heavyweight champion on the team, and he would look to poke anyone who rubbed him the wrong way—even in situations in which he wasn't directly involved. Just before the 1937 season began, baseball columnist Jack Miley of the *New York Daily News* lashed out at Dean and his wife, Pat, saying that Mrs. Dean wore the pants in the family, and that Mr. Dean wasn't capable of anything else in life except pitching and picking cotton. One day, Diz and Pat found Miley and his buddy, writer and ex–pro football player Irv Kupcinet, coming out of a lounge in the Tampa Terrace Hotel. After confronting him about the story he had written, Diz reached for Miley's coat collar when Kup intervened. "No one picks on a reporter while I'm around," he scowled at Diz. Kup reached for his throat, but not in time to see a right cross from Medwick, which sent him sprawling back into a group of potted plants against the wall. Swinging a pair of baseball spikes, Cardinal infielder Pat Crawford took care of Miley, opening a gash on his forehead—much to the delight of the other Cardinal players in the lobby at the time. In Miley's column the next day, he referred once again to the "Powerful Patricia" and that "these fellows are taking their Gas House ballyhoo too seriously."

Despite his brother's ill-will towards Medwick, Paul Dean appeared to enjoy friendship with him well beyond their playing days. Paul's only recollection of a dispute with Joe came on a train ride in 1934. The two were involved in a high-stakes poker game, including Martin, Whitehead, and coach Mike Gonzalez. After accusing Paul of loading the deck, Medwick jumped him, landing the junior Dean on his back in the corridor of the train. As Martin stood by watching and cheering both on, others separated the two. Afterwards, mutual respect was reestablished between them, and despite Paul's lifelong devotion to his brother, he did not share Dizzy's lack of fondness—or perhaps more accurately, lack of tolerance—for Medwick.

Pitcher Ed Heusser would be another Medwick victim in 1937, with Heusser also being a teammate at the time. Having his own reputation as a fighter, he accused Medwick of loafing to a catchable single hit his way. Joe promptly proceeded to drop him with a hard right in the dugout, immediately after the inning in which the play occurred.

It was evident that, at times, the team was not big enough for both Medwick and Diz. Each commanded marquee status, although Dean's self-marketing made that issue no contest. Medwick's jersey #7 and Dean's #17 were often found running into each other, and on June 4, 1935, in Pittsburgh, the two had one of their more notable disputes.

With the bases loaded and two out in the fifth inning, Diz was

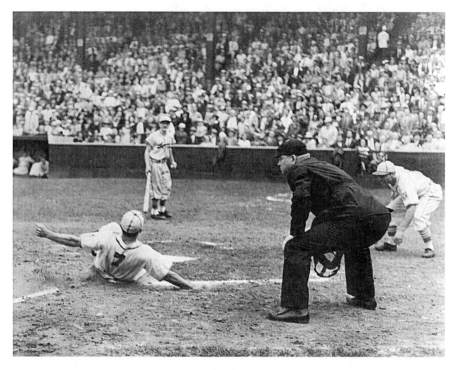

Medwick slides across home with another run for the Cardinals. (From the collections of the St. Louis Mercantile Library at the University of Missouri–St.
Louis.)

laboring on the hill, working to preserve a 2–1 Cardinal lead. Pirates
hitter Arky Vaughan looped a weak fly ball to left off of a sizzling Dean
fastball. Medwick, apparently in an uninspired attempt, allowed the
ball to drop in front of him. Two runs scored, and the Pirates took the
lead. When Dean retrieved the ball, he walked halfway between the
mound and left field, put his hands on his hips, and glared angrily at
Medwick. Joe popped his mitt twice, put his hands on his knees, and
stared in at home plate, unconcerned. The next inning, Medwick rock-
eted a pitch deep over the left field wall for a three-run homer. Upon
returning to the dugout, he had some words for Diz.

"See if you can hold *that* lead, gutless," and proceeded to the drinking fountain where he filled up his mouth with water, came back, and
spat all over Dean's shoes. Paul, who was sitting nearby, rose to his
brother's defense, and they both started moving towards Medwick. In
the days before bat racks were utilized, teams would simply lay all of

their bats on the ground in front of the dugout. Medwick grabbed one, waved it strongly in both arms, and said, "Keep on a-comin', brothers Dean—I'll separate ya real good." Fortunately, cooler heads were able to step in before Joe got in a swing.

Perhaps Diz said it best about Medwick when he once noted, "All that Hungarian bastard wants to do is fight."

Despite these displays of temper, Medwick's hitting with a baseball bat gained him greater prominence. As the line drives smoked off his bat in the hot summer of '34, he explained his torrid hitting to J. Roy Stockton, the sportswriter who primarily covered the Cardinals for the *St. Louis Post-Dispatch*: "I just smell the lettuce," Medwick said. "I have two good friends in this world: buckerinoes [money] and base hits. If I get base hits, I will get buckerinoes. I smell World Series lettuce, and I'll get my two or three a day."

Despite a stocky build, Medwick was a fast runner and adequate outfielder, at least when he wanted to be. He had decent arm strength, and few tested him on the bases. Although never a basestealer, he was a quick first-to-third and second-to-home runner. Unfortunately, he was also a careless baserunner, constantly taking unnecessary risks and foolish leadoffs. He would often get picked off, which would cause Frisch to dent the dugout wall with the heel of his shoe. The mental facets of Medwick's game would improve with experience, but, unfortunately, after his days with the Cardinals had ended. Typical of his policy on star players, Rickey sold Medwick to another team at the pinnacle of his career—it was Brooklyn in 1941, after Durocher was named the player-manager of the Dodgers. Leo was always fond of Medwick's hustle and, of course, his hitting ability. He made it a priority to get him in his lineup, and Medwick teamed with Pete Reiser, Dixie Walker, Dolph Camilli, and Mickey Owen to lead Brooklyn to the National League pennant in 1941.

Medwick may well have been the best "bad ball" hitter in the history of the game. At times, in fact, it seemed his favorite pitch was a running fastball inside, a pitch seemingly headed for his front shoulder. With a quick, tomahawk action from his short frame, he would "chop" the ball into the left field gap. Several Pittsburgh Pirates players claimed that once at Forbes Field, Medwick hit a ball into Schenley Park—an area behind the left field wall, about 450 feet from home plate—on a pitch that was above the bill of his cap. The strike zone was a non-entity for him; any pitch, any place was fair game. A pitcher could not blow a fastball by him on the inside corner, for his powerful forearms

were too strong and quick. Trying to trim the outer half would not suc-
ceed either, as Medwick would routinely step at a 45-degree angle on
such pitches (much like Roberto Clemente in later years) and drive the
ball to right field.

His exploits of bad ball hitting gained national fame. In his July
11, 1934, column, Dan Daniel wrote, "When Joe Medwick got that
home run yesterday [in the All-Star Game at the Polo Grounds in New
York], he hit a ball high over his head. How anyone can get so much
power on a ball at that height is a mystery." Five days later, when Medwick hit two homers off of Dodger pitching, Brooklyn outfielder Buzz
Boyle said he hit the first one "off his ear." "The only way to fool that
guy," said Boyle, "is to throw right over the heart of the plate. His first
home run went to left, and the second he hit over the right field fence.
What can you do with a fellow like that?" Afterwards, it was rumored
that Medwick would be a likely candidate to be the first to hit the ultimate mythical home run—that of the batter leaning over the plate to
hit the fourth pitch of an intentional walk.

Van Lingle Mungo of the Dodgers, one of the league's top hurlers
of the day added, "I'd rather pitch to any other hitter in the league."

"Forbid Medwick to carry a bat to the plate—make him hit with
his fists," chimed in Mungo's teammate and fellow pitcher, Dutch
Leonard. "Then he'd only get singles."

Of Snake Hunting, Sneezing Powder, and Stolen Bases

"Pepper Martin plays baseball with a spirit of adventure," Branch Rickey proclaimed in 1932. When he broke into the big leagues in 1928, Martin quickly became one of baseball's most intriguing characters. He did not get a starting role until the middle of the 1931 season, when Rickey noticed that he could save $10,000 by dealing the Cardinals' regular centerfielder, Taylor Douthit, to Cincinnati. Martin's hustling soon became famous. Once while shagging flies during batting practice in Pittsburgh, he pursued balls off the bat which such fury that one Pirates writer likened the scene to "a herd of elephants stampeding through the jungle." Furthermore, his practical jokes could strike anyone at anytime. Nobody could figure Martin out, nor predict what he would do next. He was a strongly-built, fireplug of a man. He played the harmonica in the clubhouse, loved to eat his mother's home cooking back in Oklahoma, and hunted rattlesnakes for the St. Louis Zoo in the off-season—arming himself with only a forked stick and a canvas bag.

He was born Johnny Leonard Martin on February 29, 1904, in Temple, Oklahoma. "A true product of the West," the *Philadelphia Inquirer* described him. "A bronco buster, a hunter, a plainsman, who has not been tarnished by the East." After joining the Cardinals for brief stints in the 1928 and 1930 seasons, he thereafter became a fixture at Sportsman's Park. He preferred the informal, easygoing lifestyle, as he carried "baggy trousers, an open shirt, and a front piece that has only casual interest in a razor," according to famed sportswriter Grantland Rice.

Pepper loved everybody, and everybody loved Pepper—even those with personalities quite different from his own. Rickey, who was known for honesty, temperance, and having a disdain for profanity, used substitutes for bad words when he became upset. Pepper followed this lead, as he burst into Rickey's office once early in his career to complain about a lack of playing time. "*JOHN BROWN*, Mr. Rickey, play me or trade me!"

Blessed with immense raw physical talents, Martin coupled his natural ability with a fierce competitiveness. His steel-clad forearms were full of strength, and provided him with a quick, smooth swing from the right-handed batter's box. He was also the fastest player in baseball in the 1930s. "People talk about Cool Papa Bell in the Negro Leagues, and he was pretty quick, for sure," said Owen, Martin's teammate on the Cardinals later in the 1930s. "But he was no match for Martin. Pepper was by far the fastest man in the game. And he would out-run any of the modern players today." In addition to his baseball skills, he was also a natural-born entertainer. Performing well before game time, he would delight fans by exercising his famous juggling act, in which several Cardinal teammates would join. To amuse himself and onlookers, Martin would also bounce a ball off the end of a bat while walking all the way from center field to the dugout. Still bouncing the ball on the bat with one arm, he would tip his hat to the fans in the first row and disappear down the dugout steps. He was one of the biggest pranksters on the club, constantly getting the Cardinals kicked out of one hotel or another. His favorite form of mischief was dropping a bag of water out of a hotel window, scaring and dampening some innocent passerby.

"One time," Durocher recalled, "Frankie [Frisch] was the target. He was talking to someone outside our hotel in New York, and Pep let him have it. Good Lord—if it had hit Frank directly, it probably would've killed him. But it exploded a few feet nearby, and Frisch was soaked. He charged up the stairs to Pepper's room, where he was sitting by an open, wet windowsill. Wide-eyed and innocent, Pepper said, 'Gee Frank—you don't think *I'd* do that to you, would you?'"

Always looking for a dare, he was also the ringleader of group tomfoolery on the club. One night, Martin, Medwick, and Dean busted into a hotel banquet dinner for a boys' club, posing as repairmen. They announced that the purpose of their visit was to "re-do the place." Diz said to the emcee, "Just keep going—you won't bother us." The speaker tried to continue, but the three made all kinds of noise; especially Martin, who was banging away on a perfectly good wall with a sledgehammer. Medwick was using a knife to pointlessly cut into the floor, and Dean was weaving his way around the tables, carrying a stepladder and bumping into everybody. With all of the commotion, the emcee finally stopped talking. When this happened, Diz walked up to the microphone and said, "Well, if you're not going to talk, I will. Let me handle this." Within seconds, the boys recognized him, and were overjoyed. Martin and Medwick also came over, both smiling from ear to ear. The audience had the time of its life. Still afterwards, Durocher noted, the Cardinals were again kicked out of their hotel.

Another favorite gag of Martin's was to put sneezing powder on the blades of ceiling fans in hotel lobbies. He would sit behind a newspaper, peeking out every so often to view his carnage of bothered patrons. Whenever the Cardinals checked out, it became standard procedure for Frisch to be called into the hotel manager's office—to explain why garbage cans had been set on fire, why underwear was hanging out the window, or why somebody had billed $25 worth of beer to Frisch's room.

What was not a laughing matter to Pepper, however, was anything that involved competition. One of his hobbies was race-car driving, and Martin had been challenged by a neighbor one day to tour the local streets at an unlawful pace. The result was Pepper being an hour late to the locker room for the game that day, upon which the manager exploded.

"Where the hell have you been?" Frisch blared, as Martin tried to sneak quietly over to his locker.

"But Frank, this guy bet he could beat me, and I had to show 'em," Pep said.

"Well," grumbled Frisch, relenting a little. "How much did ya beat the bum for?"

"A gallon of ice cream."

Martin ducked as a Frisch-propelled chair flew from across the room.

Martin's burning desire to win carried over the to baseball field as well. As he made the switch to third base later in his career, he began to develop a sore back. Knowing this, opposing teams began to bunt on him incessantly. This continued until he became so angry he called time-out in the middle of a game, and called first baseman Rip Collins to the pitcher's mound for a conference.

"Ripper," he said, "the next time those bastards bunt, forget about the bag and back up the runner. I'm gonna plunk him right in the noggin."

And sure enough, the next opponent to bunt dropped like a ton of bricks about two-thirds of the way down to first, the victim of a rocket shot to the head that came from across the infield. Word soon after spread around the league about the fate of would-be drag bunters in Sportsman's Park, and the strategy ceased to exist.

He actions were indeed unpredictable. "Pepper Martin has developed a new eccentricity which has everybody guessing," observed W.H. James in the middle of the 1934 season. "When he takes a healthy swing at the ball his bat is apt to slip out of his hands and go in any direction. Sometimes it just misses the umpire, and a few days ago it grazed the shins of the coach at third." James went on to suggest that Martin look into using the rosin bag.

He remained a favorite with Cardinal followers until his retirement in 1944. In the ultimate compliment, Frisch once told the press, "The best thing a manager could have is nine Pepper Martins on the field."

Lip Service

Nothing ever meant more to Leo Durocher than winning a baseball game. He summarized his approach as succinctly as possible. "If I was playing third base, and my mother was rounding third with the winning run, I'd trip her. Oh, I'd pick her up, dust her off, and say, 'Sorry, Mom,' but *nobody* beats me."

It was, unfortunately, a freak accident that brought Durocher to St. Louis as the Cardinals shortstop. Staggering in with a .217 batting average with the Cincinnati Reds at the end of the 1932 season, Durocher envisioned at least another year for himself in the Queen City. It was during that off-season, however, that misfortune hit St. Louis. Regular Cardinals' shortstop Charley Gelbert, an avid hunter, was tracking game in a wooded area of Pennsylvania in the fall of 1932. Slipping on some wet ground, his gun discharged accidentally, and shot through his left leg. He would not play baseball for another three years, as he filled his time as a football coach at Gettysburg College before attempting an unsuccessful comeback with the Cardinals in 1936.

Rickey was willing to pay a heavy price to get Durocher, and pay he did. After toying with the idea of moving Frisch to shortstop (and placing an aged Rogers Hornsby at second, who was reacquired after his stint with the Cubs), he sent infielder Sparky Adams and pitchers Allyn Stout and Paul Derringer to the Reds for Durocher. Derringer would become one of the dominant National League pitchers of the 1930s. In Leo, however, the Cardinals received solid defense up the middle.

No one in baseball was a finer dresser, pool player, or defensive shortstop than Durocher. His pool hall run-ins would include many of

The slick-fielding, quick-witted shortstop of the Cardinals, Leo "The Lip" Durocher. (From the collections of the St. Louis Mercantile Library at the University of Missouri—St. Louis.)

the day's finest billiards players such as Frank Taberski and John McEhelleny. As for his handling of a baseball stick, Frisch would say, "Any hitting that Leo gives us is a bonus. He'd be a big help to any club if he couldn't hit a lick." Despite his lack of ability as a batter, Durocher did not lack confidence in himself. Before the 1934 season began, he bet Frisch a whole wardrobe of autumn clothes that he would hit .300 for the year (he would wind up at .260 with 30 doubles, figures he and Frisch were nonetheless pleased about). A genuine leader, Durocher was Frisch's on-field captain, agile double-play partner, and vocal neighbor in arguments with umpires. A common sight at St. Louis games was the two standing ear-to-ear, spitting disgruntled words at the men officiating the bases.

Durocher's fiery demeanor would fuel him through six major league decades as a player and manager, a tenure that few have matched. His playing career began as a backup to Mark Koenig on the powerful Yankee teams of the 1920s. For a short while, Leo's roommate on that club was Babe Ruth. The Bambino would be the one to later dub Leo "The All-American Out" (referring to his capabilities as a hitter), but the two remained close friends. Unable to supplant Koenig at shortstop, he moved on to Cincinnati in 1930 before moving once again to become the Cardinals' regular shortstop three years later in the 1933 season.

The media seemed to take great amusement in labeling Durocher's hitting skills. Printed in St. Louis, *The Sporting News* called him "the most dangerous .250 hitter in either league." During a hot-hitting stretch in August of 1934, St. Louis papers referred to him as "Captain Slug." Due to his brash personality, Durocher was generally disliked but respected around baseball, both within and outside of the Cardinals organization. The on-field authority that Frisch delegated to him was not always appreciated by the other St. Louis players. Once at a game in Cincinnati, Collins narrowly missed being tagged out on a play because of refusing to slide, and Durocher exploded on him, saying that he should be fined for such an act. When Collins angrily yelled back, Frisch stood by Leo's side, stating that he was given authority to make such comments. Durocher was not slow to point out when a player was letting the team down. One of Leo's greatest dislikes was when pitchers on his team took long amounts of time in between pitches. From his shortstop position, he would kick the dirt harder and harder with each passing second. "Show me a guy who takes his time on the mound," he observed, "and I'll show you a damned loser."

Despite his tremendous intensity and appetite for winning, a major rift developed between Durocher and other team members for these types of things. Another example was when he bore witness against Dizzy Dean (on the side of Frisch) in a later incident in 1934, in which Dean destroyed his uniforms in the clubhouse and walked off the team in protest of a fine. On this occasion once again, the players felt that Durocher was a pawn of the management (Breadon, Rickey, and Frisch).

At times, Frisch and Durocher did not see eye-to-eye on baseball matters, and the St. Louis papers exacerbated the situation—as if a larger power struggle was taking place between the manager and the captain. "Nonsense," Durocher said later. "Frank was a fine manager, one of the best. He and I argued all the time, but it was only with mutual respect for each other." However, it was speculated that because of these disagreements, Leo was shipped off to Brooklyn in 1937. In fact, some of the Cardinal players did indeed feel that Durocher was a better baseball tactician than Frisch. Regardless of the authority in charge, however, team loyalty was the bottom line for Leo. "The '34 Cardinals were the best club I've ever been associated with," he said. "We fought amongst ourselves, yes, but God forbid if anybody picked a fight with *us*, because then they'd have to lick all twenty-three Cardinals."

Despite being a team leader, however, Durocher had his own problems with the Cardinals' management. Like so many other players around the league at the time, Leo was asked to take a salary cut before the 1934 season began due to the struggling economy. His cut, however, was quite drastic: about 40 percent less than his 1933 pay. He regarded the request as "most unfair," he told the *St. Louis Star-Times*. "I realize that conditions require most of us to accept smaller salaries," he admitted. "But when you ask a man to take $5,000 instead of $8,500—that's too much.... I don't think the Cardinals can be serious in asking me to accept that kind of salary." This type of salary bickering was going on, interestingly enough, while Branch Rickey was refusing to budge on his own $40,000 rate.

The one player on the Cardinals that Durocher could not figure out was Martin. From his shortstop position, Durocher would need to constantly yell to Martin to get ready for the next pitch. Often, Pepper would have his glove tucked under his arm as he loaded a fresh wad of tobacco in his cheek, and then gaze aimlessly into the stands—all while the pitcher was beginning his delivery. Also, Durocher would point out years later that Martin never wore a protective cup, armor that is normally donned by men who play the perilous third base position. "I've seen him get hit by the ball in every corner of his body, except the important one," Leo noted. "He was just a lucky man, I guess. But that's the way Pepper was—never wore a cup, an undershirt, or sanitary socks, neither—just his cap, jersey, pants, stirrups, and shoes. I suppose he was comfortable that way." Despite the differences in backgrounds, personalities, and social acquaintances between Martin and Durocher, they together formed an iron-clad tandem; few balls would get through the left side of the infield at Sportsman's Park. John Lardner of the *New York Post* wrote of the pair, "Between them they have more energy and fire than you'll find in the entire rosters of many clubs." Durocher could go either direction as quickly as any shortstop in the game, and Martin, in adjusting to his switch from centerfield, maintained his cat-like quickness and powerful arm. Not blessed with soft hands, Martin would frequently play a hard liner off his chest, recover, and fire a laser beam across the infield to barely nab the runner at first.

Durocher always asserted the Martin was the toughest player he ever saw. "Pepper played with a broken finger and nobody knew it until he threw the ball across the diamond and yards of bandage came following behind it," he remembered. "When the writers asked him about it after the game, Pepper said, 'It's only a small bone.'"

Leo always found time to keep up with the elite social scene of the day. He was seen everywhere around town, and usually with friends of great influence. During the 1934 season he married Grace Dozier, a highly-respected St. Louis businesswoman. This was Durocher's second marriage, the first ending with a divorce settlement just before the start of the '34 season. The first marriage, to a woman named Ruby Hartley, had all of its troubles well-documented in the St. Louis newspapers. She had been accused, by Durocher and his attorney, of romantically visiting Crosley Field peanut vendor Charles McDonald during her stay in Cincinnati. Leo also contended, in court, that she possessed a serious drinking problem. Mrs. Durocher charged him with physical abuse and financial nonsupport. The key witness for Leo turned out to be his mother, Clara Durocher, who happened to be a maid in the hotel where Ruby was sharing a room with McDonald. Upon this new-found revelation, the attorney for Mrs. Durocher panicked, and charged Leo with having his own extramarital affairs. This was evidenced, he said, by letters signed by girls' names addressed to him. Leo dismissed the letters by referring to them simply as "fan mail."

Judge Charles Hoffman of St. Louis County Domestic Relations Court granted a divorce decree to Mr. Durocher, although custody of the couple's three-year-old daughter Barbara was given to Ruby, as agreed upon by Leo. "Just happy to have it behind me," he said afterwards. "Now I can concentrate on helping the fellas to a pennant."

Despite devoting the best days of his playing career to the Cardinals, Leo got a chance to truly showcase his leadership skills when Larry MacPhail of the Brooklyn Dodgers hired him as player-manager in 1939. When he would bring the Dodgers back to Sportsman's Park for a series in St. Louis, the stands would be full, with eyes curious in anticipation—waiting for Durocher to once again display his fiery temperament. They were not disappointed.

"You can't be a nice guy in his business," he remarked forcefully. "Nice guys finish last."

Harpo and the Supporting Cast

While the centerpieces of the Gas House display were Dean, Medwick, Martin, and Durocher, the remaining players filled their specific roles to make the team a functioning, furious unit. Frisch had a deep offensive bench at his disposal, including pinch hitters from both sides of the plate and ample defensive replacements at the necessary positions. Perhaps the team's only shortcoming was a relatively weak bullpen, which lost Frisch's trust over the course of the season. Indicative of this was the fact that Paul and Dizzy Dean combined to appear in 89 games, or 58 percent of the season total.

At the plate in 1934, Medwick was actually outdone statistically by an obscure first baseman named James "Rip" Collins. Coming out of the coal fields of Pennsylvania, the switch-hitting Collins came to the Cardinals in 1931. After the popular Jim Bottomley was dealt to the Reds in 1932, few expected Collins to be able to fill his shoes. "Sunny Jim" was the darling of the media and fans in St. Louis; he also produced a record of 12 runs batted in in one game, a mark that was tied in 1993 by another Cardinal, Mark Whiten. Collins, however, soon won his own respect in the fifth slot of the Cardinals' lineup. He was often criticized for being slow afoot in the field, but he gloved the ball with soft hands and handled low throws well. The home folks of Altoona, Pennsylvania, became so proud of Jimmy that they once offered him a lifetime membership to the local Lions' Club when the Cardinals came to Pittsburgh for a series with the Pirates. Collins was very popular with his teammates, and usually was second only to Martin in practical jokes played on his colleagues. He was also one of the few switch hitters in the major leagues in the early 1930s.

The rightfielder was Jack Rothrock, the only player in the National League in 1934 to play in all of his team's games. Furthermore, his 647 at bats was second only to the 649 of the Philadelphia A's' Doc Cramer in all of baseball. These statistics help illustrate how Rothrock provided a sense of stability for Frisch amidst the eccentricities of the other players. Rothrock was simply a quiet, polite, handsome, likable man who gave everything he had to baseball each day on the field. He batted in the two-slot nearly every day, and moved Martin from the leadoff spot effectively around the bases by pulling the ball from

Jack Rothrock, the Cardinals' steady rightfielder who played in all of the team's 153 games in 1934. (From the collections of the St. Louis Mercantile Library at the University of Missouri–St. Louis.)

the left side of the batter's box. Possessing good speed and a powerful arm, he was easily the Cardinals' best defensive outfielder as well. Beginning in 1925, he spent eight years in the American League with the Boston Red Sox. In his final season with the Red Sox in 1932 he hit .196 and was sent to the minors. Rickey saw something in him, however, and stole him away from Boston for a song.

In centerfield was a platoon of fast-legged but weak-armed defenders, Ernie Orsatti and Chick Fullis. Spectators at Sportsman's Park constantly expected Orsatti to crash into the concrete wall; his reckless abandon caused him to always look for a dare. "The Showboat," as he was called, carried a 5'8", 150-pound frame that was commonly seen flopping somewhere in the outfield. A slap hitter, Orsatti was a consistent high-average batter due to his speed and the ability to hit the ball on the ground. During the off-season, he maintained a modest acting career, actually becoming quite well known in Hollywood circles for his willingness as a stunt man. His brother was a casting agent in Los

Angeles and would receive frequent wires from Ernie inquiring about possibilities for roles. While obnoxious and over-confident on the field, he was just as personable and pleasant off of it, and was a favorite among the other Cardinal players. Like Durocher, Orsatti found himself in the middle of salary negotiations with Rickey before the 1934 season began. "Mr. Rickey insisted that I take a 25 percent cut [from his 1933 rate]," Orsatti told the *St. Louis Star-Times*. "That's too much." Rickey was reported as responding, "If Orsatti's prospects in the movies are as encouraging as he outlined to me, he would be foolish not to quit baseball."

A competent right-handed batter and a good outfielder, Fullis was acquired in a trade from Philadelphia in the middle of the 1934 season. He was discovered by John McGraw while playing in an amateur game in Macon, Georgia, in 1927. Though striking out three times in the game, Fullis impressed McGraw so much with his defensive skills that he was signed on the spot to a Giants contract. In addition to sharing centerfield with Orsatti, Fullis would occasionally sub for Medwick in defensive situations. His moments of hitting glory were few and far between, although he did deliver a 4-for-4 performance in a crucial game in the early pennant drive of late August, 1934. Gene Moore also found some duty in the outfield.

The Gas House Gang was adequately stocked at the catcher position. Virgil "Spud" Davis was acquired from the Phillies in spring training, as he yearned to leave after Philadelphia's dismal 60–92 record in 1933. Now with a "first division" club, the veteran arrived at camp eager for the '34 campaign to begin. "Who wouldn't throw his arm off for this bunch after getting away from the Phillies?" he proudly stated during workouts in March. A fearsome hitter and a gifted receiver, he was pictured to be an able replacement for Jimmie Wilson, who was shipped to Philadelphia for his lack of hitting and dissension with Frisch. A big target at 6'1", 200 pounds, the Cardinals' pitchers loved to throw to the soft hands that Davis offered. The Alabama native kept to himself most times and was one player for which everyone on the team had genuine respect. He was also superstitious, often asking pitcher Dazzy Vance to chant a Seminole Indian prayer over his bat.

Davis, however, lost his job in the middle of the 1934 season to a heavy-hitting rookie named Bill DeLancey. A left-handed batter with a powerful throwing arm, DeLancey was being hailed the game's next great catcher. He finished the 1934 season with a .316 batting average and 13 home runs in only 253 at bats. Before the season even began,

Rickey asserted that DeLancey had the talent to start for any team in the league; toward the end of the year, J. Roy Stockton noted, "When the star rookies of the league are named, Bill should be near the head of the list." His career, however, was cut tragically short. He contracted tuberculosis in 1936, and his playing days would end at the age of 23. Bill DeLancey died on his birthday, November 28, 1946, at the age of 35—ending prematurely, perhaps, what could have been the greatest career any catcher may have had.

The strongest aspect of the Cardinals' bench was at the infield positions. Whitehead played superb defense at third as well as second and short, and batted .277 in 332 times at bat. In addition to the distinction of being the only Phi Beta Kappa scholar in baseball, he was also a 1931 graduate of the University of North Carolina. The *Philadelphia Enquirer* once said of him, "He probably could answer every question you asked on philosophy, psychology, and astronomy and then tie you in knots with a few of his own. If you seated him at a banquet table he probably would not make one mistake if they put seven different forks in front of him." Whitehead would later be sent to the Giants in 1936 to secure his own starting position. He was one of Dizzy Dean's closest friends on the Gang—which is ironic, for on July 11, 1936, at Sportsman's Park, the new Giant Whitehead hit a line drive back at Diz, striking him on the forehead, and rendering him unconscious in front of a terrified crowd. Diz was fine after a few moments, and the two would later laugh about it. Late in his life, Whitehead testified that Dean was the greatest pitcher he had ever seen. Also useful to Frisch as a left-handed batter was Pat Crawford, and he too played strong defense at each of the infield positions.

"I figure it'll take 95 wins to take the pennant," Dizzy Dean proclaimed in spring training 1934. "I know I'll win 30, and Paul's good for 25. That leaves the rest of the fellas only having to take 40 altogether—piece a cake." Paul Dean had perhaps more marketing done to promote his name—and all done by one person, his brother—than any pitcher yet to throw a strike in a major league game. Granted, he went 22–7 for Columbus of the American Association in 1933, the Cardinals' top farm club. But who was he to be holding out for more money before even playing in a single game, the Cardinal bosses wondered? Of course, they understood that Diz had a lot to do with Paul's thinking. But Rickey knew that such an attitude could be contagious, especially along bloodlines, and it wouldn't be long before Paul had his own ways and means of commanding attention.

During his first two weeks in St. Louis, the newspapers placed the nickname of "Harpo" on Paul. Harpo, of course, was the Marx brother who never spoke. (Really, when speaking of Deans or Marxs, what was left to be said when the other brother was finished?) Every preseason stop Diz made, every public appearance, speech, or media shoot, Harpo was there to give a quick, affirming nod to his brother's proclamations— be they baseball-related or not. The general forecast was, in fact, that Paul would eventually be even better than Diz. He already had his brother's fastball, and delivered it with a sidearm motion which produced a tailing action. Unfortunately, injuries stemming from a lack of care for his arm (as with Diz) would shorten Paul's career.

The third pitcher in the starting rotation was James Otto "Tex" Carleton of Comanche, Texas. A lean, strong man at 6'1", 190 pounds, Carleton relied on his curveball which, like Paul, came from the side. He joined Whitehead and Frisch as the only other college graduate on the Cardinals' roster, coming from Texas Christian University. Always at odds with Diz, Medwick, or somebody else on the club, the 27-year-old righthander had a surly disposition. In particular, he was not fond of Dizzy's boasting, the organization's coddling of Diz, nor was he sold on the talent level of Paul. "A busher," Carleton described him (alluding to the term "bush league" often used in those days, referring to one of only minor league ability). "He won't last a month in the big leagues," Tex said of the junior Dean in spring training of 1934.

During the 1933 season, Carleton involved himself in one of the greatest-pitched games in baseball history. The Cardinals had marched into the Polo Grounds in New York on July 2nd, and Carleton was matched up against ace screwballer Carl Hubbell of the Giants. The two pitched a scoreless battle into the sixteenth inning, when Carleton was lifted for pinch-hitter Crawford. Hubbell would continue on to the eighteenth inning when the Giants scored to take home a 1–0 win. "King Carlos" struck out 13 and walked none, en route to an MVP season with a league-low 1.66 earned run average. Carleton would finish the '33 campaign with 17 wins, and was third in the league in strikeouts behind Hubbell and Dean.

Lefthanders Bill Walker and "Wild Bill" Hallahan comprised the fourth and fifth spots in the starting rotation. Walker, a local product from East St. Louis, Illinois, enjoyed modest success. Walker was nearly Durocher's equal as a dresser (allegedly possessing, at one time, 30 tailor-made suits), and had been a Giant for the previous six years before coming home to the Cardinals. He would contribute a 12–4 record with a 3.12 ERA in 1934, but a chronic sore shoulder limited his throwing to 153 innings.

Hallahan was the enigma of the staff, if not the entire roster. The starting pitcher for the National League in the first All-Star Game the year before, he would slump to an 8–12 record in '34, and was extremely fortunate to maintain a 4.26 ERA. League batters lighted him up for 195 hits in 163 innings, and control problems (which gave birth to his nickname) continued to plague him. The press in rival cities had no sympathy. "Hallahan's toboggan slide has whittled Frisch staff down to the Dean brothers," wrote Bill McCullough of the *Brooklyn Times-Union* as early as mid–June in the 1934 season, "and nowhere do the books show a team winning the pennant with two pitchers."

The relief corps offered little true relief, but at least a veteran presence occupied the area. Called upon frequently were 44-year-old Jesse "Pop" Haines and the 43-year-old Vance. They providing some quality innings, but unfortunately, were not able to atone for the poor performance of the rest of the unit. Cardinals starting pitchers labored through a league-high 78 complete games in 1934, as Frisch's confidence in the bullpen dwindled down the stretch. Haines' longevity was due in large part to his knuckleball, a pitch that would make him one of the National League's most formidable starters during the 1920s. A Cardinal for the previous 14 seasons, Haines entered the '34 season relegated a relief-only role for the first time in his career.

Vance may well have been the best pitcher in the National League during the 1920s. He led the circuit in strikeouts for seven consecutive seasons (1922–28) while with the Brooklyn Dodgers, and had been in the major leagues since 1912. Pitching in Ebbets Field in Brooklyn, Vance used the surroundings to his advantage. He would wear a tattered, long-sleeve white shirt under his jersey, which would flap like a flag when he pitched the ball. In Brooklyn, the whites from the morning wash would hang on the clotheslines from the nearby apartment buildings and be in direct view of the hitters from centerfield. Batters complained that Vance's shirt added to the confusion, but no prohibition was made against it. He was picked up in a mid–1934 trade with the Cincinnati Reds, and the Homasassa, Florida, native would end his career the following year back in Brooklyn, totaling lifetime sums of 197 wins and over 2,000 strikeouts.

The only lefthander out of the bullpen for the Cardinals was 27-year-old Jim Mooney. The former school teacher from Mooresburg, Tennessee, endured a tough season in 1934, with a lofty 5.47 ERA and only two wins. Burleigh Grimes, Flint Rhem, and Jim Lindsey—with an average age of 34—rounded out a venerable and generally ineffective relief staff. Dizzy Dean got the call quite often, making 17 relief appearances in addition to his 33 starts. Even Martin would make an appearance on the hill in 1934, throwing two innings of scoreless, one-hit ball (he would talk Frisch into letting him throw one particular game, on August 19 against the Boston Braves. Pepper said, "I've got a high hard one, Frankie, and I think it will fool the batters"). Martin claimed to have a variety of pitches, all of which had great velocity, but none of which had any control—just like his throws from third base.

How such a diverse collection of individuals coalesced as a great team is indeed mysterious. Some tried to explain it, but most were resigned to the fact that it was simply a group of people who hated to lose. "In Medwick, Whitehead, and Martin," the *Philadelphia Inquirer* brought as an example, "we have three types of men as far apart in temperament, education, and social standing as one can hope to find."

Part Three

The Season

"...They [the Cardinals] possess playing qualities
that catch the eye. Flash and dash, speed,
and an ostentatious aggressiveness."

—Gary Schumacher,
New York Evening Journal, May 9, 1934

Opening Day, 1934

Professional baseball was like any other business in the United States during the 1930s. Public buying power was at an all-time low, and no matter how good the product was, cash-paying customers were in short supply. As the 1934 season began, owners once again toyed with the idea of night baseball, though the mere notion of playing after dark was blasphemy in the minds of most. Television would not make its appearance for another fifteen years, and even the revenue generated from radio broadcasts was scant. New, creative measures were needed to bring fans to the ballpark, and to assure them that their hard-earned money would be well spent. To make the marketing matters worse, the league became somewhat pitching-heavy in '31, '32, and '33, and the owners, fearful of losing more money from the Depression, were compelled to return more of an offensive product to the field for the fans. During the Cardinals' championship season of 1931, no team in the National League batted .300, which was a stark contrast to the season before. It was assumed that an offensive game was what the fans wanted to see, so adjustments were made.

The National League, ironically, offered the idea of having a tenth hitter in the lineup who would bat for the pitcher. The extra man would be called the "designated batter," but the American League did not agree to the experiment. Of course, it would be the American League who would introduce the designated hitter to the baseball world in 1973.

In one effort to boost attendance, the so-called "New Deal" baseball made its appearance in the major leagues in 1934. Named after the Depression-era social policies of President Roosevelt, the new ball was designed to help bring the game out of its own economic doldrums. The ball was wound tighter, which would supposedly create harder hit balls and more of them. The idea was that a more offensive game would cause more people to come to the ballpark. However, some observers weren't so sure. "It takes more than a home run to bring out the fans," asserted the *Post-Dispatch*. "Such as a little pocket money." How would it affect the pitchers? Dizzy Dean, of course, wasn't fazed. "Look for fastball pitchers like me to make that new white apple sail," he said. By July of 1934, however, the National League batting average was up over twenty points from the previous season.

At the close of the 1933 season, the Giants had marched to their first pennant in nine years and their first world championship since 1922. Player-Manager Bill Terry led the club with a .322 average and Mel Ott hit 23 home runs, but those were two of the few offensive bright spots on a club that relied heavily on its starting pitching. Carl Hubbell, Hal Schumacher, Freddie Fitzsimmons, and Roy Parmalee each started at least 32 games, as Hubbell recorded 10 shutouts, a 1.66 earned run average and took home the league's MVP award. Because their offense was so sporadic, however, few expected the Giants to hang in the pennant race. The team batted .263, good for only a fifth-place tie among the eight National League clubs in that category. Third baseman Johnny Vergez joined Ott as the only other Giant with double figures in home runs (16), as Lefty O'Doul joined Terry as the club's only other .300 hitter (.306) in having just 229 at bats.

What the Giants did have, however, was a stellar defense to go with their outstanding pitching. Blondy Ryan filled in ably for the injured Travis Jackson at shortstop, and little Hughie Critz from Starkville, Mississippi, displayed great range at second. At the age of 24, Jo-Jo Moore was emerging as a supreme flychaser in left field, and with his speed would ultimately push centerfielder Kiddo Davis out of a job at that position.

Basically the same Giants club would take the field in 1934, with one notable exception from their bench. During the '33 season, a 27-year-old first baseman named Sam Leslie was having trouble cracking the lineup—which is understandable, with the great Terry manning the position. Leslie had been with the club for four years, and McGraw could not find another position for him. He was released in the middle of the 1933 season, and picked up by the Giants' crosstown rivals, the Brooklyn Dodgers. In 364 at bats for the Dodgers for the rest of the season, Leslie batted an unimposing .286. Better things were to come, however. By the end of the '34 campaign, Leslie checked in with a .332

mark, which placed him near the top of the National League batters, and he led the Dodgers with 102 runs batted in.

Most believed that Chicago and Pittsburgh would give the Giants the most trouble in 1934, with the Cardinals teetering between being a "first division" and "second division" club. Chicago improved their offense tremendously after the '33 season in acquiring outfielder Chuck Klein from the Phillies. While playing for a Philadelphia team that finished 60–92 in 1933, Klein won the Triple Crown in the National League, finishing first in home runs (28), runs batted in (120), and batting average (.368), as well as hits (223) and slugging percentage (.602). Some predicted that his numbers would even be greater in '34, as he would be playing half his games in hitter-friendly Wrigley Field. Like many of the other teams, the Cubs had a manager who was also a player in 35-year-old Charlie Grimm. Grimm split time at first base with a hot new player acquired from Philadelphia, Don Hurst. In exchange for Hurst the Cubs, like the Giants the year before, gave up a truly gifted first base prospect in Dolph Camilli. Camilli went on to great things with the Phillies and Dodgers (including an MVP award with the latter in '41), while Hurst hit a paltry .199 in 151 times at bat for Chicago in 1934.

The Cubs were strong and deep all around, and it looked like their offense would carry them. Billy Jurges and Woody English split time at shortstop, and they were the two mediocre hitters in otherwise solid lineup. Leading the hitting attack, along with Klein and Grimm, were fleet-footed centerfielder Kiki Cuyler (.338) and third baseman Stan Hack (.289). Billy Herman batted .303 while playing an exceptional second base, while the spiritual leader of the club was catcher Gabby Hartnett, who chipped in with 22 home runs, 90 RBIs, a .299 average, and superb defense behind the plate. Hartnett would rise to greater fame in the second half of the 1938 season, when he took over the managerial duties from Grimm and nailed the legendary "Homer in the Gloamin"— a dinger in the darkness of early evening at Wrigley, as the Cubs beat the Pirates in extra innings to jump into first place on the second-to-last day of the season. On the mound, the Cubs had the "Arkansas Hummingbird," Lon Warneke, to lead the way. Later finishing his career with the Cardinals (and becoming a major league umpire after retiring as a player), Warneke notched 22 victories in '34, followed by Guy Bush (18), Pat Malone (14), and Bill Lee (13).

An unstable pitching staff made the Pirates an unknown commodity before the season began. Everyone knew they could hit, for they possessed the Waner brothers, Paul and Lloyd, known as "Big Poison" and "Little Poison" respectively. The Waners turned out to be so good, in fact, that their hometown—Harrah, Oklahoma, with a population of 753 at the time—became the smallest to have two Hall of Fame players. Dizzy Dean said that Paul Waner was the toughest hitter he ever faced, and that Lloyd was much the same. Along with them, young shortstop Arky Vaughan (with a .333 average) made a strong impression around the league, and Gus Suhr continued to be one of the finest all-around first basemen in the game. Cardinal castoff Tommy Thevenow solidified the infield with adequate play at second base.

On the mound, the Pirates struggled to find throwers. Waite Hoyt, who was the top pitcher on the famed '27 Yankee club (that beat the Pirates in the World Series), wound up with good numbers but had the stamina to start only 15 games, with 33 other appearances out of the bullpen. Larry French, Ralph Birkofer, Bill Swift, and Red Lucas all recorded double-digit victories in '34, but all also had more hits allowed than innings pitched. With an uncertain pitching staff heading into the season, Pittsburgh was aware that they would need to outslug their opponents.

Also flirting with the first division was the Boston Braves, who sported superstar centerfielder Wally Berger and his power hitting. In Brooklyn, Casey Stengel had taken over for the departed Max Carey, as the struggling Dodgers tried to regain a winning form that led them to an impressive third-place finish in 1932 with an 81–73 mark. Stengel had a good on-field leader at his disposal in catcher Al Lopez, and a fast outfield of Buzz Boyle, Len Koenecke, and Danny Taylor to go along with the heavy hitting of Leslie. The pitching staff was led by the hard-throwing, whiskey-loving youngster with the unique name of Van Lingle Mungo, who would start 38 games in 1934 to lead the National League.

Forecasters expected the final two positions in the standings to belong to the Cincinnati Reds and the Philadelphia Phillies, in no particular order. The Reds were led by former Cardinals Jim Bottomley and Chick Hafey, as well as a developing young catcher named Ernie Lombardi. Bottomley had been pushed out of St. Louis with the arrival of Collins at first base, but "Sunny Jim" still held the National League record for RBIs in a game at that time. Hafey, one of the other stars of the Cardinal pennant winners of 1928, '30, and '31, was known for his bespectacled eyes on the field and his fleetness of foot. Mark Koenig was a veteran of the great Yankee teams of the late '20s, and provided more experience at second base. But Cincinnati could not overcome a porous defense and a pitching staff that had only one bona fide starter in former Cardinal Paul Derringer. In fact, the top three starters for the Reds—Derringer, Benny Frey, and Silas Johnson—combined to lose a staggering 59 games over the course of the season.

The Phillies' .284 team batting average was third-best in the league in 1934, but they too suffered from a thin mound staff. Rookie Curt Davis from Greenfield, Missouri provided 19 wins in 51 appearances and sparkling ERA of 2.96, but he didn't receive much help. Phil Collins, Snipe Hansen, and Euel Moore were usually knocked out of games, and the midseason acquisition of Camilli for the first base job did not help much.

The indomitable Giants waltzed through spring training of 1934 with a swagger, and opened the season as 8–5 favorites to repeat as World Series champions. Before spring workout began, however, reporters had already received an ominous tidbit from Giants manager Terry in January. The last National Leaguer to hit .400 (.401 in 1930), Terry possessed a very cool confidence on the outlook for his club. The reporters circled around "Memphis Bill," and they were interested to know his thoughts on the upcoming season. "Anyone want to bet a hat we don't win it again?" he challenged them with a smile. No takers, so the questions moved on. Who would give the Giants the most trouble in '34? "Probably Chicago, the Pirates, and maybe St. Louis." One writer asked if local foe Brooklyn would pose a threat. Terry squinted his eyes in a puzzled state, scratched his head, and answered, "Brooklyn? Are they still in the league?" This drew a collection of laughs from the reporters, but none from the borough of Flatbush. Stengel, the newly-installed leader of the Flatbush club, immediately took exception to Terry's comment. "The first thing I want to say is that the Dodgers *are* still in the league," he told the *New York Herald-Tribune*. "Tell that to Bill Terry. And I don't care what you fellows call my club—the Daffiness Boys, the Screwy Scrubs, or anything, so long as they hustle."

Some of the New York writers knew what was in store for Terry and his Giants. "It doesn't take much to start a baseball war in Brooklyn," observed Dan Daniel of the *World-Telegram*. "Bill Terry's remark the other day about the Dodgers was like the shot that rang out on the bridge at Concord." Added Harry Nash of the *New York Post*, "It is amusing how quickly a Brooklynite can be aroused by a slur against the Dodgers. And if Bill Terry is as thin-skinned as some say he is, he is due for a miserable season so far as Giant-Dodger games are concerned."

But that was part of the personality of the Giants, much to the National League what the Yankees were to the American. They were the powerful, wealthy uncle, impervious to any challenge. Themselves underdogs in the previous season, the club now had placed the chip on its shoulder. Terry had made a smooth transition to managing the team from the legendary John McGraw, but this should have alerted him to another factor: a second McGraw graduate was running the team in St. Louis. Frankie Frisch had promising news for the St. Louis writers from the Cardinals' Bradenton, Florida, training site. "Fire [is] in the eyes of my players. I've never seen more aggressiveness in a team—and that goes for the New York Giants teams I played on in 1921, 1922, 1923, and 1924." McGraw, called by many the greatest manager in the history of the game, had recently passed away (February 25, 1934) and it was going on two years since he had relinquished control of the Giants to Terry. McGraw had ten National League pennants under his belt; now, the two disciples of the master were looking to lead their teams to the championship.

McGraw had stepped down as Giants manager on June 3, 1932, the same day that Lou Gehrig became the first player to hit four home runs in a single game; it was the McGraw story that grabbed all the headlines. He was 59 years old, had a variety of health problems, and could no longer handle the rigors of the job. The Giants were in last place, and he felt that the time was right. Typical of his surly disposition, his last official act as leader of the club was to file a protest with the National League over a disputed play. Terry, his beloved first baseman, was his hand-picked successor.

By Opening Day 1934, 40 of the 97 baseball writers polled across the land picked the Giants to land in first place once again, while only eight forecasted that the Cardinals would win the pennant. The New Yorkers would fire Carl Hubbell at the Phillies for the opener, and the Cardinals had their own star leading them off. Dizzy Dean, entering his third full season in the majors, had become the newest wonder of the game. In 1933, he had 26 complete games and 199 strikeouts, both league-highs. Nonetheless, the Cardinals ranked only fourth in the preseason National League poll, not expected to overtake the Giants, Cubs, and Pirates picked ahead of them.

The Cardinals made their 1934 debut on April 17 in St. Louis against the Pirates. Threatening skies in the St. Louis area had scared away many fans, while the lingering economic woes discouraged others from purchasing a ticket. To be sure, the Great Depression was continuing to wreak its havoc on baseball, and most clubs would once again, as in the several years preceding, experience a financial loss in 1934. A paltry assembly of 7,500, and along with a few hundred "knot-hole" boys, wandered into Sportsman's Park to see the Cardinals open the season. Among the attendees was St. Louis mayor Bernard Dickmann, who threw out the ceremonial first pitch. The home team did not disappoint.

They started off fast on Pittsburgh pitcher and St. Louis native Heine Meine, getting four runs in the first three innings. The assault continued on reliever Waite Hoyt, as Rip Collins smashed a run-scoring double in his first action since having back surgery on April 6, causing him to miss much of spring training. Pepper Martin added a pair of two-baggers of his own.

The witnesses saw Dean dominate the Pirates in the later innings, although he struggled slightly in the early going. After the fourth inning, no Pirate runner reached second base. He limited them to six hits in a complete game victory, 7–1. Charles Doyle, who covered the Pirates for the *Pittsburgh Sun-Telegraph*, noted that Dizzy's fastball "was smacking like a pistol in Spud Davis' mitt in the closing rounds." Medwick was another batting star, going 3-for-4 with two singles and a monstrous home run to left. Aside from the Medwick's round-tripper, a small brass band that played throughout the game was all that kept the sleepy group of spectators on its toes.

In other notable games on the first day of the season, Warneke fired a one-hit shutout for the Cubs as Chicago beat the Reds 6–0 in Cincinnati, and Hubbell beat Philadelphia 6–1 at the Polo Grounds in New York, yielding four hits which included a home run by Jimmie Wilson.

After a successful launch to the season by the senior Dean, great things of Paul Dean and a great crowd were expected for day number two; neither would surface. Fifteen home runs were hit across the league on the second day of the season, and four were in Sportsman's Park. The Pirates exacted revenge on the Dean family with a 7–6 beating of the Cardinals before a small meeting of 5,000 fans. Paul started strongly, fanning Lloyd Waner and Freddie Lindstrom to start the game. But that was followed by a Paul Waner single and Pie Traynor's homer to put Pittsburgh ahead 2–0. After falling behind 4–0, the Cards battled back to a 6–6 tie in the eighth inning. At that point, a solo home run by Harry Lavagetto, better known as "Cookie," won it for the Pirates. The blast was hit off of a weak inside fastball by Cardinals reliever Burleigh Grimes, who suffered the loss for the Redbirds.

The St. Louis newspapers viewed Paul's debut as a moderate success, considering he was facing the powerful Pittsburgh lineup in his first major league game. Some observers were concerned that Paul had only pitched six total innings in spring training, and that his lack of work had stunted his development. Diz put an end to any fear by adding, "Nah, don't worry 'bout Paul none. He may even be a greater pitcher than me, if that's possible."

In the finale of the opening series, it was Bill Hallahan's turn to take the mound. Frisch was confident that the southpaw could subdue the Waner brothers, Arky Vaughan, and Gus Suhr, all strong left-handed hitters for the Pirates. But "Wild Bill" was blasted from the field, leaving the Cardinals with a nine-run deficit after five innings, and was succeeded by Flint Rhem, another aging veteran from the bullpen making his first appearance in Sportsman's Park since 1932. Rhem gave up four runs in the sixth, three runs in the seventh, and Jim Mooney followed ineffectively. The Pirates banged out 19 hits, including six doubles and a triple in what turned out to be a 14–4 Cardinal loss. The St. Louis offensive effort was sporadic, as mediocre Pittsburgh starter Ralph Birkofer changed speeds effectively en route to receiving the outstanding run support. The Cardinals were also inept on defense, as Pirates third baseman and manager Pie Traynor was hit in the back by two throws on the same trip around the bases—once sliding into second and again sliding into home, two of five St. Louis errors on the day.

The next contest saw the Birds leave 12 runners on base, including six in scoring position, as the Cardinals dropped a 2–1 decision to the Cubs (despite 11 strikeouts from Tex Carleton). There was now a question as to whether the Cardinals were even a first-division team. "They're hustlin' and getting' dirty," Frisch would say in the clubhouse, wiping his graying temples and giving a sigh. "That's all I can ask for. Things will start coming our way." One of the Chicago runs came on a homer by Cubs pitcher Charlie Root in the third inning as Carleton grimaced in disbelief from the mound. Root had permitted the Cardinals to reach base in eight of the nine innings, but a lack of clutch hitting plagued the St. Louis men. The Cubs were off to a hot start, now 4–0 on the young season. The Giants were even better at 5–0.

An encouraging Sunday crowd of 14,000 on April 22 convened hoping that Dizzy Dean would start the Cards off on a winning streak. Interestingly, almost half of the spectators were sitting in the far-away seats for the affordable admission price of fifty cents. This was the Cubs' first real crack at Dean since last July when he struck out a record 17 batters at Wrigley Field in Chicago. It was during this game that Dean had made enemies with the Cubs, as he taunted the Chicago dugout (and Cubs pitcher Guy Bush in particular) during the entire affair.

So before their first meeting in 1934, Diz once again began strutting in front of the Chicago bench, and scowls were returned by the Cub players. But as events would unfold, the Cubs would get the revenge they sought—twice over. They chased Dizzy from the mound after eight hits and six runs over three innings, "The first victim of this wholesale batting orgy," announced the *St. Louis Globe-Democrat*. Brother Paul was offered up to the hungry hitters for six hits and two runs of his own in two innings of work. Diz gave gestures in reply when the Cubs whistled their good-byes in the third, as he trudged off the field with his head down and his mouth agape. Meanwhile, Warneke was throwing his second straight one-hitter of the season, completely thwarting the St. Louis attack. Five days earlier (on Opening Day) Warneke had 13 strikeouts and a lone base hit allowed in his 6–0 shutout of the Reds. He allowed two Cardinals to reach second base, and the final score was 15–2 with the Cubbies pounding out 22 hits. The Chicago assault was so complete that they could even afford to leave 13 runners on base. The onslaught was led by Chuck Klein's 4-for-6 performance, including a meteoric home run to right field which landed on Grand Avenue, barely grazing the top of the right field pavilion.

To add injury to insult, Medwick had to leave the game in the fourth inning, when he was spiked by teammate Gene Moore. Moore, a reserve outfielder, crashed into Medwick as the two pursued a flyball in the left-center gap off the bat of Babe Herman. The collision opened a gash on Ducky's leg, and he hobbled off the pasture as Herman coasted into third with a triple.

Traveling to Pittsburgh and needing a lift, the Cardinals faced the Pirates again on April 24. Taking the mound this time would be Jesse Haines, one of only six starts he would get all year. He pitched well, taking a 4–2 lead into the ninth. Then, in that final stanza, Freddie Lindstrom belted a three-run homer to win it for the Bucs 5–4. Although only six games into the season, word of dissension had leaked to the St. Louis newspapermen, and was printed. Frisch, however, vehemently denied any mutiny from the players, and the club responded with a 10–1 win two days later. In this game, Bill Hallahan had what would be one of his few strong outings of the year, and catcher Virgil

Davis supplied the offensive punch. "Spud" went 3-for-4 with a double and a home run.

The Cardinals went to the Windy City to play the Cubs on April 27. With a lot of bad blood still circulating between Dizzy and the north-siders, every hard slide and tight pitch created tension. Tex Carleton started the opener of the series for St. Louis, but Hallahan suffered the loss. Carleton was firing on all cylinders, but had to be lifted for a pinch hitter in the eleventh inning with the score tied 2–2. Cubs catcher Gabby Hartnett promptly singled home a run off of Wild Bill, and Warneke prevailed again—going all 11 innings for his fourth win in as many starts for the year.

The Cubs got second helpings of the Dean brothers the next day. In an almost carbon-copy of their last outing against Chicago, the visits of both Dizzy (three innings) and Paul (two) were short. Once again, Klein hit a mammoth home run, and Cubs pitcher Guy Bush got credit for the victory. After the game, Bush was quoted as saying, "The only thing those Deans are good for is pickin' cotton, and you can print that as loud as you want."

The Cardinals limped out of April with a 4–7 record. Much of the preseason hope had rested on the right arm of Paul Dean, and he had yet to respond. The Cardinals' offensive production for the first two weeks was led by Spud Davis, whose .395 average (15 for 38) was second only to the Giants' Mel Ott, batting .405 as May began. Virgil would not have to carry the St. Louis offensive attack for long, however. With Cincinnati in town on May 1, Rip Collins pounded two home runs onto the Sportsman's Park roof in an exciting 3–2 St. Louis victory in 11 innings. Collins and Medwick would develop a huge appetite for pitchers in May, as the move that sent Jim Bottomley to Cincinnati was starting to pay dividends. Pepper Martin added four hits, and the Cardinals used 17 players in the contest. Frisch was becoming more and more respected as a field tactician, and the Gas House aura was taking root.

On May 1, two weeks into the season, the National League standings looked like this:

	W	L	Pct.	GB
Chicago	10	2	.833	—
New York	8	3	.727	1.5
Boston	6	5	.515	3.5
Pittsburgh	5	5	.500	4

	W	L	Pct.	GB
Brooklyn	5	6	.455	4.5
St. Louis	4	7	.364	5.5
Cincinnati	3	8	.273	6.5
Philadelphia	3	8	.273	6.5

Paul Dean finally got his first major league win on May 3rd in St. Louis, as the Cardinals beat the Phillies 8–7, their third victory in a row, and lifted themselves to a .500 record (7–7) for the first time since April 18. It was actually a lame-duck victory for Paul as he relieved starter Flint Rhem in the sixth inning. Harpo was hit hard once again, and he was relieved by Jesse Haines. Philadelphia pounded out 14 hits. The Cardinals had 11 themselves, and Martin Haley of the *St. Louis Globe-Democrat* noted that "Of the twenty-five hits that drenched the premises one stood out above all the others." He was speaking of Medwick's Herculean blast to left in the fourth inning, a grand slam that broke a 2–2 tie. The Cardinals, however, needed a two-run double by Collins in the sixth to have enough for the victory. Medwick ended the day with three hits and five RBIs, and the Cardinals' bullpen came to the rescue to secure the win. At this point, Frisch was very skeptical about starting the younger Dean, fearing that another poor showing in such a role might severely damage his confidence. He felt that using Paul as a reliever, at least for the time being, would take a lot of the pressure off him.

While in town, Phillies manager Jimmie Wilson gave his side to the controversy that had presumably sent him packing from St. Louis— his argument with Frisch in July of 1933.

"All I know is that Frisch, right after being named manager, held a meeting and told us all he was going to run the club and wanted no suggestions from anyone," Wilson told the St. Louis papers. "Right after that I was taken out of the game for reasons unknown to me.

"Later while we were playing a game in Pittsburgh, an argument arose at the plate. The usual crowd assembled and I went up to the plate from the dugout and said a few words to Manager Gibson of the Pirates. Then Frisch turned to me and told me to get back on the bench and that he could run the game without me, or words to that effect. I then told Frisch a few things and that was the last that was said between us."

The Cardinals desperately needed a pitcher to step to the forefront, as the bullpen was already fatigued from overwork. On May 9, a taker was found. The Giants were in town, and Frisch handed the ball to Diz. Dean tossed a five-hitter and fanned seven—all in the first four innings—in beating the New Yorkers 4–0. It was the first shutout for a Cardinal pitcher on the year, as he allowed one Giant runner to reach third base. For New York, 20-year-old rookie Johnny "Jack" Salveson was making his first big-league start, and the Cards responded with a cascade of hits in the first three innings, in which they scored all their runs. Rothrock began the attack in with a double off the rightfield screen, and was promptly driven home by a Medwick single. After Orsatti walked in the Cardinals' second, Martin slashed a ball down the rightfield line that blew up chalk in barely landing fair, and scored Showboat Ernie with a double of his own. The loss knocked the Giants out of first place, as the Cubs assumed the top position.

Then, the following day was perhaps the most frightful and ominous of the summer—both in terms of baseball and the weather. The infamous Dust Bowl had been creeping its way from the Great Plains across the midsection of the country. Its storm reached St. Louis on May 10, having "swept southeastward from Nebraska and the Dakotas to envelop this town in a murky haze," wrote Tom Meany of the *New York World-Telegram*. Rising 10,000 feet into the air, the storm eerily obscured the sun as if to portend future evil. Men in the bleachers covered their mouths with handkerchiefs, and the game against the Giants that day was played in an unusual twilight for three o'clock. Less than five miles to the east, the mighty Mississippi River had desiccated to a modest creek. The dust would ultimately drift across most of the nation, sweeping into its clutches a total of 19 states and leaving destruction and sickness in its path. On a less important scale, it would also contribute to a Cardinals victory this day. Durocher hit two pop flies that Giants fielders would misplay into errors. These miscues prevented pitcher Hal Schumacher from picking up the win; he had been shutting out the Cardinals for five innings when the blunders began. St. Louis players seemed to navigate the inclement conditions ably, while the men from Harlem appeared to be lost at every turn. Although Medwick had his hitting streak snapped at 11 games, Martin, Rothrock, Frisch, Davis, and Durocher all had two hits apiece as the Cardinals won, 5–4, their 11th victory in their last 12 games. In losing a half-game to the idle Pirates, the Giants slipped behind Pittsburgh to third place.

Perhaps the atmospheric phenomenon was a supernatural sign—a sign that a storm had risen in the West, where a group of 23 angry men from St. Louis were preparing to rage over the eastern National League cities in a wave of ferocity.

Sunny, Sultry St. Lou'

On May 11, Paul Dean came to a professional crossroads. His early-season doldrums had led to speculation that he would be reassigned to the minors for further training. Why hadn't he succeeded? Didn't he have the same great ability as his brother? Now, in front of a Friday crowd of 6,500 at Sportsman's Park (about 2,500 of which were freely-admitted customers on "Ladies' Day"), he was matched up against the great Carl Hubbell, the left-handed screwball artist of the Giants. It was the prediction of most that Paul would wilt under the pressure. Among the rest of the Cardinals' pitching staff (with the exception of brother Dizzy, of course), the general sentiment was that he didn't have big-league stuff, and that the only reason he was up with the Cardinals was as a marketing ploy. This day would emit a telltale game, perhaps pointing the direction Paul's immediate future would take.

Hubbell rivaled Dizzy Dean as the best pitcher in the National League in the early 1930s. Red Barber, the longtime radio voice of the Reds and Dodgers, said this of him: "If I had a ballgame to be pitched, and my life hung in the balance, I'd want Carl Hubbell to pitch it."

The Cardinal batters were initially unimpressed with Hubbell's presence, however. A triple by Frisch, a Pepper Martin double, and a single by Rip Collins translated into a 2–0 Cardinals lead at the end of one inning. After the Giants fought back to a 2–2 tie in the fourth (the result of Hubbell's sacrifice fly with the bases loaded), Paul held fast against the World Champions, and the game remained deadlocked into extra innings. The young, unproven Paul Dean was staying stride for stride with "King Carlos." Finally, when New York shortstop Blondy Ryan miscommunicated with outfielder Lefty O' Doul on a pop fly, the ball fell free—and Martin scampered into third with the potential winning run. On the next pitch, Rothrock knocked one to the left field wall, and the Redbirds and Paul went home with an inspiring 3–2 win. Paul Dean had proven that he was here to stay, and gained some more respect from the rest of the Cardinals for his performance.

On May 15, the Cardinals finished up their longest homestand of the season; they would not play in Sportsman's Park again until June 5. In the previous two weeks, their 14 wins in 16 tries had lifted them from the cellar of the National League to third place behind the Cubs and Giants. Collins had the hot bat, with six homers since the first of the month. The fifteenth of May was also the last day in a Cardinal uniform for Burleigh Grimes, who was the only legal remaining spitball pitcher in the major leagues. The spitball had been outlawed in 1921, but because the careers of several veteran pitchers hinged on the weapon (17, in fact), exceptions were made for these individuals. By 1934, Grimes was the only one of those 17 remaining in the majors. For one month of work in his final season, Grimes won two games and lost one for the St. Louis club.

The Cardinals did not send themselves out of town on a good note, as Casey Stengel's Dodgers beat them 6–5 despite a 5-for-5 day from Jack Rothrock. Jim Mooney, chosen by Frisch to start the game because of his strong relief efforts in recent days, lasted until the eighth inning. He was pulled in favor of Dizzy Dean after loading the bases on singles while defending a 5–3 St. Louis lead. Dean and Jesse Haines allowed all the runners to score, and the "Bums" held on for the victory by spoiling a Cardinal rally in the bottom of the ninth inning.

The newspapers of May 16 listed the National League in this order:

	W	L	Pct.	GB
Pittsburgh	15	7	.682	—
Chicago	18	9	.667	—
St. Louis	15	10	.600	1.5
New York	15	11	.577	2
Boston	12	11	.522	3.5
Brooklyn	9	15	.375	7
Philadelphia	7	15	.318	8
Cincinnati	5	18	.217	10.5

After taking two out of three from the Braves in Boston, the Cards came calling on the Giants again. The showdown began on the 20th of

May, with a packed Sunday house of 38,782 on hand to see the duel between baseball's two best pitchers, Dizzy Dean and Carl Hubbell. Hubbell was anxious to get on the hill again versus St. Louis, and avenge the recent loss to Dizzy's rookie brother.

Dean allowed an unearned run in the bottom of the third, the result of a wild throw by Durocher (off a Gus Mancuso grounder) that landed ten rows behind the first base dugout. The Cardinal bats came out swinging in the fourth, however, as Medwick's single was followed by Collins' seventh home run of the year, a drive that hit the upper tier in the leftfield stands. In the fifth, Frisch tripled with the bases loaded to give St. Louis a 5–1 lead, and Medwick followed with a solo homer, his sixth of the year. The Cardinals knocked Hubbell out of the game in the seventh—the first time he had been removed that season—and hammered away on the New York bullpen in carving out a 9–5 victory. The win, coupled with a 16–1 Pirates loss to the Phillies, allowed St. Louis to creep past Pittsburgh into second place, one game behind the Cubs. After Hallahan lost 5–2 to Joe Bowman the following day, however, it looked as if the Cardinals had lost the momentum. Fortunately, Medwick delivered in the series finale. With the score tied 4–4 in the ninth inning, the Hungarian blasted a bases-loaded triple over the head of Giants' centerfielder Jo-Jo Moore, and Paul Dean had suddenly picked up his fourth win of the year.

The urban folks were indeed impressed with the country Deans. "Does anyone appreciate the resentment small town people hold for citizens of big cities?" asked Jimmy Powers of the *New York Daily News*. "This explains more than anything the success of the Dean brothers. When you hand Paul or Jerome a baseball and then they are to pitch a nine-inning contest they more or less mechanically turn in an excellent job. If you tell them to pitch against the New York Giants their eyes glow fanatically, they snatch the horsehide and stride to the mound, nostrils breathing fire."

Seemingly recovered from their early-season lethargy, the club was poised to take a strong hold of first place in the National League. Medwick had been burning up the opposing pitchers through the first six weeks of the season, batting at a .366 clip which was bolstered by a 5-for-5 outburst on May 30 at Cincinnati.

The Cardinals had been playing well away from home, a major factor in their success to this point. With long train rides, the toll taken on the player of the 1930s is not felt by the modern professional ballplayer. "We have shown better on the road than any other Western club," Frisch announced. "And that's something. With such a good record in the East we are bound to go just as well at home, if not better, and at such a pace I don't see how we can lose this year."

The big story, however, became the Dean brothers' near "strike" toward the end of the month. Diz, as was well-documented in the St. Louis papers, had felt from the start that Paul was underpaid. While Paul always seemed grateful to simply be in major league uniform, Dizzy believed that he should command much more money because of his surname. The allegiance of Paul to his brother overtook his modesty, and he grudgingly agreed to place his job in Dizzy's hands.

Their threats ranged from going to play semi-pro ball for $500 an appearance to going back to Arkansas to buy a farm. Whatever Dizzy decided to do, Paul would agree. Cardinals management recognized Paul's impressionable nature whenever they would discipline him, knowing that Diz had an omnipotent influence. Originally, Diz made his own salary out to be a secondary issue in the dispute, but used the opportunity of Paul's pay to draw attention to his once again. He pointed out that several comparable stars—namely Foxx, Klein, and Lou Gehrig—were making twice as much as he was.

It was no secret around the baseball world that Breadon and Rickey were among the league's most stingy penny-pinchers. Joe Williams of the *New York World-Telegram* once noted that "a third base coach in New York is likely to be paid more than a star in St. Louis or Cincinnati. Mr. Dizzy would be getting twice as much pitching for the Giants, and he would be worth it." Rickey, as the general manager, was notorious for selling players to other clubs before they reached their primes (as noted earlier, Medwick would be sent to the Dodgers in the early forties, and later, Cardinals slugger Johnny Mize would be dealt off and have big years with the Giants). Speculation in the newspapers at this time pondered what Dizzy's salary would be if he pitched in New York or Boston—twice, or even three times his current pay, some thought. Another writer remarked, "You can say what you want about the dopey Deans, but they're the only reason people still come to the ballpark in St. Louis." Later in life, Diz would still make reference to "that cheap bunch in the Cardinals' front office" and what he felt to be disrespect shown to him by the club. For the time being, however, all his ranting and raving (and Paul's supportive nodding) would gain him was further dislike from the other Cardinal players.

Most of Dizzy's complaining to J. Roy Stockton, the only St. Louis writer to regularly travel with the club, took place on the night of May 26;

the very next day he was on the mound against the Philadelphia Phillies. He allowed the Phils only two unearned runs, and hit a home run in the tenth inning—the longest of his career, and against a 40 mile-per-hour wind—that broke a 2–2 tie. The blast took the wind out of the sails of Philadelphia starter Phil Collins, who to that point had been pitching an excellent game himself. "When Dean smote his home run into the left-field seats," wrote Raymond Smith of the *St. Louis Globe-Democrat*, "Collins seemed to lose all interest in the game. To have a rival pitcher smack a home run at a critical time is enough to unnerve any pitcher hurling fine ball, and Fidgety Phil was no exception." Diz wound up with a 5–2 win. Hallahan turned in a splendid performance the following day, shutting out the Phillies 10–0 as Whitehead, Medwick, and Durocher had three hits each. Wild Bill left nine Phillies stranded in gaining only his third victory of the season.

Traveling to Cincinnati, the Cardinals swept a doubleheader from the Reds on a rainy Memorial Day at Crosley Field. The ground was soaked, but St. Louis marched on to their fourth and fifth wins in a row, 9–6 and 9–2. In the first game, Paul Dean lasted until the eighth inning when he gave way to brother Dizzy, who saved the contest for him. Tex Carleton needed no help in the nightcap, as he went the distance, allowing seven hits. They closed out May the following day with a 3–2 win over the Reds behind the pitching of Jesse Haines, the winning run coming in the top of the tenth inning when Frisch lifted a fly ball that Cincinnati outfielder Linc Blakely misjudged and dropped, allowing Rothrock to gallop across the dish. The Cardinals had ended with a sparkling 21–6 record for the month of May. The standings in the National League as of June 1:

	W	*L*	*Pct.*	*GB*
St. Louis	25	13	.658	—
New York	25	15	.634	1
Chicago	25	16	.610	1.5
Pittsburgh	20	16	.583	4
Boston	20	16	.583	4
Brooklyn	15	22	.405	9.5
Philadelphia	11	24	.314	12.5
Cincinnati	8	26	.235	15

Everything seemed to be clicking for the St. Louis club. The defense was solid, as Frisch and Durocher were turning more double plays than any other combination in the league; the pitchers had adjusted

to Spud Davis' catching; and the hitting was steadily improving, pro-
ducing an average of over five runs per game to this point. The long
road trip was coming to an end, and optimism was high as they entered
Pittsburgh for a three-game set with the Pirates. Unfortunately, Hallahan blew a 3–1 lead in the ninth inning of the first game and lost, 4–3.
As a result, the Giants and Cubs had closed back to within a half-game
of the Cardinals' lead. Then, out of the blue, Dizzy cornered Frisch in
the Cardinals' hotel and raised the issue of Paul's salary again—as well
as his own. Observers had noticed that Diz spent the last half of that
day's game in the grandstand, perhaps the first sign of protest.

Dizzy's tactics in protesting were often very subtle, as was the case
here. He complained of a chronic "sore arm," and he told Frisch that he
would be unable to make his scheduled start on June 2, in the first game
of a doubleheader with the Pirates. Frisch did not believe him, but Diz
still refused to take the mound. Manager Frankie then suggested that
both Dizzy and Paul turn in their uniforms and leave the club for good.
Breadon was wired of the situation at his farm in Fenton, Missouri, but
issued no immediate statement—he had sent Rickey to Columbus,
Ohio, the previous day to watch the Cardinals' minor league club there,
and wanted to wait until they both returned to St. Louis to decide what
to do. The whole matter, however, blew over before the Cardinals
returned home. Fortunately, Dizzy's complaint once again was short-
lived. Secretly, he and Frisch buried the hatchet, and Dean readied himself to take the hill the following day, and promised to make no more
of the issue.

Diz himself told the press that all was well. "You know there must
be something wrong with anybody who wouldn't pitch his arm off for
Old Frank. Show me a guy who says a word against Old Frank, and I'll
bash his face in." Dizzy won the first game in a laugher, 13–4, as "Old
Frank" played in his 2,000th National League game and Dean was the
beneficiary of 18 Cardinal hits. However, they dropped the last game
of the series 6–3, and in doing so had lost three out of four to the
Pirates. Thus, the Cardinals gained no ground during their stay in Pittsburgh and neither did Paul Dean in terms of salary. It was finalized by
Breadon that his pay would stay at $3,000. "Hard for a guy to make a
dollar these days," he sighed.

As the Cardinals returned home to open a three-week stretch at
Sportsman's Park, they found themselves in a three-way tie for first place
in the tight National League standings. The Giants and the Cubs were
even with them, and the Pirates and Braves were only two games back.

Over in the American League, the Browns were raising eyebrows with a strong start to the season. As June began, manager Rogers Hornsby had been victorious in 13 of his last 20 games, and had the Browns only three games behind the front-running Yankees and a half-game ahead of the defending league champions, the Washington Senators. It was the first time, locals could remember, that both St. Louis teams were threatening to take the pennant in the same year.

Even though it was only early June, the grass at Sportsman's Park was already worn, and the infield dirt was in poor condition. As the Browns and Cardinals shared the premises, players always expected the field to be among the worst in the major leagues. The recent weather, however, was also affecting the quality of the playing conditions.

The city of St. Louis was blitzed with scorching heat in June of 1934, with a record-setting stretch of 30 consecutive days of 100-plus degree temperatures. On such days, with the fans at Sportsman's drowning in their own perspiration, Diz would provide some comic relief. He might be seen on the dugout, frying real eggs on the skillet-like roof; a few innings later, he would cheerfully beckon the vendor for some hot chocolate; or he would gather kindling and warm himself by an imaginary (or sometimes real) self-built fire in the on-deck circle. He would bow to hearty laughs and some lighthearted applause at such acts. Laughing was perhaps the only defense in a heat wave that, combined with drought and depression, was killing people across the country. Fortunately, safe oases were found in ballparks, where entertainment and ice-cold drinks were available to those who could afford to get in.

Perhaps due to the oppressive heat, only 4,800 fans welcomed the Cardinals back home for the first game with the Cubs. Behind a home run from Collins and excellent defense, Paul Dean ran his record to 6-0 as St. Louis won, 6–3. An episode of vintage Gas House lore occurred the next day on June 7. The large, heavy-drinking, and intimidating Pat Malone was pitching for Chicago, and Carleton took the mound for the Cardinals. The teams fought to a 6–6 tie into the twelfth inning, when St. Louis appeared headed towards victory. Medwick, with two out, was on first when Collins lined a double through the right field gap. Charging hard around third, Medwick slid across the corner of home plate with the winning run—or so it appeared to him. Umpire Charles Rigler hoisted his thumb into the air, indicating that a tag was indeed applied by Cubs catcher Gabby Hartnett, and Medwick was out. Frisch shot like a dart out of the dugout, and gave Rigler a two-handed shove with full force. Rigler, in obvious self-defense, swung his mask and grazed Frisch's cheek. Medwick and Frisch launched a counter-assault, but were buffered by Hartnett and third base coach Mike Gonzalez. A wave of boys and young men from the grandstand then stormed the field, forming a circle around the batter's area where the melee was occurring. After Frisch was ejected, Rothrock had to come in and play second base, and the Cubs put six runs on the board in the thirteenth inning as they posted an easy 12–6 victory. For the Cardinals, the loss knocked them out of first place.

Frisch pointed out after the game that even Hartnett thought Medwick was safe, as Gabby headed towards the dugout after the play in assumption that the run had ended the game. "What am I supposed to do when I get a bad decision? Am I supposed to laugh it off?" Both Rigler and Frisch were fined $100 for the incident, which the latter gladly accepted in lieu of being suspended.

Rigler was surprised about being fined. "You're kidding me," he responded after learning the news. "Well, it's not the first time I've been fined. I guess the telegram telling me about it arrived at the hotel after I left." He also announced to the St. Louis papers the next day that he would react similarly again if needed, as he was only defending himself. National League president John Heydler decided the fine amounts for Frisch and Rigler after hearing both of their accounts of the situation. Rigler was quizzed further by the St. Louis papers about Heydler's investigation. "You must have gone pretty strong on yourself in the report," one writer asked him. "I just told the truth," Rigler responded. "Frisch rushed me and I hit him."

People noticed the next day that Rigler had a broken finger, but it was not from the fight; Pepper Martin caught it with his bat on a swing in the seventh inning. This would not be the first or last such incident for the Cardinals, and "those dag-gum umparrs"—as Diz called them— were always on their toes with the Gas House Gang in town.

The next day, big Jim Weaver became the first pitcher to shut out the Cardinals in '34, 1–0. Weaver had been released by the Browns just three weeks before, but entrenched himself as a strong member of the starting rotation for the Cubs behind Warneke, Lee, Bush, and Malone. The Cardinals had a chance to tie the game in the ninth, but Weaver quickly nabbed a hot shot off the bat of Medwick that seemed destined for center field while Rothrock was waiting on third. The gathering of 3,800 spectators spent most of the game scurrying from the uncovered portions of the grandstand to protected seats, as intermittent rain lingered in the St. Louis area all day.

Diz took the mound once again on June 10 in Sportsman's Park. Before a crowd of almost 13,000, he faced Pittsburgh a day later than he was supposed to. The much-needed rain that had been pelting St. Louis the past few days washed out the contest for June 9, but a new National League rule forbid any Sunday doubleheaders until after the fifteenth of June. Dean beat the Pirates for the third time of the year, scattering nine hits in a 3–2 complete game victory. He fell behind by scores of 1–0 and 2–1, but a home run by Collins knotted the game at two, and Ripper later scored the winning run on a hit by little-used outfielder Kiddo Davis, acquired from the Giants in spring training. Being so unimpressed with the Pirates, Diz said after the game, "Why, those palookas are lucky whenever they get a run off me and Paul."

After an off-day, the Cardinal bats came back again in force. Martin and Collins had three hits apiece—each with a single, a triple, and a home run—as Paul Dean shut down Boston, 7–3, in front of only 2,800 at the ballpark. Frisch had given Pepper a break during the previous week, using Burgess Whitehead at the hot corner to rest Martin's sore elbow which was preventing him from making accurate throws. Collins' home run in the seventh inning was his third round-tripper in as many games. It was the fifteenth win of the year for the Dean brothers, and Paul's seventh.

Durocher nearly claimed the single-game error record the next day in the second of the four-game set with the Braves. He kicked a ground ball in the second inning, booted another and made a wild throw in the sixth, and booted another in the ninth for four miscues on the day, falling one short of the league mark. Ironically, his shortstop counterpart from Boston, Bill Urbanski, equaled another major league record by not receiving an official at bat in six trips to the plate. He was walked four times by Cardinals pitchers and sacrificed twice, part of a Braves' attack that mustered a 9–0 victory and snapped a three-game St. Louis winning streak. The Gang managed only six hits against ex–Cardinal Fred Frankhouse, who went the distance for the shutout.

On June 16, the Cardinals received some insurance for their outfield, acquiring Chick Fullis from the Phillies. Fullis had been the Phillies regular centerfielder in 1933, hitting .309 in 151 games. His playing time had lessened in the current year, however, and Breadon was worried that he might be damaged goods, even though Philadelphia officials assured him that Fullis was fit to play. In return, the Cardinals sent Kiddo Davis to the Phils, who was not seeing regular time in the outfield stocked with Medwick, Orsatti, and Rothrock. Davis was the starting centerfielder on the Giants' championship club of '33, but had been unable to crack the Cardinal lineup.

The standings on June 17:

	W	L	Pct.	GB
New York	36	19	.655	—
St. Louis	31	21	.596	3.5
Chicago	32	23	.582	4
Pittsburgh	27	23	.540	5.5
Boston	27	24	.529	6
Brooklyn	23	31	.426	12.5
Philadelphia	19	31	.380	14.5
Cincinnati	13	36	.265	20

Amazingly the Dean brothers would appear in two-thirds of the Cardinals' games in June, combining for an 11–3 record during the month—while the rest of the staff would go 2–11 over the same stretch. These statistics were testimony to the Deans' priceless value to the ballclub. The offense was humming along, with Medwick leading the National League with a .373 average on June 16. Frisch however, was quick to relay his dissatisfaction with the rest of the pitching staff. "My gang should be pitching hay instead of baseballs," he quipped. "At least they'd be earning their pay. We're not going any place unless Carleton and Hallahan win some games, and they might as well start now." To make matters worse, Bill Walker was knocked out of action on May 6, when Medwick lined a ball off of his pitching arm during batting practice, breaking the bone. Even with all that was occurring, some St. Louis sportswriters were speculating that Dean was being overworked, though he himself mentioned nothing about it.

"Dizzy has had a sore arm," claimed Martin Haley. "That is, there has been a kink in it, but he says it works out when his arm warms up. Yesterday [June 18] was an off day for the boys, but Diz spent part of the 'holiday' getting his arm treated by trainer 'Doc' Weaver.

"Three trips to the hill in four days with an ailing fin, and it's only mid–June. We recall that after the Birds flopped last season it was said that Dizzy Dean, Carleton, and Hallahan had been worked too often in the first half of the race, and were 'all in' during the stretch drive. Is Dizzy working too often now?"

Haley was not questioning the managerial moves of Frisch; for, if one recalls, Gabby Street was the Cardinals manager in the first half of 1933 when the three pitchers mentioned were overused. However, others noticed that Dean seemed to be tiring, and were concerned that the staff would have nothing left come August and September.

In a way, it was becoming as if people expected Dean to be the one responsible anytime the Cardinals won. On June 23, Diz was credited with a victory he did not truly earn, or at least one that would not have been given to him under today's scoring rules. Against Brooklyn, he took over for an ineffective Hallahan in the seventh inning. The inning before, during which Hallahan was lifted for a pinch-hitter, the Cardinals rallied from a 4–0 deficit to take the lead 5–4. Under contemporary guidelines, those St. Louis runs would have been to Hallahan's credit, giving him the win, and bestowing on Diz the modern "save." However, during the 1930s, the official scorer was given the latitude to credit victory to whomever he felt most deserving. Thus, in light of the fact that Dean was the most effective Cardinal pitcher on the day, he was given the win. He held the Dodgers scoreless in the seventh, eighth, and ninth innings to preserve the triumph, and Haley, the official scorer for the Cardinals at Sportsman's Park, made his appeal to the National League office on Dean's behalf.

When the Giants arrived in St. Louis on June 24 to open a four-game series with the Cardinals, they found themselves only two games ahead of the Redbirds and three-and-a-half above the Cubs. The Cards had just taken three out of four from the Dodgers, and were ready to reclaim the top spot in the National League. The first game of the Giants series took place on a Sunday, with sunny and hot weather accompanying 15,000 fans in the ballpark, the largest crowd in Sportsman's Park for the year to that point.

Tex Carleton took the mound for the Cardinals, and he was opposed by Fred Fitzsimmons. The bats took off in high gear for both clubs. The teams pounded out a combined 23 hits in the first five innings, but had only one each in the final four. Bill Terry had the biggest bat on the day, knocking an RBI triple along with a bases-loaded single as the Giants chased Carleton from the hill and won the opener 9–7. Mooney and Haines were effective in relief, but the Cardinals could not launch a counter-attack against New York relievers Hi Bell and Dolf Luque. The Cubs, meanwhile, swept a doubleheader in Brooklyn and climbed to within six percentage points of the second place Cardinals.

The Cards officially acquired Dazzy Vance the next day, picking him up for the waiver price of $7,500 from the Cincinnati Reds. Rickey was confident that the veteran could provide some needed stability to the pitching staff, particularly in the bullpen. Dizzy Dean was scheduled to start this day, but Frisch went with Hallahan instead. Dean complained of stomach problems before the game, and when public address announcer Jim Kelley made the announcement to the throng of 3,300 at Sportsman's through his megaphone, a reply of "boos" met his news. Hubbell threw for the Giants, and the fans were expecting to see the two great pitchers face off against one another. King Carlos worked through the St. Louis batting order with ease, not allowing a score for the first six innings. Hallahan, meanwhile, was shelled with a barrage of hits and did not finish the second frame. He was followed to the mound by Lindsey, and the Giants ran up seven runs on seven hits in the second. A large dust storm blew into the ballpark in the fifth, followed by a brief rain shower. The Cardinals attempted to stall the game in the midst of the rain, as Pepper Martin refused to enter the batter's box to take his turn. Umpire George Barr ordered Hubbell to pitch, and Hubbell threw a ball with no hitter present. Upon seeing the action, Pepper jumped from his seat, grabbed a bat, and got to the plate.

When the Cardinals looked at the scoreboard in the seventh inning, they found themselves trailing 9–0. Rothrock then homered with two on to make it closer, but it would not help. Mooney and Walker relieved after Lindsey—with Walker making his first appearance since May 4— and allowed three more Giant tallies. The final score was 10–7, and with the Cubs winning again in Brooklyn, the Cardinals fell into third place.

Before the third game of the series the next day, it was revealed that the Giants were trying to acquire outfielder Babe Herman from the Cubs. Herman, considered one of the better hitters in the league but notoriously bad on defense, had starred for the crosstown Dodgers for several years before moving on to Chicago. His antics in left field were well-documented in Brooklyn; when a flyball went into his vicinity, no one could guess what the outcome would be. "If a ball ever hits me on the head," he once proclaimed, "I'll quit the game." Herman would remain with the Cubs through the 1934 season, however, and the failure of the Giants to pick him up certainly altered their pennant hopes as they possessed a gaping hole in center field. George Watkins manned the position for the most part, but was doing an inadequate job in the eyes of the New York management.

Game Three saw another offensive explosion, as the teams combined for 28 hits this time—all of the Giants' 15 coming off of Paul

Dean—and the Cardinals and Paul prevailed for a 13–7 victory. The Redbirds had built an overwhelming 13–2 lead after five innings, aided by the four-hit effort of Rip Collins and eight walks issued by New York lefthander Al Smith, a St. Louis native.

The other of Dean's controversial wins during the 1934 season came on June 27, in the final game of the series with the Giants and just four days after the first disputed victory. With 115-degree heat on the field, the teams found themselves in a 7–7 tie in the ninth inning. Dean loaded the bases on singles and gave way to Mooney. The Tennessee southpaw promptly retired the third out, and the Cardinals won in the bottom half of the ninth on a home run by DeLancey. Once again, the victory was given to whom the scorer felt most deserving—not who was in the game when the winning run was scored. When sportswriters across the country heard the evidence, they were even more convinced that Dizzy Dean was the unquestioned monarch in St. Louis. "In St. Louis the Deans rule," said Will Wedge of the *New York Sun* after the game.

There were even rumblings around the Cardinals' clubhouse about the decisions. Anti-Dean sentiment was always present on the pitching staff, but it peaked with these incidents. These feelings were present despite the fact that, without Dizzy and Paul, the Cardinals would be a sub–.500 ballclub at this point, over sixty games into the season.

Diz revealed after the game that he had pitched with a broken finger on his throwing hand, sustained in batting practice a few days earlier. He did not tell Frisch, he said, for he wanted to make sure that he was allowed to pitch in this important series.

The Cards entered a series at Cincinnati on June 29 with a perfect 6–0 record against the Reds for the year. Their streak was snapped, however, at the hands of crafty pitcher Paul Derringer. A six-run fourth inning boosted the Reds to a 7–1 win, as home plate umpire Beans Reardon was forced to leave the game in that frame from the intense heat. The Cardinals and Reds split the next two games, sending the Cards off to Chicago to face the Cubs with a 1–2 record on the brief road trip.

The National League standings before the day's play of June 30:

	W	L	Pct.	GB
New York	42	21	.636	—
Chicago	40	26	.606	3.5
St. Louis	38	26	.594	4.5

	W	L	Pct.	GB
Pittsburgh	34	28	.548	7.5
Boston	34	30	.531	8.5
Brooklyn	26	40	.394	17.5
Philadelphia	24	41	.369	19
Cincinnati	20	43	.317	22

"The St. Louis Cardinals called at Wrigley Field today," the *Globe-Democrat* reported on July 3, speaking of the previous day's game, "But were requested to leave the premises in wholesale quantities." Assigned to work the series was Bill Klem, a National League umpire since 1905 and considered among the best in baseball history at the job. On this date, however, Frankie Frisch and some other Redbirds did not think so.

In the seventh inning with the Cubs already leading 4–1, Paul Dean had loaded the bases and only one out. He had been engaged in a tough duel with the Cubs' ace, Warneke, and needed to get the Cardinals out of the inning to give their bats a chance to come back. The powerful Chuck Klein was up for the Cubs, and he took a mighty swing that lifted a high pop-up between home and first. A strong wing was blowing off Lake Michigan, and had fooled players on flyballs all day long. Catcher Bill DeLancey threw off his mask and took charge of the play. Unfortunately, a gust swept the ball from foul to fair territory, and it dropped safely. Klein was called safe at first by Klem, as well as Warneke at home who had crossed with Chicago's fifth run. Frisch hollered from the dugout that Klein should have been out under the infield fly rule, added an obscenity, and was tossed from the game by Klem. At this point, Diz and coach Mike Gonzalez came out of the dugout and after Klem, and they too were ejected. The Cubs went on to win the game, 7–4, and Warneke had gained his third victory of the season over the St. Louisans. Afterwards, Klem's position was that the play wasn't a routine pop fly for DeLancey, the primary fielder on the play, as is stipulated in the infield fly rule. Klem also questioned whether the ball would have landed in fair territory, another requirement for the rule to take effect.

Later that same week Rudolph Hess, the chief secretary for Adolf Hitler's Nazi Party, defied any nation in Europe to invade Germany; after the game, Frisch defied National League president John Heydler to find one good umpire. Frisch was fined $100 by Heydler for "extremely bad conduct in defying a league umpire by repeatedly refusing to resume play," and Gonzalez $25 for "unreasonable delay of game and threats to punch an umpire." Upon hearing of the verdict, Frisch reportedly told

Heydler, "You're making a joke of the National League by permitting your umpires to assume a belligerent attitude. I can't understand why you don't make your umpires stay awake, attend to business, and call plays right." After another run-in with the blue shirts back in St. Louis a week later, Frisch added, "Something must be done with these temperamental umpires. They refuse to listen to a fair discussion... The club owners should convince President Heydler that his system is making a sissy game out of baseball."

Ironically, that same week, a similar incident occurred at a Cardinals minor league game. Ray Blades, who would take over as manager of the Cardinals in the late 1930s, was suspended by the American Association on July 5 for "abusing" an umpire. Blades was in charge of the Columbus, Ohio, team in the league, and his suspension was indefinite; as it turned out, he would not return to the Columbus bench until July 9.

Medwick homered the following day, helping to lift his league-leading average to .365, which contributed to a 13-hit attack for the Cardinals, resulting in a 7–3 St. Louis win over Chicago. Durocher added three hits, as he was proving to be a viable offensive threat for the first time in his career.

The two teams took the train to St. Louis, and met in a July 4 doubleheader the following day. The largest crowd for the year at Sportsman's, 24,500, anxiously filled the stands to see their Cardinals gain ground on the second-place Cubs. It was also the largest crowd at Sportsman's since the Cubs and Cardinals played another doubleheader in 1933 before 27,500. Attendance all around the major leagues was good on the holiday, as baseball witnessed a one-day oasis of financial windfall. Every major league city had a doubleheader being played, as the total attendance surpassed 200,000 for the date. The largest gathering was at the Polo Grounds in New York, where 42,000 came out to watch the Giants take on the Braves. Elsewhere in the National League, games involving the Reds at the Pirates (14,000) and the Dodgers at the Phillies (12,000) also saw above-average numbers. The top figures in the American League included 40,000 to see a twin bill at Detroit between the Tigers and the Cleveland Indians, while 35,000 witnessed the games in Boston's Fenway Park between the Red Sox and the Yankees. The Browns even drew well on the road for the special day, as 20,000 showed up at Comiskey Park in Chicago to watch them take on the White Sox.

The crowd in St. Louis saw the Cardinals split with the Cubs, with both teams winning games by the score of 6–2. In the second contest, Jim Weaver executed another fine performance against the Birds, dispersing nine hits over the course of a complete game triumph. He was now 6–0 on the season, with two of those victories coming with the Browns before the club sent him to their Newark farm team. It was from there that the Cubs picked him up. Kiki Cuyler provided the offensive muscle for Chicago, lashing four hits including a long triple to the right-center field gap. Cuyler, one of the fastest players in baseball, had just been named the starting centerfielder in the All-Star Game to take place in New York six days later.

Frisch decided to rest both of the Deans for an entire week, choosing to not send them to the mound until a home doubleheader with the Reds on Sunday, July 9. He noted to the press, "It will be an attraction to have them work the doubleheader." On July 1 in Cincinnati, Diz pitched an unbelievable 17 innings of an 18-inning contest, and Paul had not pitched since the disputed game in Chicago on the second. For the first two-and-a-half months of the season, Dizzy's record stood at 12–3, while Paul was 11–3. They had been responsible for two-thirds of the Cardinals' victories, and Frisch was concerned that another lapse like the one in '33 was imminent.

Frisch held to his plan, as the Cardinals used a National League–record seven pitchers in the opening game of the Cincinnati series on July 6—but no Deans. Diz had to pinch-hit, however, for five other substitute batters had already been used. Carleton, the final pitcher, had to bat for himself in a crucial situation as the Reds won a wild one, 16–15. Hallahan and Paul Dean were the only Cardinals who did not play, and the two-hour, 41-minute game (which would be normal by today's standards) was called by an observer "probably the longest nine-inning game of the season." Ernie Lombardi, the slow-footed, large-nosed catcher of the Reds, was the offensive star of the day. He collected five hits, including a homer and a triple, the latter coming on a play in which Cardinals rightfielder Rothrock tripped while pursuing the ball. Lombardi finished the day with six runs batted in, and scored three more himself.

Bill Hallahan gained his second straight complete game victory the following day, 10–4, setting up the series-ending doubleheader for Sunday, the all–Dean show, which would send the teams into the All-Star break. The Cards split with the Reds, with Dizzy winning the first game 6–1 over Bennie Frey and Paul losing the second 8–4 to Paul Derringer. The big blow in the nightcap was the grand slam off the bat of

Cincinnati outfielder Harlin Pool, which caused Paul to fling his glove from the mound in disgust. He then turned to home plate umpire Cy Pfirman and told him that the previous pitch should have been strike three to Pool, not ball three as was called. Durocher then started in on Pfirman as well, and Leo was thrown out of the game. After things had apparently cooled down, Paul had something shouted at him from the Reds dugout. He turned and jogged towards the Cincinnati bench, looking for the origin of the slur. He challenged the tormentor to come out of the dugout and fight him (which turned out to be Reds pitcher Ray Kolp), but no one emerged. Unsatisfied, Paul proceeded to enter the dugout but was restrained by Rip Collins. By that time, Diz had also sauntered over to the dispute, and he too invited the entire Reds bench to a sparring session. The scene did finally dissipate, and Paul let in two more runs as he continued his work on the hill.

With the split, the Cardinals entered the All-Star break with a 43–31 record, four games in back of the first-place Giants and two behind the Cubs for second place.

Meanwhile, in the American League, the powerful Detroit Tigers and their player-manager Mickey Cochrane were gaining ground in the pennant race. Their success was earning them notice in periodicals across the land, as evidenced by this stanza in a Midwestern newspaper which reminded fans of the Tigers' glory years:

> *Mickey Cochrane on the job*
> *Recalls the days when Tyrus Cobb*
> *With his Tigers did an act*
> *That kept the baseball circus packed*

11

Star Gazing

With the success of the inaugural 1933 edition, it was evident that the All-Star Game was a fan's delight and would be a worthy annual event. The Cardinals added their own flavor to the first contest with Hallahan as the starting pitcher for the National League. It was perhaps most fitting, however, that the game was won for the American League on a homer by Babe Ruth, which brought cheers from the crowd at Chicago's Comiskey Park. The game was not an offensive affair, as many had expected; the final score was 4–2.

For the 1934 game, most of the traditional stars made the roster once again, with fans balloting in their time-honored favorites. Some onlookers, particularly in the media, had hoped to see younger players take the stage. "The complete results of the poll, announced today [July 2], reveal a conspicuous lack of support for freshman luminaries of the game who have flashed into the headlines for the first time this year," complained one writer. "Experience, the public seems to have decided, will be a valuable asset for both teams." Indeed it would, as a cast of veterans—and one veteran pitcher in particular—would take part in the most memorable feat in All-Star history.

It was a mostly sunny, pleasant day on July 10 at the Polo Grounds in New York. The horseshoe-shaped home of the Giants sat at the foot of Coogan's Bluff, a hill that overlooked the stadium along the Harlem River. It was announced in the newspapers that a capacity crowd of 52,000 was expected, but league officials were hoping for even more with the sale of standing room tickets. Gate revenue from the game was expected to be $60,000, all to be donated to the Players' Benevolent Fund, a trust set up to assist disabled former ballplayers. In addition, further proceeds were to be gathered from the national radio broadcasts of the game over CBS and NBC. On a more mischievous note, it was also estimated that approximately $1 million was being wagered on the game in underground parlors.

Because his Giants were the 1933 World Series champions, Bill Terry was given charge of the Nationals against the Washington Senators' Joe Cronin and his American League squad. Frisch, Martin, Medwick, and Dizzy Dean were on the roster for the National League, although Terry led all players with 123,600 fan votes. Going into the All-Star break, Terry was also leading the league in hitting with a .367 average; Medwick had slipped to fifth with a .349 mark, behind Terry, Paul Waner, Cuyler, and Sam Leslie. The only man in baseball still eclipsing the .400 mark by the break was Heinie Manush of the Washington Senators, the starting centerfielder for the American League. He arrived at the event in New York smacking the ball at an awesome .403 clip.

The top American League choice among the voters was Detroit Tigers second baseman Charlie Gehringer, outdistancing Ruth, Cronin, and Gehrig with 121,000 tallies. Frisch was third overall with 120,141. The top vote-getter among pitchers was the Giants' Hubbell with 86,000, and he would start the game for the Nationals. Lefty Grove of the Yankees got the nod for the American League with his 84,000 votes leading the way for AL moundsmen. Behind Hubbell in the National League, the pitchers finishing next in order of votes were Diz, Warneke, Van Lingle Mungo of the Dodgers, Guy Bush, and Paul Dean.

Frisch had been bothered during the past week by a deep thigh bruise, but was determined to play. "I wouldn't miss this game," he told reporters on the train to New York City, as they passed by some rolling countryside in the Empire State. The Cardinals had just completed an exhibition game at Rochester, and Frisch, Dean, Medwick and Martin went separate ways from the team to come to the All-Star Game. With their teammates headed to the Polo Grounds, Hallahan, Vance, and Mooney would pitch the rest of the Cardinals to a 3–1 win over their Elmira farm team in the New York–Pennsylvania League.

"Look at those green hills out there," Frisch continued, as the train rolled along. "How could a fellow help but like baseball when he can get around and see things like this? Baseball players ought to play their heads off to have the advantage of traveling." Pepper Martin was also hurting from a sore throwing arm, but was ready to play if the Nationals called on him.

Two seats over on the train, Dean mentioned that his arm was feeling better. "There was a catch in the elbow and it kinda had me worried a little," he said, looking down at his right arm while giving it a twist. "But Doc Weaver put some hot stuff on it and it feels pretty good today."

Hallahan got the start in the 1933 game, as John McGraw decided at the last minute to name him over Hubbell. This was done, it was reported, at the request of Bill Terry. For just a couple of days earlier was the incredible doubleheader that the Giants played against the Cardinals, in which Hubbell lasted the 18 innings in out-dueling Carleton 1–0 (Roy Parmalee defeated Diz by the same score in the second game), and Terry believed that Hubbell needed extra rest after the marathon contest. So now in 1934, it was Hubbell's turn to shine. Diz, who had more respect for Hubbell than any other opponent in his career, was disappointed in not being chosen to start (with his 62,000 votes), but resigned himself to the National League dugout to watch the show begin.

Meanwhile, that same day, legendary manager Connie Mack of the Philadelphia A's was being honored in his hometown of North Brookfield, Massachusetts, for his fifty-first year in baseball.

The starting positions for the 1934 All-Star Game were as follows:

AL	NL
1B—Gehrig, NY	1B—Terry, NY
2B—Gehringer, DET	2B—Frisch, STL
3B—Higgins, PHI	3B—Traynor, PIT
SS—Cronin, WASH	SS—Jackson, NY
LF—Manush, WASH	LF—Medwick, STL
CF—Simmons, CHI	CF—Berger, BOS
RF—Ruth, NY	RF—Cuyler, CHI
C—Dickey, NY	C—Hartnett, CHI

And the reserves included:

AL	NL
Ruffing, NY (Pitcher)	Warneke, CHI (Pitcher)
Bridges, DET (P)	J. Dean, STL (P)
Harder, CLE (P)	Mungo, BRK (P)
Russell, WASH (P)	Frankhouse, BOS (P)
Foxx, PHI	Martin, STL
Dykes, CHI	Vaughan, PIT
Chapman, NY	Herman, CHI
Averill, CLE	P. Waner, PIT

AL	*NL*
West, STL	Ott, NY
Cochrane, DET	Klein, CHI
Ferrell, BOS	Lopez, BRK

Grantland Rice, in relaying his thoughts the day before the game, put together his own all-star roster from players of "yesteryear." His list included Ty Cobb, Walter Johnson, Christy Mathewson, Honus Wagner, Tris Speaker, and others, and Rice was convinced of the superiority of his team. "My vote would go to this team against any outfit that might be named today," he offered. "Gomez, Hubbell, Dean, and others can handle their share of pitching, but that old-time staff, in its prime, would be even harder to hit or break down—even with Gehrig, Foxx, Ruth, Gehringer, Terry, Klein, Ott, and Manush taking their cut at the ball."

As the game got ready to begin at 2:30 in the afternoon, umpires Brick Owens and George Moriarity from the American League and Charles Pfirman and Dolly Stark from the National League took their positions. In the first inning, Hubbell allowed a single to Gehringer and a walk to Manush. Next was Ruth, the living god, looking like a ogre as he traipsed from the on-deck circle towards the batters box. With a 1-2 count, Ruth watched a Hubbell screwball whiz by, catch the outside corner, and the Sultan of Swat was out on strikes. Batting fourth was Gehrig, and he struck out swinging on a full count on another screwball from King Carlos. Jimmie Foxx pinch-hit for Pinky Higgins as the next batter, and when he air-conditioned the park with a vicious cut for his third strike, the partisan New York crowd roared its approval. Hubbell had pitched his way out of a jam by fanning the AL's top three guns.

Frisch had mentioned before the game that he would be aggressive at the plate. "They usually put that first one over in a big game like this," he predicted. When he batted in the bottom of the first inning, however, he took his first pitch for a ball. The next offering from Gomez was in the zone, however, and he launched a long home run into the grandstand in left to give the Nationals a 1–0 lead.

In the top of the second frame, Hubbell returned to the hill amid scattered cheers and whistles. He promptly struck out Simmons, a player who had hit over .380 in four separate seasons in his career. Cronin went down next on three straight strikes, and the incredible stretch was complete. In five consecutive strikeouts, Hubbell had sat down five Hall of Famers and a total of 2,218 career home runs among the group. It is often left untold that he also whiffed Lefty Gomez next for six in a row; this was ironic because Gomez, though a stellar pitcher, was one of the weakest hitters in the history of the game. The ever-modest Hubbell would later simply recall, "I guess I just had some pretty good stuff that day." Ruth, however, was more impressed. "I couldn't even see the ball when Carl threw it," the Babe admitted.

On some accounts, the game became uninteresting after the string of strikeouts. Wrote Ed Neil of the Associated Press, "Rarely, in a match of such magnitude, has the play ever denigrated so quickly and so completely from the sublime to the ridiculous as it did after Hubbell's magnificent display."

A three-run homer by Medwick in the third inning gave the Nationals a 4–0 lead. The Cardinals had the oldest and youngest players on the entire all-star roster (with Frisch at 36 and Medwick at 23), and now they had both gone deep. However, the American League stormed back with two runs in the fourth off Warneke, and then blitzed Mungo for six runs in the fifth inning.

Dean entered the game in the sixth to enthusiastic cheers. He was always the enemy in the Polo Grounds, but today he was an ally. He pitched three innings, and the 8–7 deficit he inherited would eventually wind up a 9–7 American League victory. Some used the result to augment the notion of American League superiority, such as W.H. James. "The most we can make out of that all-star ball game is that 16 Americans can beat 20 Nationals," claimed James. "Bill Terry shot the works to the limit of his quota, while Joe Cronin still had four men in reserve when the game was over. It seems his machine took less manpower, as the technocrats would say." On the other hand, James had this to offer about the fine showing of the Cardinals' representatives:

> *Joey Medwick and Frankie Frisch*
> *Served them up a juicy dish,*
> *And Dizzy would have done the same*
> *If put in early in the game*

A final tally of the crowd listed 48,363 spectators, and the following day's newspapers praised Hubbell for his unbelievable feat. "Of all the stars on the field, Hubbell was the brightest," wrote Paul Gallico of the *New York Daily News*. "When Foxx struck out swinging, the crowd lifted the Polo Grounds six feet off the ground with a roar, and then set it down again."

12

Not Goin' to
Detroit—Not Yet

The Cardinals returned to league play the following day, a July 11 date with the Phillies in Philadelphia. After their strong showing in May, the Cardinals had only broken even with a record of 18–18 since June 1. Now, after the two-day layoff, they commenced one of their longer road trips of the year, with stops in Brooklyn, Boston, New York, Pittsburgh, and Chicago before returning home to Sportsman's Park on August 3. Frisch was still unsure about starting Martin at third, as Pepper was still suffering from a sore arm. So instead, Burgess Whitehead was the choice for the opener in Philadelphia. Frisch had aggravated his bruised thigh in the All-Star Game, so little-used Pat Crawford took his position at second base. Crawford, showing no signs of rust, handled 11 chances without an error and socked three singles at the plate. It wasn't enough help for Tex Carleton, however, as he lost to Phil Collins 5–2. Carleton believed he was in for a strong second half of the season after his victory over the Cubs on the Fourth of July. The Phillies, however, pounded him for 12 hits in the defeat.

The next day, the Cardinals' pitching staff incurred an injury it could not afford. Pitching in the first game of a doubleheader with the Phils, Paul Dean sprained an ankle while running the bases in the third inning. Mooney and older brother Diz came to the rescue, and they were able to finish out an 8–5 win. Frisch was still nursing his hurt leg, but managed to get thrown out of the game anyway. He protested a sixth inning call by umpire Dolly Stark in which Crawford supposedly missed second base on a force play. The Cards lost the nightcap, 8–3 (with

DeLancey being ejected from this one for arguing balls and strikes), and all of a sudden, the lowly Phillies had taken five out of their last six contests with St. Louis.

Although the X-rays of Paul's ankle were negative, he was out of action indefinitely. The team rode the train to Brooklyn on an off-day on July 13, where a long five-game series awaited with the Dodgers.

Meanwhile, in a game in Detroit against the Tigers, Babe Ruth slugged the 700th home run of his career, a two-run shot in the third inning that proved the difference in a 4–2 Yankees' victory. At this point, Lou Gehrig's physical condition was already beginning to deteriorate from the early stages of Amyotrophic Lateral Sclerosis, the disease that would eventually bear his name. "Gehrig's acute cold in his back struck hard after he had singled in the second," reported the Associated Press after the game, "And Lou found it hard to breathe and almost impossible to stand erect. His 'iron man' string reached 1,426 consecutive games with today's contest." Gehrig, who earlier in his career had been nicknamed the "Iron Horse" for his indestructible body and clean living, had not been scratched from the Yankees' lineup since June 1, 1925.

In light of Paul Dean's injury, the Cardinals hoped that Bill Walker would be ready to pitch in the Dodgers series, but he hadn't received a starting assignment since breaking his arm in early May and had only a few relief appearances in recent weeks. "Hallahan and Carleton demonstrated in the Philadelphia series they still are unreliable," wrote Martin Haley, "But if Walker were to come back he may tend to bolster the morale of the staff, and the morale as well as the physical end needs strengthening. In fact, the entire team's *esprit de corps* could stand much bulwarking. What with injuries, player fines for training rule violations, lack of dependable pitchers, poor morale and the fact that they are dropping farther back each day, the Cards are in a sorry plight."

But, as the character of the team so often revealed, they responded when the chips were down. They took three out of the five games from the Dodgers, including a doubleheader victory on July 15. Dizzy Dean started the day off with a 2–0 blanking of the Brooklynites, his second shutout of the season, his sixteenth win, and his eighth triumph in a row. He also nailed an eighth-inning homer off Ray Benge for the second of the Cardinal runs. Diz was becoming the one-man wrecking crew of the Cardinals' pitching staff, and hadn't been beaten since June 16 against Philadelphia in Sportsman's Park. Despite having pitched in five of the previous ten games, Diz dominated the Dodgers with an overpowering fastball and devastating curve. Game Two wound up a

6–3 victory for Carelton that was bolstered by a pair of Medwick homers that produced five runs. Medwick was perhaps venting some latent anger, as he was ejected the day before for protesting a call with first base umpire Beans Reardon. Joe had hit a squibber to Dodgers shortstop Lonnie Frey, and believed that he had beaten the play out. Reardon disagreed.

Medwick was all rage and fury on the ballfield, and he was letting his bat do all the work. In the five games in Brooklyn against the Dodgers, he had four homers, a triple, two doubles, ten hits total, and eleven runs batted in. "Thank goodness the National League schedule permits him to play 11 games in Flatbush each year," cited Brooklyn sportswriter Bill McCullough about Jersey Joe afterwards.

The standings on July 16:

	W	*L*	*Pct.*	*GB*
New York	52	30	.634	—
Chicago	50	32	.610	2
St. Louis	46	34	.575	5
Pittsburgh	41	37	.526	9
Boston	41	42	.494	11.5
Philadelphia	35	48	.422	17.5
Brooklyn	34	49	.410	18.5
Cincinnati	26	53	.329	24.5

In a remarkable turn of events, John Heydler decided on July 16 to uphold Frisch's protest of Bill Klem's infield fly call in Chicago on July 2, and ordered that the game be replayed on July 31 (when the Cardinals and Cubs next met) from the point at which the dispute arose—in the bottom of the seventh inning. Heydler ordered that the two teams take the field with as close to the same lineups as possible, and replay the contest before the regularly-scheduled game began.

Despite playing in the Midwest and garnering a meager salary, Diz was beginning to gain prominence on the national stage. One of his biggest admirers was Grantland Rice, and the renowned sports columnist dedicated his July 20, 1934, newspaper space to the brightest new star in the game. "How many pitchers has baseball known," asked Rice, "with more color than Dizzy 'Gunga' Dean—who happens to be a great ballplayer on the side?" Rice responded to his own query by constructing a new version of a famous Rudyard Kipling piece:

Dizzy Gunga Dean
(If Mr. Kipling Doesn't Mind)

You may talk of throwing arms that come up from Texas farms,
  With a hop on the fast one that is smoking;
But when it comes to pitching that keeps the batter twitching
  I can slip you in a name that's past all joking;
For in old St. Louis town, where they called him once a clown,
  There's a tall and gangling figure on the scene.
And of all that Redbird crew, there's one bloke that pulls 'em through,

  Just a fellow by the name of Gunga Dean.
  It is Dean—Dean—Dean
  You human coil of lasso—Dizzy Dean!
  If it wasn't for old Dizzy
  They'd be worse than fizzy-wizzy,
  Come on and grab another—Gunga Dean.

He told 'em what he'd do, and they labeled him a screw,
  Just a blasted mug who took it out in boasting;
And one day they sent him back to the cattle and the shack,
  With a fair amount of panning and of toasting;
But the tall and gangling gawk, with a fast ball like a hawk,
  Keeps them standing on their heads along the green—
Brings back color to game with a flash of crimson flame,
  So I'm slipping it along to Gunga Dean—

  Yes—it's Dean—Dean—Dean—
  He's a beggar with a bullet through your spleen.
  Though at times some bat has flayed you,
  By the Texas sun that made you,
  You're a better man than bats are, Dizzy Dean!

Perhaps as a coincidence or perhaps not, Dean was reported in the St. Louis papers the next day to be asking for an $11,000 raise for the 1935 season. "Here's some good news for Sam Breadon," announced the *Globe-Democrat*. "Dizzy Dean says he is going to demand only $18,500 for next season. Asked how he came to arrive at that figure, he pointed out that the highest paid Cardinal player since Diz joined the team received $18,500 for a single season, hence Dizzy reasons that he is worth at least that much. Dean says his salary for this year is $7,500, but he disclosed the Cardinal club paid him a bonus of $2,500 at the close of the 1933 season."

In addition to the landmark Heydler-Frisch-Klem case, more history was made in Chicago on July 22. John Dillinger, the world's most famous gangster, was shot down and killed by 15 agents of the U.S. Justice Department as he left a movie theatre in the center of the city. The agents, led by Mel Purvis, waited outside the theater for two hours after they witnessed Dillinger buying a ticket. Upon leaving the movie house, Dillinger, whose plan to see the film had been revealed to Justice Department officials the day before, noticed that he was being watched, and drew his pistol. This commenced a barrage of gunfire from the agents, which killed Dillinger instantly and wounded two innocent passersby. Dillinger was reported as being heavier than usual, and wearing a mustache. "The end of the greatest man hunt in contemporary criminal annals came in the swift tempo in which the notorious outlaw had lived," announced the Associated Press.

The Cardinals, meanwhile, were struggling to match guns with the National League's best. After leaving Brooklyn, the Gang traveled to Boston to open a series with the Braves. On the day that Dillinger was cornered, the Gas House Gang found themselves in third place, a game behind the Cubs, and four behind front-running New York. And much like the attack on Dillinger, the Braves were relentlessly pinned down by the booming bats of the Cardinals. The Cards won all five games of the series with the Bostonians, including a doubleheader on the final day in front of 14,000 spectators, to lift their record to 53–35 on July 24. However, they gained little ground on the Giants, who were continuing to play outstanding baseball themselves.

The Cardinals knew they needed to take as many head-to-head games with the Giants that they could. Another opportunity presented itself as the Cardinals marched into the Polo Grounds on July 23 to open a four-game set with the Giants. They trailed New York by four games, and the second-place Cubs by a single contest. In the first game, Diz matched up against righthander Hal Schumacher. It was a hot, sultry day at the "Horseshoe" (the nickname in correlation with the unique shape of the Polo Grounds), and the usual Cardinals-Giants intensity was present on the field. Even though Frisch's leg injuries had healed, he kept Whitehead in his place in the lineup; he did not want to break the momentum of his streaking team, which had won eight of its last nine. The Cards built a 5–1 lead by the fourth inning, and knocked Schumacher from the hill. When the Giants batted in the bottom of the fourth, Diz was struck for three runs, narrowing the St. Louis lead to 5–4. Diz settled in after that, and cruised in to a 6–5 victory. Medwick had to leave the game in the fifth inning, when he dove for a ball off the bat of Bill Terry and landed on his right shoulder. Unable to make the catch, Medwick recovered and fired the ball into second base, which hurt the shoulder further. Fullis took his place in left field, but Joe vowed to return to the next day in the critical series. In the ninth inning, pinch hitter George Watkins and Hughie Critz of the Giants watched six Dean fastballs whistle by them for the final two outs, with the "Great One" apparently throwing harder in the last frame than he was in the first.

It was the tenth straight win for Diz, and his fourth against New York to that point in the season. Before suffering the defeat, Schumacher himself had nine victories in a row entering the game. Dean was his ever-confident self as he addressed the *St. Louis Post-Dispatch* after the game. "It's just payday for Diz and the Redbirds. Give ol' Diz a lead of a run or two after five or six innings, and the other fellows might as well fold up."

But Tex Carleton lost 5–0 the following day, due in part to a tremendous home run by Giants slugger Mel Ott. Ott's blast, which caromed off the upper deck in right field, netted his 100th RBI of the season. Meanwhile, Roy Parmalee tossed a four-hit shutout at the Redbirds while striking out seven. Parmalee, who missed the first ten weeks of the season with appendicitis, allowed no Cardinal runner to reach third, and only three batted balls to reach the outfield. In the process, the Giants' outfield tied a major league record by not recording a putout or assist all day. Frisch put himself in the lineup for the first time since July 8, spelling Pepper Martin at third who was still suffering from a sore arm.

The loss had snapped the Cardinals' streak, and things seemed like they'd get worse. A rainout on July 25 moved that day's game into a doubleheader the following afternoon, and Paul Dean was to face the great Hubbell once again in the first contest—played in front of a surprisingly large Thursday crowd of 30,000. Paul had not pitched in a game for two weeks after spraining his ankle in Philadelphia. Furthermore, nobody expected Harpo to duplicate his magnificent performance on May 11, when he beat Hubbell in St. Louis; nobody, that is, except Paul. "I hope they pitch Hubbell against me," he had said earlier in the week in a Diz-like tone. "We'll win for sure."

Fortunately, the Cardinals would manage one of their few productive offensive outings against the great lefthander on this day, and Hubbell was gone after only four innings. In that stanza, Rothrock hammered a three-run homer after an error by Giants shortstop Blondy Ryan allowed the inning to continue. Paul went seven strong innings, allowing six hits and two runs. He got relief help from brother Dizzy and gained the victory, 7–2. Like Diz, he now had four wins against the Giants for 1934, and it ran the siblings' record to 29–7 for the year.

Bill Walker, however, could not outduel New York knuckleballer "Fat Freddie" Fitzsimmons in the second game, bowing to the Giants, 6–3. Fitzsimmons yielded only two hits over seven shut-out innings, with Bill DeLancey providing a little pop in the eighth with his sixth home run.

Hence, with the 2–2 split in games, the Cardinals left the Polo Grounds with no territory gained in the standings. Nonetheless, they did gain the respect and peek-over-the-shoulder of the Giants. The Redbirds headed to Pittsburgh with an 11–6 record under their belts for their tour of the eastern seaboard, which was precisely the Giants' ledger in playing at home for the previous two weeks.

Despite the strong trip along the Atlantic Coast, the Gang lost two out of the next three when they moved on to Pittsburgh. Diz's ten-game winning streak was stopped in the middle contest, as he was unusually wild. He walked six and gave up a home run to Paul Waner and lost to veteran pitcher Waite Hoyt, 5–4. The Cardinals left July in third place, a game-and-a-half behind the Cubs, and a full five behind the first-place Giants.

Meanwhile, the Cincinnati Reds had replaced Bob O'Farrell as manager with Charley Dressen in an effort to shake up the lethargic team. Dressen claimed that swift changes would be made in the operation of the team. "All I ask is that the boys bear down every minute," he told the writers. "If they don't, there will be quick displacements." The Reds were firmly entrenched in last place, as the National League standings showed in the newspapers on the morning of August 1:

	W	*L*	*Pct.*	*GB*
New York	61	36	.629	—
Chicago	58	38	.604	2.5
St. Louis	55	40	.579	5
Boston	49	49	.500	12.5
Pittsburgh	45	48	.484	114
Philadelphia	42	55	.433	19
Brooklyn	40	55	.421	20
Cincinnati	33	62	.347	27

A series to begin August in Chicago was a chance for the Cardinals to make up some more ground, and the Gang sought to take advantage. Dizzy was particularly anxious to work, as he had not beaten the Cubs since July 30, 1933, when he established the single-game strike-out record of 17. Walker lost the opener to Lon Warneke on July 31 (before the regularly-scheduled game, the Cardinals also lost the "replay" game that was completed from Frisch's earlier protest; a large crowd of 25,000 gathered to see the extra ball played). Paul Dean came back the next day, however and pitched masterfully in shutting out the Cubs, 4–0. He raised his season record to 12–4 while allowing only four hits and striking out seven. Once again, Jim Weaver proved to be a worthy adversary for the Cards, stubbornly allowing only two hits over seven innings. However, a two-out walk to Durocher in the eighth led to his demise, as four singles and a wild pitch followed. The next day, in the final game of the long road trip, Hallahan was tormented by four Cardinal errors in a 6–2 loss. Wild Bill had not made an appearance since July 21 in Boston when he injured a finger on his throwing hand.

As the Cards were struggling in Chicago, Hubbell fired his fifth shutout of the season, a 2–0 whitewash of the Phillies in Philadelphia. The Giants' lead had stretched to five games over the Cubs and six-and-a-half over the Redbirds.

Frisch's confidence in pitching staff began to wane even further save the Deans. Coming back to St. Louis on August 3 (the Cardinals' first home game in four weeks), Diz avenged his loss from previous week to the 35-year-old Hoyt in beating him and the Pirates, 9–3. Helping at the plate, Diz also smacked a triple and a double to the wall, as did Orsatti and Durocher. It was Dean's 19th win, and speculation once again began to rise about the Dean family gaining 45 victories for the season as Diz had predicted in spring training. He came to the rescue the very next day as well, preserving a 6–4 victory for Carleton. He had pitched a full nine innings the day before, but still blew through the Pirate hitters in the eighth and ninth on this day with relative ease.

For a change, the baseball news out of New York on August 4 came from the Bronx, not Harlem. Gehrig, still fighting through the fatigue that had plagued him all season, hit his 34th and 35th home runs to take the major league lead away from Jimmie Foxx. More significantly in the eyes of the baseball world, however, was that Gehrig was ahead of Babe Ruth's pace of 60 home runs in the 1927 season. It was quickly forgotten, however, that Ruth went on a tear of 17 home runs in the final month of the '27 season to smash the 60-dinger barrier, a pace that Gehrig would not maintain.

Back in St. Louis, yet another Dean was set to make his major league debut on August 10. Elmer, who had been toiling in the minor league stands as a peanut vendor, arrived at Sportsman's Park anxious to become goober king of St. Louis. "Elmer comes well recommended," announced the *Globe-Democrat*. "He served his peanut apprenticeship for a year and a half at the Cards' baseball farm team in Houston, Texas.... Elmer, who was born about 28 years ago, will pitch peanuts and catch attention as well as nickels." Elmer had been recently rediscovered by the Dean family after a four-year absence. Wandering off on his own after the family separation at the train tracks, Elmer wound up in Texas when his brothers' exploits got him to speak to his coworkers about his surname. Fred Ankeman, president of the Houston club, sensed that he may have caught lightning in a jug; as soon as Elmer's roots were ascertained, he was immediately given a tryout as a pitcher. He did not seem to have the same stuff as his brothers, however, and was relegated to grandstand duty.

Meanwhile, the Cubs were in town to open a four-game set with the Cardinals. The Redbirds needed to win all four to jump ahead of the Cubs, who led St. Louis by three-and-a-half games while trailing the Giants by two.

As high winds and threatening storm clouds engulfed the ballpark during the first game, it was the Cardinal bats that launched a storm. They pounded out 21 hits, including four each by Frisch and Durocher, as the Chicagoans were drubbed 17–3. The Cards exacted revenge on Warneke, who won both contests in Chicago on July 31—the end of the disputed game, and the regularly-played affair as well. Warneke was lifted during the Cardinals' nine-run third inning, a Cardinals' season high for one frame. The Gang followed up with a tough 6–4 win behind Bill Walker the following day, powered by Rip Collins' 25th homer of the season. With both Deans slated to start in the Sunday doubleheader to finish the series, the momentum—and an assault on second place— appeared to favor the men from St. Louis. A full house of 36,073 gathered on Grand Avenue on this hot St. Louis Sunday in August, expecting to see a command performance by Dizzy and Paul.

Paul started crisply in the first game. He was snapping off curves and fastballs, and held on to a 1–0 lead into the sixth inning. Unfortunately, at that point the roof caved in. The Chicago bats came alive and knocked Paul out, the result being a 7–2 Cubs victory. Diz would try to salvage a win in the second game, and he also began the game well. He fanned Cuyler and Billy Herman to start the game, but soon ran into trouble. He claimed to feel some arm stiffness in the middle of the game, and in the latter innings relied on curves and changeups for the most part. Sensing his shifted strategy, the Cub bats once again exploded in the eighth inning. Four unearned runs plagued the Cardinals, and Diz moped off the field with his fifth loss of the year, a 6–4 defeat.

The morbid St. Louis locker room was full of players sitting at their benches, heads between their knees, wondering what happened. They had blown a great chance to take second place, and also to gain on the Giants. Everything was silent, when someone suddenly played the radio. Medwick shouted, "Shut that damn thing off!" and all was silent again. The Gas House Gang now faced a seven-and-a-half-game margin between them and New York. In the middle of the despair, Frisch walked in the room, and told the players that they needed to shower and dress quickly. Their train was leaving Union Station soon, bound for Detroit, where the Cardinals would play a scheduled exhibition game against the Tigers the next day. At this announcement, Diz rolled his eyes and shook his head; it was the last thing he felt like doing. Both he and Paul had just lost two tough ballgames—games the Cardinals desperately needed—and now he was being asked to ride in a train for eleven hours to play one of those games that "Don't count none," as he put it. After showering, he went over to Paul's locker and said something, to which Harpo nodded. The two then left the clubhouse together, but did not go to the train station; instead, they went home and went to sleep, as the rest of the team lumbered wearily across Illinois on the rails.

When word got back to St. Louis that they were not on the train, Breadon did not rush to judgment. "They were on the list to go Sunday morning," he revealed, "but whether Manager Frisch excused them from the trip later in the day is something I do not know now. If they were not excused by Frisch, then it will be up to Frank to handle the case as he sees fit. I will see him this morning after he returns to St. Louis." It was noted in the papers that Diz was fined $100 the previous season by then-manager Gabby Street, which might set a precedent for this scenario. With the rest of the team out of town, and Breadon's statement already secured, the press focused their attention on Dizzy's side of the story.

"We [he and Paul] did not have our coats or bags with us at Sportsman's Park so we figured we'd stay in St. Louis," he explained. "The team left right after Sunday's second game and we came back to our hotel. I did not see any reason to make the trip. Besides, I hurt my arm Sunday. That's the reason I lost my fastball.

"I pulled something loose in my right elbow while pitching to Babe Herman in the fourth inning," he added. "I didn't have my stuff after that. I'm not going to pitch again until the arm is healed. Other pitchers don't work if they have sore arms and I'm not going to, either. If I went out there with the arm feeling the way it does I might ruin my career." Interestingly, this was Paul's 21st birthday—rather than a day he might be considered a grown man, he was still having Diz make his decisions for him. When the reporters asked for his story, it sounded remarkably similar—no coat or bag at the ballpark, and the need to rest an injury that recently developed (he claimed his ankle was hurting once again). Breadon even acknowledged Dizzy's influence over Paul, as he considered fining the former $100 and the latter $50.

The brothers weren't concerned when the tired team returned from Detroit two days later. The Philadelphia Phillies were in St. Louis to play the Cardinals, and the Dean boys got plenty of cold looks from the other players as they entered the clubhouse. Diz once again brought up the idea that he had a sore arm, with that being the reason why he didn't make the trip; nobody bought it. Dizzy expected the superstar treatment and didn't receive it. Frisch then walked in, and told Diz that he was being fined $100 for missing the train, and that Paul would be levied the lesser citation of $50. "You shouldn't have walked out on us," Frisch snapped. When he said this, Dizzy started jumping up and down, ranting and raving. He kicked over stools, cursed the entire ballclub, and punctuated the display by tearing both of his Cardinal jerseys to shreds. He vowed to everyone in the room that he would never again play for St. Louis. Frisch then hollered, "You're suspended! Both of you! Nobody runs this ballclub except me!" Later, Diz was confronted by a reporter who missed the uproar from earlier in the day. Would he mind tearing a little more piece of the uniform for his photographer? Diz obliged.

When things had cooled off, Frisch tried to explain things simply to the St. Louis press. "There's no hardship in a train ride. People pay money to take train rides. Baseball is our business, and the mere fact that we worked Sunday is no excuse for running out on a Monday game just because it's an exhibition." Frisch also stated that, despite the suspensions, the Dean boys were free to rejoin the club whenever they saw fit—and paid their fines.

"We've got to have discipline," the manager added. "We can't let one or two men miss exhibition games. No team does that."

Diz watched from the press box that day and chatted with the sportswriters. They were all, of course, eager to know the nature of what went on in the clubhouse. The Cardinals beat the Phillies that day, 6–1. Only 1,100 fans turned out at Sportsman's Park, and it was reported that many of them were hollering at Frisch because of the action taken against the Dean boys. Diz was waiting to see the reaction of Breadon and Rickey; as it turned out, both naturally supported Frisch wholeheartedly. Some even suggested that Frisch's efficient handling of the incident earned him a contract for the 1935 season. Breadon, though, did not care to discuss the matter at the present time. "Frisch has been a fine fellow, and has done a lot for us and I am backing him up 100 percent in the Dean case," Breadon pointed out when asked about his manager's status for the following year. "However, with so much happening lately I have not entertained any thought relative to the 1935 contract."

Diz continued the next day (as did Paul) to watch the game in the press box, each on a "sit-down" strike until the Cardinals lifted the fines. The game was rained out anyway, so the issue rested for another 24 hours. Regardless of what the Deans decided to do that night, Frisch had already named Carleton and Walker to start the doubleheader the following day, with the second contest a makeup from the August 15 washout. While the rains fell, Diz continued to chat away with the sportswriters, although he was evidently becoming disturbed by the entire "strike" situation—especially being asked about it repeatedly. Thinking that their strike wouldn't last, a reporter sitting next to Diz turned to him and said, "Betcha you're back in uniform by tomorrow."

"Here's ten bucks that says I won't," Diz fired back, as he whipped two fives onto the table.

On August 16, the National League standings looked this way:

	W	L	Pct.	GB
New York	71	41	.634	—
Chicago	66	44	.600	4
St. Louis	63	46	.578	6.5
Boston	55	54	.505	14.5
Pittsburgh	54	55	.495	15
Brooklyn	46	62	.426	22.5
Philadelphia	44	64	.421	24.5
Cincinnati	39	72	.351	31.5

In a swift turn of events, Paul was suddenly no longer siding with Diz; he wanted to get back on the mound and pitch. Diz was not so quickly reconciled, and once again complained of his "sore arm." The other Cardinals, especially the pitchers, knew that this statement was his panacea for all of his disagreements with management. "The Deans, after their row, uttered remarks which indicated all was not rosy between themselves and some of the other players," noted Martin Haley, "...some members of the other bloc seem not unhappy that the Deans are absent." If he complained long enough, some of the other Cardinals figured, Breadon would give him whatever he wanted (however, he complained just as often about not being allowed to pitch enough). But Breadon held fast, saying that the fines would indeed stick.

Without the Deans, the Cardinals won both games of the doubleheader against Philadelphia, 4–3 and 7–2, even though darkening skies had scared away all but 1,800 spectators to the ballpark. Carleton got relief help from Jesse Haines in the first game, won by a Durocher hit to the wall in extra innings. Walker struck out six to win the nightcap, aided by Collins' 27th homer and Rothrock's ninth.

Paul announced afterwards that he was petitioning Breadon for reinstatement. After admitting guilt and losing a total of $120 on the affair (amid fines, torn uniforms, and missed games), he rejoined the ballclub on August 17. Diz, on the other hand, was planning a car trip with his wife Pat, but did not reveal a destination. When a reporter asked him if he was headed to Chicago to appeal his case to Commissioner Kenesaw Landis, he gave no comment. He also printed the following statement in the August 17 editions of the *Globe-Democrat* and *Post-Dispatch* in an attempt to explain his side of the story:

> The first thing I want to say is that I realize I made a mistake in not making the trip to Detroit. Had I known what the game up there was all about, I would not have disappointed those kids for anything in the world. But I was so disgusted about losing that doubleheader Sunday that right then I didn't care if I never saw another ballgame.
>
> You know how bad I hate to lose games. And when Paul and I both lost before all that crowd of loyal St. Louis people I was "re-gusted." It's bad enough when I lose away from home, but to go out there in that hot sun and pitch my heart out and still lose. Well, you can imagine just how I felt.
>
> Then Tuesday, when the team came home, I went out to the clubhouse, fully expecting a fine. I had already realized I had made a mistake. When I went into the clubhouse I expected Frank to call me over and tell me I was fined. But it seems as though everybody on the team was told before I was. So when they all, from the batboy up, got through telling me I was fined, I wasn't in any mood to be jumped on again. So I blew up. One word brought on another, and when the storm was over I had torn up my uniforms to keep anyone else from using them.
>
> The ball club then announced I could return to the club anytime I would accept the fines. I wanted to return today (Thursday) and I agreed to the fine, suspension without pay for two days, and to pay for the uniforms. But after I agreed to do that, the "powers that be" informed me

that I would get an extra ten days' suspension, because Paul does not care to return. Paul is 21 years old and a man with his own mind.

I have apologized and admitted I was wrong, and I want to go back to work now, not ten days from now. I'll leave it up to you and all the sports fans, what else can I do?

Sincerely,
"Dizzy" Dean

On his first day back, Paul picked up the win in a 12–2 triumph over the Phillies. He was activated by Breadon and Rickey only an hour before game time, and came to the relief of Dazzy Vance in the third inning after Philadelphia had taken a 2–0 lead.

Finally, the whole deal with the Dean strike closed on August 20, when Diz appealed to Commissioner Landis. Diz drove seven hours from St. Louis to Chicago for the hearing, which was held in Landis' private suite of the Park Plaza Hotel. The council against Dean consisted of Breadon, Rickey, Frisch, and other Cardinal players. Rickey, an eloquent and intelligent man, led off the prosecution's case, and soon everyone joined the fray. Pitcher Jesse Haines went on to confirm that Diz got a sore arm "whenever he felt like it"; Frisch testified that Diz and Paul had blatantly disappointed about 40,000 children in Detroit who had shown up to see them; and Dizzy and Breadon accused each other of being liars. Dean said that the Cardinals never finished paying all of his signing bonus money, and also were not taking care of his brother Elmer the way they'd promised. Breadon noted that the evidence pointed to Dizzy not having a sore arm at all, and that he used the ploy as an excuse to miss the Detroit trip.

Landis declared, "I feel that a suspension of ten days for Dean's failure to appear in Detroit with the Cardinals for the exhibition game last Monday is not an unreasonable penalty." This statement, however, only supported Breadon's move; it did not legally enforce it. At this point, Rickey (acting as legal counsel for the ballclub) suggested a suspension of eight days. Frisch then suggested that seven days would suffice, and it was thus agreed. Furthermore, Dizzy's request for Landis to reimburse Paul and him for the fines was denied. When newspaper photographers took pictures of the group upon completing the deal, Diz refused to smile for the cameras. Upon leaving the room, Dean also refused to shake the hands of both Breadon and Frisch.

Frisch's summation of the entire event echoed the feeling of most of the other Cardinal players. "There are ten million people out of work in this country, yet Dizzy Dean is willing to sacrifice a daily income of approximately $50 to fill the role of a play-boy." Added Sid Keener of the *St. Louis Star-Times*, "The feeling of the Cardinal players toward the Deans has dropped from the freezing point to ten degrees below zero since the latest rebellion. Some of the fellows, including Captain Durocher, especially resent the use of the term 'bushers' as applied to them by Paul, a first-year man."

The ordeal wound up costing Diz a total of $486 in fines, lost salary, and torn uniforms, in addition to a telegraphed apology to the fans in Detroit. As for the morale of the team, the incident only served to strengthen the other players' respect for Frisch, for he never succumbed to Dean's pressure. Supporters from around the country, many of whom could hardly afford to put bread on their own tables, sent Diz whatever they could to make up for the money he had lost. He sent back every dime.

Taking a break from a successful homestand on August 23, the Cardinals crossed the Mississippi River into Illinois to play an exhibition game against the Griesedieck Stags of Belleville, as 3,000 folks showed up to see the action. The Cardinals squeaked out a win against the upstart Stags, 6–5, as Pat Crawford belted a home run over the right field wall. And Jim Mooney, proving ineffective even against an amateur team, gave up 15 hits.

The Cardinals returned to Sportsman's Park the following day to open a series with the Giants as the Redbirds found themselves six games behind New York with only 38 to play. Local sportswriters tried to maintain hope for the fans, as they reminded them that on this date in 1930 the Cards were nine games back and still managed to win the pennant. The Cardinals held an admirable 9–6 record against the defending champions so far in '34, so their confidence remained high. Eight of the nine victories were logged by one Dean or the other. It was Paul's turn today, and the crowd sat back to see if he could beat the Giants again.

Paul smoked through the New York bats for the first five innings, allowing only two hits and no runs as the Cardinals had built a 3–0 lead. The lead ultimately shrunk to 3–2, and with two out in the ninth, it looked as if that was how it would finish. That was when Joe Moore of the Giants lifted a long fly to left that carried out of the ballpark, scoring himself and two teammates, which gave the Giants a 5–3 win. Paul was picked off second base in the fifth inning, and he pointed to this as an important mistake in the loss. Big brother, however, was soon coming to the rescue for Paul and the Cardinals.

"Dizzy Dean is once again the fair-haired boy," proclaimed the *Globe-Democrat* on August 25. The day before, in front of 4,900 fans who ignored dark clouds in the sky, he made a grand return to Grand Avenue with the Cardinals holding a 69–48 record, only a half-game behind the Cubs for second place but a full seven behind the Giants. Diz and Joe Bowman matched "goose eggs" for five innings, each allowing only two hits over the duration. Schumacher was scheduled to start for New York, but informed Terry before the game that his ailing back would keep him out of the lineup. In the sixth, Rothrock and Collins homered to the pavilion roof in right, and the Cards got two more runs off Al Smith in the seventh. Dean shut the Giants down for the distance, allowing a total only five hits—all singles—and also recorded his first (and only) stolen base of the season in the fifth inning after one of his two hits. The victory put the Cardinals at 22 games over the .500 mark (70–48), and was Dean's 22nd win. Even with his absence of nearly two weeks, Dean was leading the major leagues in victories by one over Lefty Gomez of the Yankees. In addition, his 145 strikeouts after the August 24 win was also tops in baseball. The Gas House Gang had crept ahead of the Cubs into second place (who had lost in Brooklyn), but still trailed the Giants by five-and-a-half games.

The next day saw the largest Saturday attendance for the season at Sportsman's Park—only 16,656. Instead of continuing their pursuit of the Giants, the Cardinals dropped behind the Cubs into third place once again, blowing a 5–0 lead in losing to New York, 7–6. After a Frisch pinch-hit triple returned the Cardinals' lead at 6–5, Diz attempted to rescue the game for Bill Walker in the seventh inning. Then, a Travis Jackson single drove in the tying and winning runs for the New York.

All the while, the Tigers were looming as an indomitable force in the American League. Their star pitcher, Lynwood "Schoolboy" Rowe, had tied the league record for consecutive victories with 16, matching the marks of Walter Johnson, Smokey Joe Wood, and Lefty Grove. The 22-year-old from Arkansas faced the A's in Philadelphia on August 28, looking for the new record in front of 33,718 fans, the largest crowd in the history of Shibe Park. Rowe would fall short, losing 13–5 in the second game of the doubleheader. It was his first loss since June 10 to the Chicago White Sox, and since that date, he had beaten every team in the league—including the Yankees four times. In splitting the day's contests, Detroit had moved out to a five-game lead over the Yankees in the Junior Circuit, and nearly everyone around baseball was beginning to formulate the matchups for a Giants-Tigers World Series.

In yet another example of the grave differences between generations in baseball, the Cardinals did something on August 30 that modern players would deem inconceivable—they played another exhibition game, against another National League team. The beneficiaries this time were the grateful folks of Oshkosh, Wisconsin, 90 miles north of Chicago. With poor transportation and no television, exhibition games were the only means for many citizens of isolated communities to see big league baseball. In the first exhibition ever played in Oshkosh, "About 12,000 packed the grandstand and all available standing room," according to reports, as the Cardinals took on the Cubs in a game that would never be recorded in professional baseball annals. Players complained of the skinned infield that bled bad hops, as both team committed three errors. The Cubs won, 12–5, and the two teams packed up and headed south to Wrigley Field to begin a series in returning to regular league play.

The standings on September 1, with only a month left in the season:

	W	*L*	*Pct.*	*GB*
New York	80	46	.635	—
St. Louis	74	51	.592	5.5
Chicago	74	51	.592	5.5
Boston	64	60	.516	15
Pittsburgh	59	64	.480	19.5
Brooklyn	54	69	.439	24.5
Philadelphia	46	76	.377	32
Cincinnati	45	79	.363	34

13

The Stretch Run

Still poised to try and overtake the Giants, the Cardinals launched their final extensive road trip as September began. Their voyage started in Wrigley Field against the Cubs, as Diz took the hill still trying to beat the bruins for the first time in nearly 14 months. With insults flying back and forth between both dugouts and the pitching mound, Dean wiped the sweat from his brow, and rocked back into his windmill motion to let "foggers" fly. His struggles against the Cubs were career-long; his 13–17 lifetime record against them was his only losing tally against any club. "That Wrigley—it's a hitter's park," scoffed Diz, excusing his poor outings in Chicago. "Any ham-and-egger could hit dingers in that crackerbox of a field."

The Cards took advantage of the tired Cubs, beating them 3–1 and 7–1 on consecutive days, and in the process landed in second place all by themselves. The opening game was Dizzy's 23rd win, as he denied Chicago rallies in the sixth, seventh, and eighth innings to hold on for the win before a Ladies' Day crowd of 27,000 at Wrigley. Hallahan pitched surprisingly good ball the next day, holding the Cubs scoreless until the ninth when Kiki Cuyler's double was followed by a Tuck Stainback single to spoil the shutout. Rip Collins again led the St. Louis batting attack as he launched his 31st homer of the year to the right field stands.

Also in the first game, Dean was hit by a line drive off the bat of Cuyler which caromed off his right leg. An X-ray after the game showed no bone break, and Frisch announced that Dean would be ready for relief work when the team moved on to Pittsburgh. The final game of the Cubs series, which had scheduled Paul Dean to face Lon Warneke, was rained out. Because of the extremely dry conditions in the Midwest during 1934, it was only the second (and final) rainout at Wrigley Field on the season. It was decided by league officials that the game would not be made up unless close standings at the end of the season warranted it to be played. The storm gave the club a pleasant, unexpected extra day's rest before heading east to face the Pirates.

If Dizzy Dean was the individual that evoked the most Cub anger, then it was Medwick who was the chief annoyance of the Pittsburgh team. As was his custom, Ducky would bother Pirate sluggers Arky Vaughan and Paul Waner during batting practice. But no one wanted the job of removing him—he would eventually waltz off on his own. Or perhaps it was his hitting that really irked the Bucs; he owned a .378 lifetime average against Pittsburgh.

It was a sunny Labor Day in the Steel City, and an anxious crowd of almost 20,000 came to watch "those Dean brothers" pitch. The Pirates record stood at 60–65, 19½ games out of first, and the club was only playing for pride at this point. But Diz and Paul were good drawing cards, and many workmen enjoyed their day off at the ballpark, scarfing down hot dogs and gulping cold beer.

Paul got the start in Game One. Unfortunately, he had no control, speed, or anything else. He was shelled for eight runs in the third inning, including a bases-loaded single by Waner who was continuing to lead the National League in hitting with a .367 average going into the day's action. After Paul was yanked by Frisch, old Dazzy Vance came in to mop up the mess. The final score was 12–2, and Cardinal spirits plummeted as they tried to inspire themselves for Game Two of the doubleheader, hoping that starter Bill Walker could give them the lift they needed.

The game was close all the way, and in the ninth inning with St. Louis trailing 3–2, Pepper Martin smacked a triple to the right field wall to drive in the tying and go-ahead runs. Medwick's sacrifice fly scored Martin, and the Cardinals needed just three more outs to secure a 5–3 victory. In the importance of salvaging a win from the day and not losing any more ground, Frisch summoned Diz to replace the tiring Walker. But like his brother, Diz didn't have his stuff today either, allowing a run, plus letting Pirate runners to reach second and third, and then was replaced by Hallahan. Pittsburgh third baseman Pie Traynor then lined a single to right, winning the game for the Pirates, 6–5. With the two losses, the Cards fell to a full six games behind the first-place Giants, and retreated to a second-place tie once again with the Cubs. Though in the middle of a dejected Cardinal clubhouse,

Frisch refused to give up hope. Ray Gillespie of the *St. Louis Star-Times* wrote afterwards, "The two defeats virtually eliminated St. Louis from the 1934 pennant scramble."

"*Are we* out of the race, Frankie?" another St. Louis reporter asked.

"Never—not until we're counted out officially. When I played for John McGraw, I was taught to fight to the finish, and you can bet your last dollar that every man playing for me will do the same." The Giants looked invincible, with 20 of their last 24 games being played at home in the Polo Grounds. "The Giants can be overtaken," admitted Gary Schumacher of the *New York Evening Journal*, "but it's a million-to-one shot."

The New York lead increased to seven games the next day, as the Cardinals were idle and the Giants swept a doubleheader from the Phillies.

Meanwhile, Tigers owner Frank Navin was so confident his club would be in the World Series that he ordered 17,000 new seats to be installed behind the left field fence at the ballpark in Detroit.

In his own latest twist to the saga of events, Diz sent his wife Pat into a frenzy, as the Cardinals were to leave Pittsburgh on a train for Greensburg, Pennsylvania, where the club was to play another exhibition game. This time, the Cardinals would be playing one of their minor league teams, the Greensburg Red Wings. He was embroiled in an intense poker game at the hotel, which he refused to leave despite Pat's pleading. Ironically, Frisch had actually given Diz this exhibition game off—information that Diz did not share with Pat. He was to meet the team in Brooklyn so that he could rest up for the important series upcoming against the Dodgers. Pat went storming into Frisch's room, worried that Diz would miss another game he was supposed to attend, and get fined and suspended all over again. Frank eased back in his chair, puffed at his cigar, and chuckled. "I think he's pulling one on you, Pat," he said.

The Cards won another of those games that "don't count none" as Jim Mooney beat the Red Wings, 10–6. The most significant baseball news that day was Hack Wilson's release by the Phillies, which effectively marked the end of his career. Wilson, at 5'6" and 200 pounds, was described by one writer as being "shaped like a beer keg, and not unfamiliar with its contents." Wilson was best known, however, for his 1930 season with the Cubs, during which he belted 56 home runs and an astounding 190 runs batted in—the latter a major league record that is unlikely to ever be broken. He had been with Philadelphia for only a month, another unsuccessful replacement in the outfield after Chuck Klein had departed for Chicago. Wilson told reporters that he was considering a new career in professional wrestling.

Diz was indeed well-rested when the team joined him in Brooklyn, and responded accordingly with a 2–1 win over Casey Stengel's club. The game was tied 1–1 in the ninth inning, when Bill DeLancey surfaced as the hero. He drove a low fastball over the right field fence for his 12th home run of the year. The other St. Louis tally came earlier on another solo homer off the bat of Rip Collins. Dean had notched his 24th win.

After a 7–5 win by Tex Carleton over the Dodgers on September 6, two days of steady rain soaked the Brooklyn area. The last two games of the series were washed out, but across town the Giants and Cubs were able to play and Chicago handed New York a 4–2 loss. The Cardinals moved on to a Sunday doubleheader in Philadelphia on September 9. Because of observance of the Sabbath, twin bills had only been recently approved by the Pennsylvania legislature, and this was to be the first Sunday doubleheader ever in Philadelphia. The Baker Bowl, home of the Phillies, enjoyed its biggest crowd of the year for the event—a modest 14,000. With the weak Philadelphia team limping to a 48–79 record, these were two games that the Cardinals couldn't afford to lose; there were only three weeks left to go, and they still trailed New York by six-and-a-half games. Any pennant hopes that remained rested heavily on these games.

Paul Dean came through with a great effort, a complete game four-hitter with Medwick and Rothrock the hitting stars in a 4–1 win. For a while, it appeared that the second game might not be completed, as darkening skies made vision a problem. Bill Walker was hurling quickly for the Cards, and he kept the Phils at bay. Collins had an RBI double and a triple, and "East St. Louis Bill" held on for a 7–3 win and a sweep for the day. And in New York, a home run by Gus Suhr in the ninth gave the Pirates a 1–0 win over the Giants. New York was starting to feel somebody breathing down its neck; the lead was five games. Not to worry, however, the New York sportswriters told their readers. Dan Daniel assured the faithful that "it is quite generally accepted that it would take a baseball holocaust to prevent a World Series between the Giants and the Tigers" (Detroit held a six-game lead in the American League race).

The following day, September 11, Diz took the mound against the Phillies. To his right, Pepper Martin smoothed the dirt in front of his third base position. Pep had mud caked all over his uniform; it hadn't been washed in weeks. But you never wash a player's shirt in a hot streak, and through the muck and mire, he smiled back at Diz approvingly. Dean fired aspirin tablets at the Philadelphia hitters, and gained win number 25. It was a 4–1 victory, as Diz allowed only five hits and struck out seven. He also scored a run on the basepaths, "a picturesque slide across home plate for the second tally," as Stan Baumgartner of the *Philadelphia Inquirer* described it. "The slide was not necessary— no play was made on him—but Dean gave it to the cash customers just the same, to give them their money's worth." It would actually turn out to be a six-game series, as the clubs had to play a doubleheader the next day to make up for a previous rainout. With the Giants losing again in New York, the Cards went into the day's play only four games back. Cy Peterman, writing for the *Philadelphia Evening Bulletin*, nonetheless claimed that "the St. Louis Cardinals, a two-pitcher outfit, is needlessly exciting the National League with a phony bid for the flag." Only 3,000 people witnessed the extra two games on this Tuesday afternoon.

Tex Carleton and the rest of the Gang were shut out in the first game 5–0 by Phillies pitcher Syl Johnson. In the second match, however, they would strike back. With Diz relieving Hallahan in the seventh, he allowed a lone run over the last three innings in holding on for a 6–4 victory. Sensing a collapse by their club, the New York newspapers began speaking of the "crumbling Giant empire" and wondered how Bill Terry could allow his club to slip so close to the Cardinals. Roy Parmalee gave the New Yorkers some relief, though, with a 3–1 win over Pittsburgh that day. As was the tradition in Harlem, the blue flag was raised in centerfield over Coogan's Bluff, signifying to elevated train riders on their way home from work that the Giants had won that day. Nonetheless, with a four-and-a-half-game margin seeming to dwindle all the time, the New York faithful were getting nervous about the situation.

Dazzy Vance lost to the Phillies the next day. Vance did pitch well, shutting out Philadelphia for seven innings. But the Gas House Gang had no offensive fuel, as pitcher Roy "Snipe" Hansen shut down the Redbird bats in going the distance. The big play came in the eighth, with the score tied 1–1. A pop fly to centerfield off the bat of Ethan Allen should have been caught by Ernie Orsatti, but instead it bounced off his glove. Two runs scored on the play, and the score ended 3–1. Everyone around the country was preparing for a Giants-Tigers World Series, the latter still enjoying a decent lead in the American League chase. The Cardinals were now five-and-a-half behind with only two weeks left, as Carl Hubbell got his 20th win against Pittsburgh, 3–2. The entire season would come down to a four-game series in the Polo Grounds beginning September 14, with the Cardinals marching into New York to take on the resilient Giants and the National League looking this way:

	W	L	Pct.	GB
New York	87	50	.635	—
St. Louis	81	55	.596	5.5
Chicago	80	56	.588	6.5
Boston	69	66	.516	17
Pittsburgh	66	67	.480	19
Brooklyn	59	77	.434	27.5
Philadelphia	50	83	.376	32.5
Cincinnati	48	86	.358	34.5

14

A Double Feature

The Gas House Gang invaded Coogan's Bluff looking for another chance to overcome the Giants. Since they entered the series five-and-a-half games down, a split of the four-game set was unacceptable; they needed to sweep, or at least win three games in the series. Paul Dean would throw for the Cardinals in the first game, facing the large-bellied Freddie Fitzsimmons, a master of the knuckleball. The young Dean matched Fitzsimmons for ten innings, each pitching a scoreless slate at the opponent. While still a 0–0 tie in the 12th inning—with cold weather and ominous black rainclouds surrounding the ballpark—the Cardinals began to make noise with the bats. Medwick singled, and was then moved over to third on a base hit by Collins. Then, when Bill DeLancey lifted a flyball to right field, Giants star Mel Ott attempted to make a big play. He caught the ball, set his legs, and let one fly towards home plate, trying to nail Medwick. The ball sailed over catcher Gus Mancuso's head, and Collins scooted into third as the 9,100 in attendance moaned. Then Durocher, with two out after Orsatti popped up, smacked a single to center to give the Cardinals a 2–0 lead.

The Giants threatened slightly in the bottom half, but Durocher made a circus catch of a line drive off the bat of pinch hitter George Watkins. Paul Dean had thrown yet another big game, a 12-inning shutout of the defending champions. It was the ninth time the Giants had been blanked that year, as it was becoming increasingly obvious that the pitchers carried the pennant hopes for the Giants despite the presence of Ott and Terry in the lineup. It was Paul's fourth shutout of the season, and his fifth win against the Giants—his only loss to the New Yorkers had come on August 23rd in Sportsman's Park. He also had increased his strikeout total to 122 for his rookie season by fanning seven batters in the game. The next day, the New York papers marveled at the Dean brothers' mastery of the Giants. "All either of the Deans have to do, seemingly, is step on the mound. Automatically handcuffs are fitted to the Giants' wrists. They're helpless, and what is worse, they know it," wrote Gary Schumacher.

All momentum the Cardinals gained seemed lost, however, when Walker dropped a 4–1 decision to Schumacher the following day and fell five-and-a-half games back once again. The Giants had entered the series with a 46–19 record at home in 1934, and their pride showed through as a crowd of 15,000 saw New York edge closer to the pennant. Diz even tried to summon supernatural forces to help the Cardinals, as he paraded a black cat in front of the New York dugout before the game. His particular target was second baseman Hughie Critz, a young, impressionable, and superstitious player. Dean, holding the cat in one arm and waving the other in a wizard-like fashion uttered, "Go on cat, get Critz!" Poor Hughie jumped up and ran towards the right field corner in a crazed frenzy, attempting to escape the bad luck. Nonetheless, neither antics from Dean nor the cat fazed the Giants on this day.

A rainout of Saturday's game left a doubleheader for Sunday, as storm clouds still loomed in the New York area. The turf of the Polo Grounds was soaked, and Diz took advantage of the off day to let the sportswriters know of his plans for 1935. "Next season? Well, like I said, I will have to get a lot more money than I am getting now or I won't play at all. Another thing: I don't play if Frank Frisch doesn't manage. He is a great manager. He's the only man who could keep a club in a pennant fight with only two pitchers."

And who would that be, he was asked?

"Me and Paul."

"I'm getting $7,500 now," Dean continued. "I'm worth $100,000 or more in a trade or sale. The Cincys offered that back in May and St. Louis refused it. If we don't get good dough next season there will be a walkout that will make Rhode Island laugh theirselves sick."

As the writers paused and reflected on what that unusual prediction might mean, one asked Diz, "Who are the four best pitchers in the National League?"

He responded without hesitation, "Warneke, Hubbell, Schumacher, and me."

"You should have named Dizzy Dean first," someone offered.

After pausing to consider the order, Diz revised his statement. "Yes, I should of," he acknowledged.

The Cardinals needed to win both games of Sunday's twin bill. In realizing this, Frisch decided to throw both Deans; Diz in game one, Paul in game two. The advance billing of the magnificent brothers caused an overflow crowd. Despite the threatening weather, the stadium stretched to its utmost capacity by game time. People were even hanging from the elevated train tracks that overlooked the ballpark. When Roy Parmalee threw the first pitch for the Giants, a National League record of 62,574 had "jammed the aisles, crowded two in a seat, and clung precariously to rafters," according to reports. The Harlem Fire Department closed the gates a half-hour before game time as thousands more attempted to squeeze in. The stage had been set: the powerful Giants against the upstart Cardinals, the Polo Grounds, Dizzy Dean, Mel Ott, Bill Terry, Joe Medwick, and a pennant on the line. Baseball in its Golden Age.

A slight rain had continued throughout the morning, but the umpires were determined to get the first game going. Home runs by Ott and Mancuso gave the Giants a 2–0 lead in the fourth, and the lead increased to 3–0 in the fifth inning. Parmalee was rolling along, turning St. Louis away at every attack. He allowed only three hits through six innings, and Diz was struggling to keep the Cards in the game, hoping for a rally by the Gang. In the seventh, with New York still holding on to their three-run lead, the rally came. DeLancey, Orsatti, and Davis all singled to score a run. After pinch hitter Pat Crawford lined out to short, Schumacher was brought in to face Pepper Martin. These were two clutch players going head-to-head in a clutch situation: two outs, the tying run on base, in the most important game of the year. Martin patiently waited for a good pitch, and finally walked to load the bases. Next was Frisch, and despite Schumacher throwing four balls out of five pitches to Martin, Frankie wasted no time and jumped on the first one. The result was a liner to right-center field that fell safely, scored Orsatti and Davis, and gave the Cardinals a 4–3 lead as loud "boos" descended from the grandstand.

Carleton wound up saving the game for Dean, ultimately a 5–3 Cardinal victory. Tex pitched three strong shutout innings, and it was the 26th win of the season for Diz, the most by a Cardinal pitcher in one season in 35 years (dating back to when Cy Young won the same number in 1899). Now, for Game Two of the doubleheader, Paul would have to face none other than the great Hubbell once again. Giant fans were confident that Carl was due; surely he wouldn't let the rookie pitcher beat him a third time.

New York grabbed a 1–0 lead in the third when Joe Moore tripled to right and was driven home on a sacrifice fly by Critz. Hubbell, meanwhile, had kept St. Louis to their six-inning totals from the first game: three hits, no runs. Then Rip Collins, who made the first out in the seventh inning of the first game before that rally came, started the rally this time as he boomed a tremendous home run to the upper deck in left to make the game a 1–1 deadlock. The game went into extra innings, when in the tenth, Medwick saved the day—defensively, for a change. Hank Leiber drove a long ball into the left field gap, which the Duck drifted back on. He retreated, retreated, leaped, and made a one-handed catch against the wall, robbing Leiber of perhaps a home run and at least a double. Medwick tossed the ball back in, and limped back to his original position, grimacing in pain as he recovered from his crash into the wall. The next batter, shortstop Blondy Ryan, doubled to the opposite side of the park. This hit would have scored Leiber and won the game for the Giants if Medwick had not made the previous play. Wanting Hubbell to continue pitching, manager Bill Terry let Carl bat for himself in the next slot, and he promptly grounded out to end the inning. Rain continued to fall, but the umpires decided it was safe to play one more round, in order to try and produce an outcome in this all-important game.

Through the fog and gloom, few people actually saw Pepper Martin connect on Hubbell's first pitch of the 11th inning. It was a steaming fastball inside, and Pepper socked it. The ball sailed through the fog, like a wind gust slicing through a cloud of smoke, and the ball landed over the wall for an opposite-field home run to right. The great lefthander was stunned as Pep gleefully galloped around the bases to the moans of the Giant faithful. Soon after, Medwick drove home Rothrock with a single, and St. Louis took a 3–1 lead into the bottom of the 11th, attempting to gain the sweep of the critical doubleheader. Paul coolly retired the New York batters in order, and the league lead for Giants was suddenly down to three-and-a-half games. This was the 12th win for the Dean brothers against New York in 1934, and Hubbell's fourth loss in five tries against the Cardinals during the season—three of them to Paul. Fans all around the borough of Harlem began to lament the fall of the Giants; they could feel the lead slipping away to the men from the West. Diz and Paul had provided a remarkable double-feature for baseball fans on this date, but it would pale in comparison to their accomplishment just five days later.

Because of continued inclement weather, the Cardinals were not scheduled to play again until September 19, with another doubleheader against Boston. The standings as they appeared after the series with the Giants:

	W	*L*	*Pct.*	*GB*
New York	88	53	.624	—
St. Louis	84	56	.600	3.5
Chicago	80	58	.580	6.5
Boston	71	68	.511	16
Pittsburgh	68	67	.504	18
Brooklyn	61	77	.442	26.5
Philadelphia	50	85	.370	36
Cincinnati	50	88	.362	37.5

Unfortunately, the Cards and Braves were washed out for the first game of their series. Needing every victory he could get for the pennant drive, Frisch petitioned John Heydler that the teams play three games the following day (September 20), but the request was denied. President Heydler stated that a tripleheader was permissible only on the last day of the season, in the event that less than four games was the difference between the first- and second-place teams. So, while the Cardinals watched the raindrops from their hotel rooms, Giants owner Horace Stoneham announced that he was now accepting applications for World Series tickets as his boys won again and increased the margin to four full games. The Cardinals had 13 games remaining to make up the deficit, and the Giants had nine left to defend it.

When the Cardinals and Braves were finally given the green light to play, Bill Walker and Tex Carleton were handed the ball by Frisch for the starting roles in the doubleheader on the 20th. Carleton fired a three-hitter in the first game in gaining the victory, 4–1. Walker would surpass him, however, shutting out the Braves 1–0 in Game Two. Frisch proved that the competitive Cardinal fire was still blazing when he got kicked out of the nightcap after disputing a call on a steal of second base by Boston's Hal Lee. "Cy Pfirman, 'quick on the trigger' ump, did the canning," reported the Associated Press. The two wins ran the Cardinals' record to 9–1 in Boston for the year, and finished their games against the Braves for 1934 with a 16–5 mark overall.

The Giants, however, managed to keep pace. They won three out of four games in their series against Cincinnati, including a 4–3 victory this day just as the Cardinals second contest had ended, and kept a three-and-a-half-game lead as the Gas House Gang traveled to

Brooklyn. Yet another doubleheader was slated for the Cardinals the very next day against the Dodgers.

The Dodgers were close to 20 games under the .500 mark, as was usually the case. The borough of Brooklyn, long the stepsister to Manhattan and the rest of the city, was always the underdog with little to call their own. What they could call their own, however, was their ballclub. The Dodgers' name came from the action of avoiding the streetcars through the neighborhood, a practice in which everyone needed to become skilled to navigate through the streets. In the days of Babe Herman dropping flyballs in the 1920s, however, the team's ineptitude would lead to another label. In suffering through loss after loss, fans would leave Ebbets Field muttering to themselves, "Those *bums*! How could they lose again today!!!" After a while, however, the term lost its negative semantics, and took on a meaning of endearment. They were still bums, but bums that belonged to Brooklyn, like their own children. The club was the one thing that wasn't the property of the Bronx, Queens, Staten Island, or any other part of the city—the title of ownership rested with the people of Flatbush.

With both Dean brothers slated to pitch, therefore, it was an extra-special day for the faithful to come watch their Dodgers on Friday, September 21. A swell total of 18,000 made it to the afternoon contests. The Cardinals were coming into Ebbets Field with growing confidence, in full belief that the Giants could still be overtaken. Continuing his bid for the Most Valuable Player award, Rip Collins unloaded in the opening act. He had two doubles and a homer (his 34th on the year) and five RBIs as part of a 17-hit St. Louis attack. The Cardinals built up a 13–0 lead, but Diz only needed one run on this day. He smoked through Brooklyn hitters with ease, not allowing any hits until there was one out in the eighth inning, when Buzz Boyle beat out a slow roller to Durocher. Diz had seven strikeouts in gaining his 27th win of the year, a new Cardinal record for one year. He laughed heartily as he walked off the mound after the final out, in which he fanned Al Lopez.

Dodgers manager Stengel was later quoted as saying, "How would you feel? You get three itsy-bitsy hits off the big brother in the first game, and then you look around and there's the little brother with biscuits from the same table to throw at you."

Indeed, Paul was "on" for his start in the second game. Brimming with confidence after just defeating Hubbell for the third time, he was pitching as well as brother Diz down the stretch drive of the 1934 pennant chase. This would be his greatest day in a career cut tragically short by injuries, resembling Dizzy's own fate. Dodger centerfielder Len Koenecke, the third Dodger batter in the first inning, drew a walk. After that, as Roscoe McGowen of the *New York Times* described, "The Stengel athletes marched to the plate and back again with monotonous regularity."

Paul would sail along through the second, third, fourth, fifth, and sixth with no Dodger batter gaining a safe hit ... sailing along until, with two out in the ninth, he was one batter away from the Cardinals' first no-hitter since 1924. The last Brooklyn hitter was outfielder Boyle, the man who broke up Dizzy's no-no in Game One. He once again tested Durocher, hitting a sharp grounder to Leo's right which he couldn't handle cleanly. He recovered, found the ball, and let it fly with everything he had over to Collins at first with the speedy Boyle racing down the line. Half the witnesses that day said he was safe; the other half that he was clearly out. But the opinion that counted was that of umpire Ziggy Sears, and when his thumb shot towards the sky, a congratulatory pandemonium swept the field. It was the first no-hitter in the major leagues since Wes Ferrell of the Cleveland Indians turned the trick in 1931, and the first one in the National League since Hubbell's in 1929. It was actually Paul's second no-hit game of his professional career, as he blanked the Kansas City Blues as a member of the Columbus Red Birds the previous August.

The only legitimate threat to the masterpiece came in the seventh, when Brooklyn first baseman Sam Leslie lined a ball over Medwick's head in left. Ducky turned 180 degrees, raced back, and reached with everything his body had to snare the drive.

McGowen reported before the first game that prophet Dizzy had announced, "[Brooklyn pitchers] Zachary and Benge will be pitching against one-hit Dean and no-hit Dean today." Perhaps he originally meant the two titles to have been reversed in their outcomes, but a remarkable prediction nonetheless. And even though another Giants win allowed only another half-game improvement in the standings for St. Louis on the day, spirits remained high.

There were handshakes and laughs all around in the Cardinals' clubhouse. Pepper Martin was blaring away on his harmonica, and Medwick joined in with a song. Paul was relatively nonchalant about the feat. "I've hear tell that you jinx a no-hit game by talking about it," he told J. Roy Stockton. "But I think that's all bunk, because somebody is sure to think about it and what's going to happen is going to happen. I never was excited about nothing. But I was pouring that ball through there in the late innings. How did you like them strikes I throwed to [secondbaseman Jim] Bucher in the ninth inning? He ain't never saw anything I thrun."

How would he have felt if Boyle reached safely in the ninth?

"It wouldn't have bothered me none. 'Course I was thinking it would be kinda nice to have the no-hitter, but if Boyle had been man enough to sock one I'd have taken it without crying."

During the celebration, Diz went up to his brother and greeted him with one of his most famous lines. "Gee Paul, you shoulda told me you were gonna throw a no-hitter. If I'da known, I woulda thrown one, too."

Still in the League

The double victory by the Deans in Brooklyn injected more life into the ballclub, while the Giants continued to look more like a club that was fighting to get out of last place than one battling for a pennant. Frisch told reporters that the Cardinals were ready to "have our sails set" if New York continued its slide in the final eight days. "We're trying to win every game possible," spoke the leader. "Anything can happen."

On September 23, the baseball writers across the land announced their choices for the all–major league team of 1934. The balloting went as follows:

	Votes
1B—Gehrig, NYY	54
2B—Gehringer, DET	67
3B—Traynor, PIT	19
SS—Jackson, NYG	36
OF—Ott, NYG	50
OF—P. Waner, PIT	45
OF—Simmons, CHIW	38
C—Cochrane, DET	61
C—Dickey, NYY	20
P—J. Dean, STLC	60
P—Gomez, NYY	57
P—Rowe, DET	42

Members of the second team included Terry (19 votes), Frisch (2), Hubbell (21), and Schumacher (6) among stars from other teams. The emergence of Dean and Rowe is most noticeable here, as Hubbell—the MVP of the major leagues in 1933—failed to make the first cut.

The Cardinals knew that whatever the Giants did wouldn't matter if they lost, so they kept their focus on their own games. Yet, Durocher and Frisch would occasionally peek over their shoulders at the scoreboard from their positions, checking the score of the New York game being played across the country. Getting rained out in Cincinnati on September 22, the Cardinals and Reds played a doubleheader the following day. The Giants were also playing a two-gamer that day in Boston.

In the Cardinals' first game, Jesse Haines got relief help from Diz, and St. Louis held on for a 9–7 win in front of 13,000 fans at Crosley Field. However, in the nightcap, the Cardinals blew a chance for the sweep. Leading 3–2 late in the game, Paul Dean seemed to be rolling towards another victory. With two out in the eighth inning, he had a full count on Reds batter Adam Comorsky, and then broke off a sharp curve ball. The pitch seemed to grab a good portion of the plate, but home plate umpire Ernest Quigley gave no gesture. Comorsky walked to first as "ball four" was the call. Paul stormed towards the plate with arms up and hands open in protest. Frisch was about to charge in also, but thought better of it with a runner now on first and time-out not being called. Diz came in to relieve soon after, but it was too late. After the base on balls, Cincinnati proceeded to score the tying and winning runs in claiming the second game 4–3. In the clubhouse, a dejected Harpo took full responsibility for the defeat—one, he was sure, that would knock St. Louis out of the pennant chase. Now slightly more confident, the New York press returned to good feelings about their club; their attitude seemed to change daily. "Although the Cardinals are the best team in the National League right now, the Giants will play Detroit because they cannot possibly blow the pennant no matter how hard they try," decided Stanley Frank of the *New York Post*.

It was a quiet train ride to Chicago for the Redbirds. Bill Walker would attempt to get them back on the winning track against the Cubs the next day at Wrigley Field, as the Giants' lead was still two-and-a-half games. Walker responded beautifully with a 3–1 win, in which he had seven strikeouts and was aided by a long home run off the bat of Pepper Martin. It was the eleventh win of the season for the East St. Louis native and his third in a row over the Cubs. The Giants had the day off, so the Cardinals had trimmed the margin to two games.

They swung back home to St. Louis after the short stay in Chicago and met the Pirates at Sportsman's Park. Frisch chose Diz as his starter, and the Great One steered the Cardinals to a 3–2 triumph. Before the game even started, however, news flashed on the scoreboard at Sportsman's of what happened in Philadelphia: FINAL—PHILLIES 4, GIANTS 0. The Cardinal fans roared in excitement, and the players began the game with renewed vigor. Many found it hard to believe that the Giants could let a poor team like Philadelphia beat them in such an important game. After the St. Louis win, the lead was down to one game. Gary Schumacher mourned, "No team in major league history ever went into September with a seven-game lead and lost it. The Giants haven't done that yet, but now it appears inevitable."

So, as the morning papers hit the newsstands on September 26 (in which Sam Breadon published a letter describing the application process for World Series tickets), they showed the standings like this:

	W	L	Pct.	GB
New York	93	57	.620	—
St. Louis	91	57	.615	1
Chicago	83	64	.565	8.5
Boston	74	72	.507	17
Pittsburgh	72	73	.497	18.5
Brooklyn	68	81	.456	24.5
Philadelphia	55	89	.382	35
Cincinnati	52	95	.354	39.5

As if someone in St. Louis had written a perfect script in April, stuck it in a bottle, and wrote on the outside, "*Do not open until September*," a storytale ending was set. The Cardinals were scheduled to face the Reds—the worst team in the league—in the final two games of the year, while the Giants would have to play their local nemesis, Brooklyn, whose very existence the Giants' leader questioned at the start of the season.

Severe pressure began to mount on the shoulders of Terry, as his Giants would have to knock off the neighboring Dodgers in both games to secure the flag. Everyone was reminded of spring training, when Terry made his infamous interrogative of "Brooklyn? Are they still in the league?" Granted, New York had beaten the Dodgers 15 out of the previous 20 meetings between the two clubs, but this was Flatbush's ultimate chance for revenge. Baseball experts were considering this pennant race to be the National League's closest and most exciting since 1908. "There has been nothing like it for some 50 or 60 years," claimed Grantland Rice.

The Tigers had already clinched the pennant in the American

League, and their slugging first baseman Hank Greenberg was relieved. "Boy, is it a great feeling to be in," he admitted.

Terry had certainly put himself in a vulnerable position as the Brooklyn "Bums" came to the Polo Grounds on September 29. In the Giant-Dodger games in Brooklyn during 1934, the home crowd had booed Terry every time he emerged from the New York dugout. Thus he was pleased that, despite having to play the team he slammed in the spring, the final games would take place in the familiar surroundings of the Polo Grounds. Dodgers manager Casey Stengel couldn't wait for the series to begin, and he had his troops ready. "My boys are fully intent on administering the *coup de grace* to the Giants," he spoke with an easy confidence. The Dodgers came in laughing and loose; the Giants were uptight, quarreling among themselves about recent losses, and well aware of what was on the line for them. "Brooklyn is more than ready for their part in [Sunday's] drama," wrote Edward Neil, "while the Giants, in the throes of a hitting slump, nerves ragged and tempers slipping, were never more poorly prepared."

Stengel spoke as if on a religious crusade. "I have a mandate from my people," he said to the press with a bold finger in the air, "I will not betray my trust to Brooklyn. I feel that I must use my best pitchers, Van Mungo and Ray Benge, to insure victory. My people have spoken. The Dodgers are ready." Sportswriters noticed a foot-high pile of telegrams and letters from Brooklyn citizens on Casey's desk, all calling for vengeance.

Terry would rather have faced any other team than the Dodgers, despite the latter's poor overall record. The Brooklyn faithful were anxiously awaiting the chance to play Davids against the Harlem Goliaths. It was, perhaps, as if the entire city, nation, and baseball world knew what was about to happen next. This was Brooklyn's World Series; and until Durocher would guide them to greater heights in the 1940's as player-manager, the next best thing to a Series appearance, for the time being, would be to knock the Giants out of one. "The big iron trough beneath Coogan's Bluff will be an absolute bughouse," smirked Paul Gallico of the *New York Daily News* in predicting a Dodger triumph.

To add more drama to the scenario, the Cardinals would open their series with the Reds on the 27th, while the Giants had to wait until the 29th to begin play with the Dodgers. The New York men could do nothing in the meantime, except consider the possibility that the Cardinals could be tied with them before Stengel and his legion even set foot in the Polo Grounds.

So although being just as important in deciding the league outcome, comparatively little attention was paid to the Cardinals-Reds games in St. Louis in the two days prior to the Brooklyn–New York series. Before the first contest got underway in St. Louis, Cardinal fans presented diamond rings to Dizzy and Paul for their fine work during the season, as a pregame ceremony for the event had been organized by the "Dean Day Committee." Admirers had sent in as little as two cents or as much as several dollars to pay for the gifts, each of whom would have his or her name on a list to be presented to the brothers.

Walker and Carleton combined to defeat the Reds 8–5, as a five-run first inning propelled the Cardinals to victory. With the Dodger-Giant series still another day away, the Cardinals crept to within a half-game of New York, with the two clubs even in the loss column at 58 and having 92 and 93 wins respectively.

A driving rain hit Sportsman's Park the following day, and most were sure that the game would be called off. The grounds resembled more of a torn-up horse racing track than a ballfield, as its everyday use between the Browns and the Cardinals began to show its early-autumn wear, as was the case each season. The two teams took the field, however, with Diz coming back on two days' rest to try and tie the Cardinals with the Giants in the standings. He rose to the occasion, allowing seven hits and no walks, while striking out seven, as the Gang beat Cincinnati 4–0 in front of only 6,500 at the ballpark. It was win number 29 for Dean and his sixth shutout of the season. The Giants groaned when they learned the news, preparing for their final standoff against the Dodgers the following two days. The win put the Cardinals' record at 93–58, exactly tied with New York. The Giants seemingly insurmountable seven-game September lead had been erased; a cold, threatening wind had blown in from the Midwest, over the Alleghenies, and right down the Giants' backs in the Polo Grounds. The prowler they had felt creeping up on them had finally jumped, and was preparing to make off with the booty. The Cardinals had two more games against Cincinnati in Sportsman's Park, and the Redbirds were flying high.

The Cardinals' work was far from done, however, and they knew it. They still needed some assistance from the Dodgers, who were more than willing to give it. The hard-throwing Van Lingle Mungo was the starting pitcher in the first game for the Dodgers in New York. In large, bold, patriotic type, the headline of the *Brooklyn Eagle* read, "DODGERS SET TO KICK GIANTS OUT OF RACE AT POLO GROUNDS TODAY." With an angry temper to match his hot fastball, Mungo was the only pitcher close to challenging Diz for the league lead in strikeouts; hence, he bore down on the Giant hitters with a personal stake involved amid the more grand pennant implications surrounding the game. The New Yorkers seemed to be losing more and more confidence with each passing hour, as reminders from the press made clear. "The Giants need these last two games more than a wanderer in the sun-baked desert needs a drink of water," added Rice to the litany of writers who proclaimed the epic implications of the contests.

"What happened to the Giants?" he continued, speaking as if the Dodgers had already claimed victory in the ensuing games. "Here was a ballclub good enough to set the pace through the greater part of 1933, and then stop the [Washington] Senators abruptly in four out of five games [in the 1933 World Series].

"Here was a ballclub that picked up in April where it left off last October to hammer out a seven-game lead over their main rivals, the Cardinals, by September 6.

"Here was a ballclub, ably managed, a ballclub strongly fortified in every position, with a fine pitching staff, smart and keen and certainly game enough. Yet this ballclub suddenly turns from a world's champion outfit to a reeling, staggering delegation that blows game after game in every known way there is.

"…the Giants were just about ready for the ax, mentally, physically, and psychologically, swaying on the tightrope, when the two Deans set off the powder explosion a fortnight ago."

When Mungo took the hill for the Dodgers, dark storm clouds hung at a 500-foot elevation, striking further chills of imminent death at the Giants. Gallico noticed that "the two white championship flags, the 1933 pennant and world championship bunting, hung for the most part like shrouds, although occasionally a south wind would set them to waving like ghostly veils." It appeared as if the Dodgers were mounting a stealth attack on the Giants, as "the Brooklyns in their gray uniforms seemed to merge with the haze and gloom on the field."

As the innings progressed, Mungo's fastball was working as a sawmill on the Giants' bats. Most of the 13,774 in attendance were Dodger supporters who made the trip across the bridge from Brooklyn, and they let Terry hear it all game long as was customary. A round-tripper by Watkins was the only offense for the home team, and Mungo outlasted Roy Parmalee, 5–1. Mungo provided a spark for the Dodger offense as well, as he singled in the fifth, took second on a passed ball, and ultimately scored on a single by Boyle. The next inning, he smacked another single to center that plated Lonnie Frey, the Dodgers' 21-year-old shortstop from St. Louis, and the "Bums" were on their way. The Giants mustered a desperate attack in the ninth, as Terry reached on an infield hit and Ott walked. Not fazed, Mungo "hitched up his trousers, hurled his fast one swiftly through the gloom," and struck out Travis Jackson, Watkins, and Lefty O'Doul in succession to end the game. It was New York's fourth loss in a row, only the second time such a streak had occurred during the season.

The entrance to the Giants' clubhouse in the Polo Grounds was in the outfield, and they left the field under a fierce swarm of boos, jeers, and thrown objects. Feeling like sinners entering a pit of doom, they shamefully covered their faces while passing spectators in the bleachers. They already knew that first place was no longer theirs—for, in St. Louis, Paul Dean dispersed 11 Cincinnati hits so evenly that they amounted to only one run, and the Cardinals provided plenty of their own offense for a 6–1 victory. Like his brother the day before, Harpo was working on only two days' rest. A Ladies' Day crowd of over 23,000 cheered as the results came in from New York—first place was for the Cardinals all by themselves. Still, they knew that the race was still not yet over, even though the papers were slightly more certain. "There is one more game to go before the rigor mortis sets in officially," conceded the Associated Press, "But as far as the world champion Giants are concerned, the situation is as desperate as it can be without all hope having departed." The Giants could still tie if they won and the Cardinals lost. Such an outcome would set up the first-ever playoff game in league history. With that possibility, there was no major celebration in the St. Louis locker room.

Not taking any chances, Frisch chose Diz as his starter in the season finale. With only one day of rest, however, there was some concern about his strength. The press, however, continued to marvel at the Deans and to chastise Cardinals management for taking them for granted. Dan Parker of the *New York Daily Mirror* had perhaps the most biting quip. "If they win the pennant for St. Louis, the Dean boys, you may be sure, will be handsomely rewarded," he promised. "Sam Breadon will probably give them a day's rest before the World Series, a pat on the back and two of the best five-cent cigars that can be bought in St. Louis."

As the regular season ended, another story was unfolding in the American League. It was assumed that the Yankees' last game in 1934 would be Babe Ruth's final curtain call. "For the last time—George

Herman Ruth said it was his final appearance as a regular—the single line, *Ruth—RF*, went into the starting lineup of a major league ball game," reported New York writer Dillon Graham on October 1. Over 10,000 fans turned out at Griffith Stadium in Washington, D.C., as the Yankees ended their season against the Senators. Ruth sent three balls into the rightfield stands during batting practice, however, and that was pleasing enough to the admirers in attendance. The Yankees lost the game 5–3, as the legend went hitless in his final appearance in a New York uniform. With his last swing, he drove Washington's star center-fielder Heinie Manush to the wall on what looked like one more home run, but the ball was caught. Ruth went on to his ill-fated stint with the Braves in 1935, and then called it quits on his playing career.

Great people seem to rise to great occasions, and Dizzy Dean did so on September 30, 1934. He was going after his 30th win, something which no one had done in the National League since 1917, and which no one has done in the Senior Circuit since; he was pitching for the chance to put the Cardinals in the World Series; and he was taking the mound for the beloved people of St. Louis—people who, like so many others in America in the 1930's, had so little to cheer about.

That was why 37,402 yearning people crowded into every nook and cranny of Sportsman's Park on this day. It was the second-largest crowd at the ballpark since 1926, behind only a 1931 doubleheader with the Cubs. With so much on the line for Dean and his teammates, the Reds didn't have a prayer. If he had thrown 15 innings the day before, Dean would probably still have shut them down. The Cardinal bats got in their final licks of the regular season, providing him nine runs of support. Finally, at 4:41 P.M. St. Louis time, he whistled a fastball on the inside corner at the final batter, and forced a weak pop-up for the last out. The Cardinals had won again, finishing up a stretch of .800 ball in the final four weeks of the season. As a celebrating mob rushed the field, Dizzy was escorted off by security personnel. The final score of the Giants' game had been flashed on the scoreboard with one out in the ninth inning, which officially ended the pennant race—New York had lost to the Dodgers again, 8–5.

The Giants actually jumped out to 4–0 lead in the bottom of the first inning, but the Dodgers chipped away, knocking out starter Freddie Fitzsimmons late in the game. The Dodgers tied the game at five in the eighth, and then won it with three runs in the tenth inning off Schumacher and Hubbell.

There was a roar at this unveiling, but the loudest cheers came seconds later when Dean ended the game in St. Louis. In the middle of the celebration on the field at Sportsman's Park, a young boy placed a four-pound chunk of ice on the pitching rubber, as instructed by Diz. "Dizzy told me this morning to put it there after the game," the youngster revealed. "Said it would be burning up if I didn't. Go ahead and feel it. Even the ice hasn't gotten it cooled down yet." Dean had become the National League's first 30-game winner since Grover Cleveland Alexander in 1917 (Dazzy Vance had come the closest until then, notching 28 victories for the Dodgers in 1924). Perhaps most amazing of all, Dizzy and Paul had combined to win seven games in the last ten days.

The Cardinals, in first place all by themselves for the last two days of the season, held that distinction for a total of only 11 days during 1934—the first nine of those coming between May 28 and June 5.

In the joyous Cardinal clubhouse, Diz smooched a big kiss on Frisch's cheek, and then joined Medwick and Martin in laughter. Things quieted down a little when the team went on live national radio, as Frisch gave his thanks for "a great group of hustlin' ballplayers." Sam Breadon described the flourishing finish to the season as "the greatest display of pure fighting grit I have ever seen." Even though the Cardinals had increased their 1934 attendance at Sportsman's Park (334,866) by almost 40 percent, the regular season financial sheet for the club still finished in the red. The extra money from the postseason would certainly be welcomed by Breadon and the players.

The celebration was raucous throughout the rest of the city as well. "Downtown Washington Avenue and its tributary thoroughfares were packed with automobiles and pedestrians," reported the *Globe-Democrat*. "Voices, horns, cowbells, dragging tin pans, whistles, and other noisemakers set up a terrific din and traffic moved at a snail's pace." It was indeed a celebration for which the Depression-laced city had been wishing. "It seemed like the windup of the 1934 National League season provided a tonic which St. Louis has been needing for a long time," said one observer. It was stated that an estimated 50,000 reveled in the celebration, with the largest crowds forming on Washington between Locust and Olive streets, as well as along Grand Avenue.

In New York, the Giants' collapse left the fans at the Polo Grounds furious. "When I stepped out there in the tenth inning with the flag money gone and everything lost they booed me," mumbled a stunned Bill Terry after the clinching defeat. "I thought I was in St. Louis." What did he think of Brooklyn now? "You can say this for me. If

Dizzy Dean receives the 1934 Most Valuable Player award on July 16, 1935, at Sportsman's Park. (From the collection of the St. Louis Mercantile Library at the University of Missouri–St. Louis.)

Stengel's team had played as hard all year as it did in the last two days, it would not be in sixth place." Terry sat by himself at a table in the center of the Giants' dressing room with his head between his knees — a place, it was noted by a local writer who covered the Giants, "usually reserved for jovial aftergame beer parties."

Meanwhile, in the Dodgers' locker room, Casey Stengel was giving his team a congratulatory address. "Farewell, my bonny men. Some of you are off to maim the gentle rabbit. Some of you will shoot the carefree deer. I bid you Godspeed, my lamby-pies, my brave young soldiers. Go with Casey's blessing upon your sweet heads." When he heard about Terry's dejection in the adjoining room, Stengel of course offered no sympathy. "So he feels bad, eh? How do you think I felt when he made fun of my ball club last spring before I even reported on the job? I wish I had his money. They could boo the ears off me. You've got to learn to take it in this business.

"So he says if we had played hard we wouldn't have finished in last place, eh? Well, you can tell him if the season lasted another month and we kept playing them, *he'd* finish in last place!"

He had one more caution for the New York players.

"The Giants thought we gave 'em a beating Sunday and yesterday," Casey said in conclusion. "Well, they were right. But I'm sorry for them when I think of the beating they still have to take. Wait until their wives realize that they're not going to get those new fur coats."

With the regular season complete, Paul Waner of the Pirates wound up the league batting champ with a .362 average, followed by Terry (.352), Cuyler (.338), Collins (.333), and Arky Vaughan (.333). Lou Gehrig won the American League title with a .363 clip, in addition to the Triple Crown with 49 home runs and 165 RBIs. Collins had tied Ott for the National League lead in home runs with 35, while Martin led the circuit in stolen bases with 23.

For the Cardinals, it was now on to Detroit and the World Series, where the waiting Tigers had just recently steamrolled over the rest of the American League.

PART FOUR

The Series

"The Dean boys admit that they are very good, and they have an exasperating knack of winning even when they aren't."

—*The Chicago Daily News*, October 6, 1934

Chasing a Championship

Tigers manager Mickey Cochrane confessed a true concern about the Cardinals, largely because his club had been expecting for the past few weeks that they would be facing the Giants for the world championship. "For a month I have had the Giants scouted," the veteran told reporters. "I have been furnished with the batting weaknesses of Ott, O'Doul, and Moore, and a chart of the rest of the hitters. I have been given blueprints of the Polo Grounds and the positions the Giants employ on bunt defense. I have even received maps marked with crosses showing how I should station my outfielders to play each New York batter. Now, I've got to heave all this stuff in the ash can."

The baseball world was looking forward to the first "all-western" World Series since the Reds and White Sox played in the infamous 1919 clash. There were no off-days scheduled as the teams were slated to play seven straight games, if necessary, from October 3rd through the 9th. As the Cardinals' Special pulled out of Union Station in St. Louis at around 7:30 P.M. on October 1, Diz passed the time by playing cards or just staring thoughtfully out the window. Paul read a newspaper, and pondered which game of the series he would start. Medwick was puffing at his bulldog pipe, and a few seats ahead, Frisch was plotting his strategy for Game One. A veteran of the postseason, Frisch entered the 1934 championship round with 40 career hits in the World Series play, the most in history. It would be his eighth trip to the Fall Classic.

Along the way, Diz tried to put the manager at ease. "Look at Frankie, boys," Dean yelled over his shoulder as he made his way through the aisle. "Deep in thought again. Don't worry, Frank, we'll win the series for you."

When the team finally got to Detroit, hundreds, and then thousands of people gathered to catch a glimpse of the National League–phenomenon Dean brothers. Finishing his card game with Durocher and a service boy, Diz was the last one to leave the train. All smiles and laughs as he departed the passenger car, he shook an endless sea of admiring hands.

Dizzy couldn't find enough to do once he arrived in the Motor City. According to one eyewitness, "He made predictions and autographed everything but the paintings on the wall of the hotel." After checking into their quarters, he and Paul proceeded promptly to the nearest eating establishment. Their whereabouts were constantly tracked by the media; they could not even leave their rooms without coverage. "The Deans are on every lip," reported Jimmy Powers of the *New York Daily News*. "The papers carry headlines of the size usually employed to announce a declaration of war. They tell hourly bulletin movements of the two grinning, roistering, record-breaking farm boys." Diz later met up with Will Rogers, and the country pair went out to Henry Ford's place for breakfast. When the pitcher met the automobile entrepreneur, Dizzy had a warm greeting for him. "Put 'er there, Henry. I'm sure glad to be here 'cause I've heard so much about you, but I'm sorry partner, I'm a-gonna have to make pussycats out of your Tigers."

The Detroit newspapermen seemed to be especially interested in Paul. Diz had made headlines during the entire year, but people still knew Harpo only as "Dizzy's little brother." Was he as good as his sibling, the folks in Detroit wanted to know?

"I'm no Dizzy, and I don't think I'll ever be," Paul responded in modesty. The brothers' support of each other was unconditional; both Dean boys were each other's greatest fan, in good times and bad. "Why, Diz is wonderful. There's nobody like him and there ain't been in years. He's as great as Mathewson, Alexander and Johnson were in their day. I wouldn't be surprised if he'll be even better than those guys. Yeah, there's only one Dizzy, I'm tellin' you. Diz is always boostin' me. Why, when I'm pitchin' and I get hit, Dizzy picks up his glove and goes right out to that bullpen. Yeah, I do the same for Diz. Any outfit that licks one of us has to lick us both."

Back west the boys' father, Albert Dean, was on a bus traveling to St. Louis from Oklahoma to see the series games in St. Louis in a couple days. Pa Dean had some more backing for Paul. "If you think Dizzy is good, just wait until Paul gets one more year of that big league pitching, and you're gonna see some real throwin'," he promised. An Associated Press reporter had caught up with the 62-year-old sharecropper along the trip, and got the inside dope on the Dean heritage. Pa Dean noted that he provided the boys' pitching instruction. "When Jay and Paul was growin' up, I showed 'em how to chunk outdrops, curves, and all that stuff."

Dizzy was not by himself on the train ride to Detroit. His wife Pat had made the trip with him, and the two were able to spend some quiet moments in conversation. Vera Brown was on special assignment to Detroit for the *St. Louis Star-Times*, and caught up with Mrs. Dean. Brown was hoping that Pat could give some insight into her pitcher-husband.

"Yes, Dizzy's wonderful. We've been married four years. I'm two year older than he, and to me he seems like a little boy. I wish you could know Dizzy as I do! He's the sweetest kid in the world. Only when he gets home does he let down. When he comes to the door I get him right to bed. In one game this summer he lost 12 pounds. Whenever he pitches, I make him rest at least an hour before he has supper. I have to watch every mouthful he takes and make him eat. I sit over him at breakfast until he has cleaned up his plate, and I feed him cod liver oil all the time. I sometimes wonder if fans realize what pitching a game does to a pitcher." As Dean's mother passed away when he was four, Pat was able to fill a nurturing void that had been missing all his life. The couple never had children, so Pat cared for him as the "little boy" she imagined him to be.

The teams had light workouts on October 2 in preparation for the first game the following day. Already bored and running out of things to do on the first day there, Diz walked right onto the field in the middle of the Detroit practice session at Navin Field, home of the Tigers. He was still dressed in a coat, tie, and slacks, and he picked up a bat from the ground. Greenberg was taking his last swings during batting practice. Diz pushed him aside and said, "Lemme show ya a *real* ballplayer at work." With some of the other Cardinals watching and snickering in amusement, Dean beckoned the batting practice pitcher for some throws, and the multitude of media members at the park that day quickly converged on the batting cage. He slashed one line drive after another into the outfield, and then took off his coat for a few more.

With the Tigers angrily waiting for the side-show to end, Dean laughed, flipped the bat on the ground and strutted off. "Boy, I love to hit," he chirped, as a few of the Detroit players continued to growl at him. Paul Gallico was there and reported, "The Cards look like winners ... Dizzy Dean is all ice."

The 1934 World Series was the first to have a sponsored commercial radio broadcast. The Ford Motor Company was the benefactor, shelling out $100,000 for transmission of the games. Ford himself witnessed each series game in Detroit from his personal box seat.

When it was announced that extra bleachers seats to Game One would go on sale the morning of the contest, "an army of dyed in the wool fans from Maine to California laid siege to Navin Field" the night before, according to the *Detroit Free Press*. Complete with camping gear, prepared meals, and cribbage boards, an estimated 12,000 hopefuls waited for the ticket windows to open.

The people in Detroit were enjoying the recent resurgence of their team. The Tigers had finished no higher than fifth in the American League since 1927. Like many owners, Frank Navin of the Tigers experienced a loss at the gate in the late twenties and early thirties mainly because of the stale economy, but his red ink was compounded by the poor play of his club. The turning point came on December 12, 1933, when he purchased Cochrane from Connie Mack's Philadelphia A's for $100,000 and catcher Johnny Pasek. Mack, coming off three straight pennants in 1931, was in the process of selling his other stars (which included Simmons, Foxx, and Grove) to pay off his bank loans that had gone sour after the stock market crash in 1929. A week after the Cochrane deal, Navin acquired outfielder Goose Goslin from the Washington Senators, champions of the American League the previous season.

It was the Tigers' first appearance in the Fall Classic since 1909, and the Detroit club came into the series on a roll. They swept the Browns in a doubleheader on the last day of the season, winning by scores of 10–6 and 6–2. Along with Cochrane, Goslin, and the slugging Greenberg (who set team records with 26 home runs and 63 doubles in '34), the other superstar on the team was second baseman Charlie Gehringer. A soft-spoken gentleman, he demolished American League pitching in 1934 (.356 average, 50 doubles, 127 RBIs, and a league-leading 214 hits), and was as sharp a keystone defender as there was in the game. Cochrane, one of the greatest catchers of all-time, perhaps summed it up best about Gehringer. "In spring training, Charlie says 'hello,' hits .380 or something for six months, and then says 'good-bye' at the end of the season. A manager's dream is what he is." Nicknamed

"The Mechanical Man" for his flawless technique, Gehringer was really the main cog in the Detroit machine.

Cochrane hit .320 on the year with 32 doubles, and was still fairly agile with a powerful arm behind the plate. He was revered in the Detroit area for bringing the Tigers back to prominence. "Cochrane is the town hero," wrote Jimmy Powers as the series was about to begin. "The waiters are bowlegged from lugging trays in and out of the banquets tossed in his honor." Despite his gentlemanly conduct off the field, he had earned the nickname of "Black Mike" for his fierce anger displayed during games. His pitching staff was led by Rowe, winner of 24 games on the season.

Although announcing the previous week that Rowe would be his choice to start Game 1, Cochrane did not want to throw him against Diz, thinking that Dean would probably win the game no matter whom the Tigers pitched.

The newspapers speculated that this move gave the Cardinals a psychological edge before the series even started—that the Tigers had it in the back of their minds that Dean couldn't be beaten. "If the strategy was to concede the first game because Dizzy's name was at the bottom of the lineup," wrote Dan Parker, "Cochrane and the boys made a complete job of it." Cochrane claimed that his decision was based upon a September 23rd doubleheader in St. Louis against the Browns when Rowe, who was going after his 25th win, was tagged for 11 hits in a 4–3 loss. The reason Cochrane gave to the writers was that Rowe had not yet regained his sharp form. So, Alvin "General" Crowder was given the ball instead for Game 1. But even though Crowder won the second game of that twin bill with the Browns, he himself gave up ten hits in a showing that was not much better than Rowe's.

Acquired from the Washington Senators on August 4 of the 1934 season, Crowder won five games in nine starts for the Tigers and the veteran gave the young Detroit staff some stability. His nickname was derived from his experience as a soldier in World War I. He had actually faced a Cardinal in a game before—Frisch, who homered and singled off him in the 1933 All-Star Game in Chicago. Crowder, who won 24 games for the American League Champion Senators the previous season (as well as 26 the year before), naturally got a pregame visit from Dizzy in the Tigers' bullpen. It was twenty minutes before game time, and Dean should have been warming up himself. "His curve ball looked as straight as the foul line," Paul Dean lamented about his brother's practice tosses on the sideline. Diz wanted to see, however, "If this

GENN-rall guy had any gravy on his chops." Interestingly, in the 1933 World Series, Crowder was hit hard by the Giants as he gave up six runs in six innings of work.

On his way back to the Cardinals' bench, Dean picked up a bat lying in front of the Tigers' dugout, and took it with him for a souvenir. "You fellows don't know what bats are for anyway," he yelled over his shoulder.

Detroit fans eagerly awaited the first pitch as they crammed into their seats, which ranged in price from $1.10 to $6.60, the same rates as during the regular season. The entire city had been waiting for this moment, and no other activity was found around the ballpark. "To a stranger unaware of what was going on Wednesday [the day of the first game]," explained the *Detroit Free Press*, "the downtown area of Detroit was not Detroit the Dynamic, but the Deserted Village. For three hours—between one and four o'clock—the business district resembled siesta-hour in a Central American town. Nobody worked. Doormen stood in front of theaters trying to look as important as their uniforms indicated." Down Michigan Avenue, the main thoroughfare that connected Navin Field to the rest of the business district, several amateur musicians could be heard strumming the tunes to "Tiger Rag," a hit by the Mills Brothers that was recorded in 1922.

Despite dealing with some understandable fatigue, the Cardinals were generally healthy heading into World Series play. Rothrock was recovering from a "slight concussion of the chest," according to team trainer Doc Weaver. He sustained the injury colliding with the right field wall during the previous week, but was expected for duty. Orsatti had a slight muscle pull in his right thigh, but he too was in the lineup for Game 1. The only minor casualty on the pitching staff belong to Carleton, who twisted his ankle stepping in a hole at Crosley Field in Cincinnati. If called upon, he would be ready to pitch in the opener. Dean was ready to take the hill, but was so thin "his clothes hung upon him like drapes," according to one reporter. He told the press he had lost twenty pounds in recent weeks, but everyone knew that he would be ready for these big games. "Baseball is his love," Martin Haley proclaimed, "and though he were down to mere skin and bones, he'd be there to answer the call."

The Cardinals came out swinging, as 11 of their first 12 batters swung at Crowder's first pitch. Early in the game, it was also evident that the Tigers were indeed intimidated by some force, whether it was Dean's presence on the field or something else. During the first three innings, all four Detroit infielders—Greenberg, Gehringer, shortstop Billy Rogell, and third baseman Marv Owen—each made errors (with Owen committing two), and the Cardinals parlayed the five miscues into three runs. Normally, the group was as cohesive as any infield unit in baseball. During the regular season, the quintet had a unbelievable streak of 144 games started together. The stretch was interrupted when Greenberg observed the Hebrew holiday of Yom Kippur late in the season, and removed himself from the lineup. As they "gummed up ground balls they would ordinarily catch in their hip pockets," the Tigers' infielders amazed everyone in the park as the vaunted group crumbled in the opening acts of the series. "Seldom can any team, even though it be the American League champions, spot Dizzy Dean three runs and get away with it," warned the *Globe-Democrat*. Added Grantland Rice, "For something like 40 minutes Greenberg, Gehringer, Rogell, and Owen sounded like a series of giant firecrackers with the fuse exposed to flame."

The writers were particularly critical of the misplay by Gehringer, who dropped a toss from Rogell with the hard-charging Orsatti sliding into him at second. Gehringer was obviously unnerved by Orsatti's furious rush, and the umpire reversed his previous call of "out" to declare Ernie safe.

After getting through their jitters, the Tigers received a gift run in the fourth, as a double by Pete Fox that scored Rogell had actually landed foul by a half-foot, according to several witnesses. Medwick added a solo homer in the fifth inning, the only earned run that Crowder allowed on the day as he was lifted for a pinch hitter in the bottom half of the inning. Greenberg homered for the Tigers in the eighth, but St. Louis promptly blasted Detroit relief pitching, building an 8–3 lead late in the game that would eventually be the final score. The Cardinal attack included doubles by DeLancey and Dean. Despite leaving ten runners on base, the Cardinals found plenty of scoring. After he set Detroit down in order in the ninth, Dean finished with six strikeouts and only two walks in going the distance for the win. He had run the count full on 14 batters, and threw 129 pitches on the day.

The newsmen noticed how, throughout the game, the Cardinals were very calm and composed while the Tigers were nervous. "Frankie Frisch handled his club faultlessly," praised Dan Parker. "There is a vast difference in temperament between the two teams, by the way. The Tigers are high-strung; the Cards, phlegmatic. Like Dean, who hasn't a nerve, even in his wisdom teeth (if any), his mates seem to regard every game as just another contest, nothing over which to get unduly excited."

Diz contacted Branch Rickey back in St. Louis with the following telegram that was printed in the *Globe-Democrat* (Diz sent the telegram collect, of course):

> Many, many thanks. This American League is a pushover. Breezed through today with nothing but my glove. If possible have Dad on airplane in time for game tomorrow. Wire time of arrival. Tell everybody hello. Henry Ford will be my guest in St. Louis Friday. Cook a good meal for all of us—sandwiches and everything. Will Rogers and Joey Brown coming, too. Thanks again.
>
> Dizzy Dean

What did Diz think of Cochrane's decision to throw Crowder against him instead of Rowe? "Mickey used good gumption," he affirmed. "You see, he knew if I was at my best, nobody could beat me. So he saved Schoolboy Rowe for another game instead of puttin' him against me ... but I'd be tickled plum pink to pitch tomorrow again. I'd have my stuff I know and I'd shut Detroit out. If they'd let me pitch all the games, I think I could probably win all four.

"Them Tigers wasn't so good as I figured they belonged to be. Why, I could take any of four National League teams and beat 'em for a World Series—if I pitched."

Dean topped off the day with a radio connection to Richard Byrd, who was on his legendary expedition through Antarctica to the South Pole.

"Howdy there, Dick Byrd, down at the South Pole," Dizzy greeted him with a hearty holler. The rest of the press was amused by his informality in addressing the famous explorer. "Dean spoke as though addressing an old Yell County, Arkansas friend of boyhood days instead of a Rear Admiral with as many decorations as he had winning games this year," it was reported in the *Post-Dispatch*.

"Well, it was a hard-pitched game," the great thrower continued. "I didn't have anything on my ball. That's why I had to work so hard. I finally staggered through. But it was a lousy, tick-flea-and-chigre bit ball game."

Diz was so pleased with his opening-game win that he also phoned Babe Ruth. According to Bill Corum of the *New York Evening Journal*, what follows is a "rough transcript of the conversation":

"Hello, is this Mr. Ruth?"

"Yes, this is Babe."

"Say, Mr. Ruth, this is Dizzy Dean. I just called up to say hello and to thank you for putting me on your All-American team this year. I was sure proud of that, and I don't know how to thank you enough, Mr. Ruth."

"Aw, that's all right, kid, you deserved to be there. What the hell, you deserved to be on there, kid."

"Well, thank you, I just wanted to say hello, Mr. Ruth, and thank you."

"That's all right, kid, I'll see you at the game."

"You mean you'll come in the clubhouse? Gee..."

"No, I won't be in the clubhouse, but I'll see you on the field."

"That'll be swell, Mr. Ruth, but I wish you'd come in the clubhouse if you get a chance."

"I'll be seeing you, anyhow, kid, and though I'm an American Leaguer, good luck."

"Gee, Mr. Ruth, that's swell. I'll be seeing you out there."

Medwick was so tired from the day's events that he retired to his hotel bed at 6:00 P.M.

The box score from Game 1:

St. Louis

	AB	R	H	RBI	PO	A	E
Martin, 3B	5	1	1	1	1	1	0
Rothrock, RF	4	0	2	2	0	0	0
Frisch, 2B	4	0	0	0	2	4	0
Medwick, LF	5	2	4	2	2	0	0
Collins, 1B	4	2	1	0	13	1	0
DeLancey, C	5	0	1	2	7	1	0
Orsatti, CF	4	1	2	0	1	0	2
Fullis, CF	1	0	1	0	0	0	0
Durocher, SS	5	0	0	0	0	4	0
J. Dean, P	*5*	*2*	*1*	*0*	*1*	*2*	*0*
Totals	42	8	13	7	27	13	2

Detroit

	AB	R	H	RBI	PO	A	E
White, CF	2	1	0	0	6	0	0
Cochrane, C	4	0	1	0	2	0	0
Gehringer, 2B	4	0	2	1	2	3	1
Greenberg, 1B	4	2	2	1	8	1	1
Goslin, LF	4	0	2	1	3	0	0

Detroit

	AB	R	H	RBI	PO	A	E
Rogell, SS	4	0	1	0	1	4	1
Owen, 3B	4	0	0	0	2	1	2
Fox, RF	4	0	0	0	3	0	0
Crowder, P	1	0	0	0	0	0	0
Doljack, PH	1	0	0	0	0	0	0
Marberry, P	0	0	0	0	0	1	0
Hogsett, P	1	0	0	0	0	1	0
Walker, PH	*1*	*0*	*0*	*0*	*0*	*0*	*0*
Totals	34	3	8	3	27	11	5

	1	2	3	4	5	6	7	8	9	R	H	E
St. Louis	0	2	1	0	1	4	0	0	0	8	13	2
Detroit	0	0	1	0	0	1	0	1	0	3	8	5

Not wanting to fall behind by two games, Cochrane knew it was time to summon Rowe to the mound. He would face Bill Hallahan who, despite having a poor regular season for the Cardinals, was a veteran of St. Louis' 1931 World Series championship team against the Philadelphia A's, and Frisch liked the experience he possessed. Hallahan had a 3–1 career record in the Fall Classic, with appearances in 1926 and 1930 as well as in 1931. Frisch also pointed out to the writers that Hallahan had already beaten the Tigers twice in 1934—albeit in exhibition games.

As the crowd of 43,451 settled in, Rowe took the mound in a confident gait with his imposing 6'4", 210-pound frame. The Cardinals were not intimidated, however, and got off to a strong start in Game Two. They nailed Rowe for two early runs on six hits, and it looked like the second contest was going to be a runaway. They could have had three runs, but Medwick committed a base-running error. He attempted to score on a Rip Collins' base hit to right but was easily gunned down by a wide margin on a throw from Tigers rightfielder Pete Fox. For good measure and consolation, Medwick needlessly plowed into Cochrane anyway, and nearly knocked the Detroit catcher out of the game. Rowe also was experiencing the misfortune of having his fiancée from Arkansas, Edna Skinner, within earshot of the Cardinals' dugout. All day long, the cry rang out from the St. Louis bench, "How'm I doin', Edna?"

After the third, however, the Schoolboy pitched seven innings of no-hit ball, and the Tigers ultimately fought back to tie the game at 2–2 in the bottom of the ninth. The score that evened the game came as a result of an error by the normally sure-handed Orsatti in center. Rogell lifted a high fly ball that Orsatti drifted on and finally lost as the ball fell in front of him, "A drive that Orsatti would pocket 99 times out of 100," according to New York writer Damon Runyon. Pinch hitter Gee Walker, batting for the Detroit centerfielder Jo-Jo White, then laced a single to drive in Rogell—on a pitch that was preceded by a dropped foul pop-up by Collins. DeLancey and Collins headed for the ball that went high in the air between home and first, but the wind carried it back towards the plate. Collins still called for the ball, however, and could not reach it. Walker then followed with his base knock.

Through all this adversity, Hallahan provided perhaps his most courageous performance of the year. He ultimately fatigued, and gave way to Walker in the ninth inning. Rowe continued on into the extra innings, and the string of hitless Cardinal frames was finally broken by a Martin double in the eleventh. Pepper was left stranded, however, and St. Louis ran out of chances in the bottom of the twelfth inning. Goose Goslin shot a single to center that scored Gehringer, and Detroit won Game Two, 3–2. Rowe had pitched the entire twelve innings, in what Cochrane called "the greatest World Series pitching performance in history." He had no walks, seven strikeouts, and also added a sacrifice bunt to the Tigers' offensive cause. It was Detroit's first ever World Series victory at home, and their second postseason win of any kind. The Tigers had gotten exactly what they needed—a command performance by their top pitcher to even the series.

In the Tigers' clubhouse, Rowe was proud of his day. "For the first few innings, I felt there was something funny inside of me. I didn't feel right," he told reporters. "Mind you, I wasn't scared. I've never been scared in my life. But after I got over that third inning I had every confidence that we would win."

Over in the St. Louis locker room, bitterness prevailed. "Frankie Frisch, the fiery little leader of the National League champions, was so enraged that he ordered newspaper correspondents out of the room until he had time to cool off, or perhaps tell some of his players just what he thought of them," mentioned the *Chicago Tribune*. "The Cardinals, red-necked and fighting mad, tossed their baseball equipment around the room in an expression of their anger." Conceding nothing, Diz wasn't impressed with Rowe at all. "That palooka is probably as fast pitchin' with the wind as Paul is throwing against it."

The box score from Game 2:

St. Louis

	AB	R	H	RBI	PO	A	E
Martin, 3B	5	1	2	0	1	1	1
Rothrock, RF	4	0	0	0	4	0	0
Frisch, 2B	5	0	1	0	2	6	1
Medwick, LF	5	0	1	1	0	0	0
Collins, 1B	5	0	1	0	12	2	0
DeLancey, C	5	1	1	0	10	0	0
Orsatti, CF	4	0	1	1	2	0	0
Durocher, SS	4	0	0	0	1	3	0
Hallahan, P	3	0	0	0	1	3	1
Walker, P	1	0	0	0	0	1	0
Totals	41	2	7	2	34	16	3

Detroit

	AB	R	H	RBI	PO	A	E
White, CF	4	0	0	0	4	0	0
Walker, PH	1	0	1	1	0	0	0
Doljack, CF	1	0	0	0	1	0	0
Cochrane, C	4	0	0	0	8	0	0
Gehringer, 2B	4	1	1	0	3	6	0
Greenberg, 1B	4	0	0	0	13	1	0
Goslin, LF	6	0	2	1	3	1	0
Rogell, SS	4	1	1	0	1	2	0
Owen, 3B	5	0	0	0	0	1	0
Fox, RF	5	1	2	1	2	0	0
Rowe, P	4	0	0	0	1	1	0
Totals	42	3	7	3	36	12	0

	1	2	3	4	5	6	7	8	9	10	11	12	R	H	E
St. Louis	0	1	1	0	0	0	0	0	0	0	0	0	2	7	3
Detroit	0	0	0	1	0	0	0	0	1	0	0	1	3	7	0

With the series tied 1–1, the next three games would be played in St. Louis; and played immediately, as there was no travel day in between. Therefore, each team boarded its train quickly after the game and spent the 12-hour ride trying to devise a way to get their team the go-ahead victory in Game 3. Since it was the Depression, extra money was scarce, and every player on both teams needed the winners' share check. That, as much as anything else, made the 1934 World Series a hard-fought struggle. "Sixty-eight hundred dollars for the winner," remembered Burgess Whitehead years later. "I needed that money to help my father, and the losers' share wasn't going to do it. It was definitely a cut-throat battle between us and the Tigers for that extra money."

"You Can't Hurt No Dean by Hittin' Him on the Head"

When the Cardinals arrived back home, the Dean brothers had a special treat waiting for them—a throng of hundreds of baseball fans from the Southwest, each one proud to say that he or she came from "Dean country." They came from Texas, Oklahoma, Arkansas, and "rural Missouri and little towns in Tennessee and Mississippi, where nothing much happens and a World Series within driving distance is not to be missed," the *Post-Dispatch* reported. And as one of the pilgrims who made the trip noted, "There isn't much to do but play ball or go to minor league games. You can't hurry cotton." With St. Louis the only major league city in the South and West at the time, the Cardinals represented their segment of the republic: rough farm boys, tobacco-chewing, with sunburnt faces, rowdy reputations, and from "true baseball country where the ball players are raised for the big city trade." This was their kind; and when Pepper Martin went head-first into the dirt at third base, all of Oklahoma went with him.

Pa Dean was one of those voyagers, and could not wait to see his boys in action. Himself a semi-pro ballplayer in the old days, Albert Dean spent his bus ride to St. Louis telling stories to the other passengers in Diz-like fashion, mostly about his exploits back in his younger days. He was as carefree as his eldest son Elmer, as stubborn as his middle son Jay, and as pensive as his youngest, Paul. "He shows in his gnarled hands that he has gone through the mill of hard work," described a writer as they traveled, and Albert was surviving (along with Elmer) partly on whatever the boys could send him from their Cardinal paychecks each month. The caravan made a stop in Joplin, Missouri, for a bite to eat, when he told everyone that there would not be a third Dean in the big leagues. "Elmer'll never make a major league player," he revealed. "He just isn't major league timber. But as for Dizzy and Paul, they'll tie the Tigers in knots once they're back in St. Louis. Paul will take them tomorrow, and Dizzy will stand the Tigers on their heads Saturday. The Cards won't have to go back to Detroit," he predicted.

After learning that ham hocks and cabbage were available, he told the person reading him the diner menu, "Don't read no further." Pa Dean and his fellow travelers filled Sportsman's Park with a raw baseball knowledge that formed a "critical gaze of the most expert class of customers in the country," according to admirer Westbrook Pegler of the *Chicago Daily News*.

A contingent also arrived at Sportsman's Park by way of Eldorado, Arkansas, the home of Schoolboy Rowe. Two full coachloads of train riders arrived at the ballpark from Eldorado, as well as another hundred by automobile. Students at Eldorado High School were dismissed early from classes to listen to Rowe's pitching in Game Two on the radio, which was broadcasted in the school's auditorium.

Paul Dean was named the Cardinals' starting pitcher for Game 3. When asked again about his youngest son would do, Pa replied, "Aw, Paul'll do just fine. Those boys got great support from each other while they was growin' up, and that's why they're such good pitchers today—'cause they've patted each other on the back when the other one needed it. I had my hands full, trying to raise my three boys, but I always tried to do what I could for them. They went to Sunday school regularly—and stayed for preachin', too."

How much were his sons worth to the Cardinals?

"That's a question for them to settle. As a baseball fan, and not a father, I would say that Dizzy would be worth $15,000 and Paul $10,000." Then somebody asked if a 30-game winner should get more than that.

"No, I believe in doing the right thing. Fifteen thousand dollars seems to be a reasonable figure."

Diz was upset that the Cardinals wouldn't pay for a plane ticket for Pa, but Albert would have declined the offer, anyway. "I'd rather see the country a little," he reasoned about the bus trip.

Curveball artist Tommy Bridges was the starter for Detroit. Bridges, at least in quantity, had actually outpitched Rowe during the regular season (275 innings to 266), and had also logged 22 victories on the year. After Paul, Diz, and Rowe posed with Arkansas governor J.M. Futrell for a photograph, Paul said, "So long, mayor," as the governor laughed at the misnomer and Paul took the hill. The Cardinals shone brightly as they took the field in brand-new white uniforms, which seemed to sparkle in the afternoon sunshine. Detroit donned their typical road grays, and a crowd of 34,073 anxiously awaited the first World Series action at Sportsman's Park in three years.

Paul afforded the Tigers numerous early chances, as he issued five hits, five walks, and a hit batsman in the first five innings, and "waded into holes deeper and darker than the mouth of a railroad tunnel." But all the attacks were stymied. A sacrifice fly by Rothrock, after Martin blasted a triple to right to lead off the game, had given the Cardinals a 1–0 lead in the first inning. Bill DeLancey added another run as he sizzled a double down the right field line, scoring Collins. After knocking Bridges out of the game with four runs, the Cardinals were shut down by Detroit reliever Elon Hogsett for the final four innings. But St. Louis already had done enough damage, as Martin would later double and score again, and the Cardinals held on for a 4–1 win. The lone Tiger score came in the ninth when Greenberg tripled in Jo-Jo White, who had singled. From the mound, Paul had been flirting with danger all day. By game's end, he would permit a total of 14 runners, and the Tigers left 13 of those on base. The final attack soon subsided, however, and Paul was escorted from the field with congratulations. Diz was the first to greet him, as the older brother put his arm around him and gave a big smile. "A grin twice the width of the old Mississippi ... the roar of the crowd, the acclaim of 35,000 fans, the headlines of the nation meant little or nothing to young Paul," said Grantland Rice, "compared to the approval and the handshake of old Diz." Despite receiving more gratitude in the dressing room, Paul tried to reconcile with himself. "I had the lousiest curve today I ever had in my life," he told reporters.

"You certainly had a fast one today though, Paul," commented Pepper Martin from across the room.

"Yeah, I was faster in the last two innings than I was at any time during the game," Paul acknowledged, half to Martin and half to the media men. "I don't hold no ballclub cheap, and that's the reason I beared down."

Pegler had the most succinct, yet accurate, summary of the game. "The Tigers ... have the look of losers, while the Deans are overbearing even when mediocre."

The box score from Game 3:

Detroit

	AB	R	H	RBI	PO	A	E
White, CF	5	1	2	0	4	0	0
Cochrane, C	3	0	0	0	6	3	0
Gehringer, 2B	5	0	2	0	3	3	0
Greenberg, 1B	4	0	1	1	6	0	0
Goslin, LF	4	0	1	0	2	0	0
Rogell, SS	4	0	1	0	1	2	2
Owen, 3B	3	0	0	0	1	0	0
Fox, RF	4	0	1	0	1	0	0
Bridges, P	1	0	0	0	0	0	0
Hogsett, P	2	0	0	0	0	1	0
Totals	35	1	8	1	24	9	2

St. Louis

	AB	R	H	RBI	PO	A	E
Martin, 3B	3	2	2	0	2	1	0
Rothrock, RF	4	1	1	2	5	0	1
Frisch, 2B	4	0	2	1	2	1	0
Medwick, LF	4	0	1	0	3	0	0
Collins, 1B	4	1	2	0	3	0	0
DeLancey, C	4	0	1	0	9	0	0
Orsatti, CF	2	0	0	0	1	0	0
Durocher, SS	3	0	0	0	2	1	0
P. Dean, P	3	0	0	1	0	0	0
Totals	31	4	9	4	27	3	1

	1	2	3	4	5	6	7	8	9	R	H	E
Detroit	0	0	0	0	0	0	0	0	1	1	8	2
St. Louis	1	1	0	0	2	0	0	0	x	4	9	1

Sixteen-game winner Tex Carleton was Frisch's choice for Game 4 the next day. Still indignant from being in the Deans' shadow, he was out to prove himself. Carleton had been a football player at Texas Christian University, and for this game he matched up against another former college gridiron performer. Eldon Auker, the sidearmed hurler and starter for the Tigers, had played football at Kansas State University. Auker, later in his career, pitched in St. Louis for the Browns, but he was the Cardinals' enemy today. With St. Louis up two games to one in the series, this was a critical contest. Auker had just completed a solid year for Detroit, during which he had a 15–7 record and a 3.42 ERA. His pitching style was sidearmed, but actually appeared to be underhanded (the result of, it was rumored, honing his pitching skills in low-ceilinged Kansas tornado shelters). His unusual technique would give the Cardinal hitters trouble all day long.

After Medwick singled in the first inning, a Collins double drove him home for a 1–0 St. Louis advantage. Auker settled down afterwards, however, and was the beneficiary of a shower of Tiger hits and runs in the third. Gehringer, Goslin, Rogell, Greenberg, and Owen all deposited the ball in different corners of Sportsman's Park, and the result was a 3–1 deficit for Carleton.

With Detroit up 4–3 in the bottom of the fourth, "disaster struck like forked lightning," wrote Paul Gallico. Virgil Davis' single had moved Durocher to third, and Frisch scanned the Cardinal bench for a pinch runner for Spud. Diz hopped up and ran out to first base, although Frisch never requested his services. Martin was the next batter, and he rolled a grounder to Gehringer. Charlie flipped the ball to Rogell at second base, and the Tiger shortstop reared back to fire to first in an attempt to complete a double play. Dean charged into second standing up "with his head in the road," and was smote in the forehead by Rogell's throw (as all good shortstops are taught to do, if the runner does not show an inclination to slide). Diz fell "like a marionette whose string had snapped," said one observer, and lay motionless on the infield dirt as the entire St. Louis dugout rushed to his aid. The ball reportedly glanced 30 feet into the air, and 100 feet away from the play—landing in Greenberg's glove in shallow right field.

There was not a sound to be heard out of the some 37,000 spectators in attendance. They all feared the worst—that Dizzy might be dead. Fortunately, he survived the ordeal "by the breath of the gods," according to Rice. After being helped to part of his senses, he was carried off the field by his teammates, including brother Paul. He soon regained consciousness in the locker room and immediately asked, "Did they get Martin at first?" to the astonishment of his caretakers.

Despite his brave effort, Dizzy's contretemps would not inspire the Cardinals. Carleton, Vance (in his first World Series appearance since his professional career began in 1912), Walker, Haines, and Mooney could not stem a later Detroit assault, a six-run barrage in the seventh and eighth innings. In a complete game 10–4 win, Auker did give up ten hits and four walks, but was able to record the big outs in clutch situations. Martin committed three errors at third, and sat dejectedly as he stared into his locker in a somber Cardinals clubhouse. Martin thought that his performance may have been affected by the quart of ice cream he quickly downed the night before.

"We played like a lot of sandlotters," Frisch told the press, leaning back against a wall and wiping the sweat from his graying temples. "There was no one especially to blame. We all had a finger in the pie.

"I do not think the injury to Dean had anything to do with our collapse in the late innings of the ball game. It was just a case of weak pitching and missing grounders and easy pop flies."

Then, reporters began questioning him about the play at second base. Frisch was denounced for putting Dean in the game, although it was never fully confirmed that Dizzy had Frisch's permission to enter the game. Frisch did acknowledge that he gave his consent for Diz to go in the game, but Diz was not the selection he was about to make for a pinch runner; Diz was on the field before he could be stopped. "Yesterday we saw what was probably the greatest managerial World Series boner in the history of baseball," Gallico still declared after listening to Frisch's side of the story. "Frankie Frisch took a million-dollar asset and used him on a ten-cent job... In the press box reporters looked at one another, puzzled. Dean to run? What for? The bat boy can run."

The box score from Game 4:

Detroit

	AB	R	H	RBI	PO	A	E
White, CF	4	2	1	0	2	0	0
Cochrane, C	5	2	1	0	1	0	0
Gehringer, 2B	4	2	2	0	4	4	1
Goslin, LF	3	2	0	0	3	0	0
Rogell, SS	5	1	2	4	4	3	0
Greenberg, 1B	5	1	4	3	10	2	0
Owen, 3B	5	0	2	1	1	2	0
Fox, RF	4	0	1	0	2	0	0
Auker, P	4	0	0	0	0	2	0
Totals	39	10	13	8	27	13	1

St. Louis

	AB	R	H	RBI	PO	A	E
Martin, 3B	4	0	1	0	1	2	3
Rothrock, RF	5	0	0	0	3	0	0
Frisch, 2B	5	1	1	0	2	4	0
Medwick, LF	3	1	2	0	0	0	0

St. Louis

	AB	R	H	RBI	PO	A	E
Collins, 1B	4	0	2	2	9	1	0
DeLancey, C	2	0	0	0	8	1	1
Orsatti, CF	4	1	2	1	2	1	0
Durocher, SS	4	1	1	0	2	1	0
Carleton, P	1	0	0	0	0	0	0
Vance, P	0	0	0	0	0	0	0
V. Davis, PH	1	0	1	1	0	0	0
J. Dean, PR	0	0	0	0	0	0	0
Walker, P	1	0	0	0	0	0	1
Haines, P	0	0	0	0	0	0	0
Crawford, PH	1	0	0	0	0	0	0
Mooney, P	0	0	0	0	0	1	0
Totals	35	4	10	4	27	11	5

	1	2	3	4	5	6	7	8	9	R	H	E
Detroit	0	0	3	1	0	0	1	5	0	10	13	1
St. Louis	0	1	1	2	0	0	0	0	x	4	10	5

As he left the ballpark, Diz was greeted by his personal squad of bodyguards who had been hired by Breadon for the rest of the series. The day before, Dean had accepted a ride from strangers, and Breadon feared that he would be abducted by gamblers, Tiger supporters, or whomever. After Breadon witnessed Diz getting into the car, he ordered the guards to watch him 24 hours a day. Strutting along with his hands in his pockets, Diz peeked back over his shoulder at his protective mercenaries. "You guys wanna grab a bite to eat?" he suggested.

To be absolutely certain nothing was permanently wrong, Breadon had Dizzy spend the night in the hospital, but he was cleared to play in the next game. The mythical headline the following day supposedly read, "X-Rays of Dean's Head Show Nothing." As accurate as that may have been, however, no newspaper had it. The question was apparent: Would Diz be able to pitch in the critical fifth game? "Hellfire, yes!" he exclaimed. "You can't hurt no Dean by hittin' him on the head."

Before the game the next day, Rogell posed with Diz for photographers. He presented Dean a World War I doughboy helmet, and Diz gave the camera a pained smile out the side of his face as he shook Rogell's hand. "Yep, ya plunked me good," he admitted as the cameramen finished their work. He patted the Detroit shortstop on the back, and both men trotted back to their respective dugouts.

Still a little woozy from the incident but having no serious problems, Diz took the mound before the largest crowd of the year at Sportsman's

Park, 38,536. With the series tied 2–2, the winner of this game would be only one victory away from the championship. Tommy Bridges came back on only one day's rest, as Cochrane wanted to save Rowe for later use.

Detroit opened the scoring in the second inning, in part the result of a change in the Cardinal lineup. Chick Fullis had been inserted into center field for Ernie Orsatti, as Frisch believed that Fullis would play better defense in the strong wind gusts that were present this day. However, when Pete Fox hit a line drive into the right-center gap, Fullis let the ball scoot by him, and Fox's double allowed Greenberg to score the game's first run. Fullis misplayed another ball on the ground in the sixth inning, as a routine single went between his legs and the batter Rogell was able to hustle into third. "Manager Frisch's theory on the replacement of Ernie Orsatti by Chick Fullis proved to be half right, which wasn't enough," John Kieran stated after the game. "Chick was better out there on flyballs, but Manager Frisch's theory didn't cover ground balls. Neither did Fullis."

Fullis' second error was preceded by a home run by Charlie Gerhinger, as Dean tried to blow a full-count fastball by him on the inside corner. Charlie was able to turn on the ball and launch a prodigious blast into the right–center field stands, and Greenberg later added a sacrifice fly. The Cardinals could not hit anything off Bridges this time, and after six innings the Cardinals trailed 3–0, still unable to figure out Bridges' elusive curveball.

The only St. Louis run in the game came in the seventh when DeLancey lifted his own round-tripper into the seats, making the game 3–1. The Cardinals threatened again in the eighth, but Tigers centerfielder Jo-Jo White made a spectacular catch off the bat of Martin with Spud Davis on first. The Tigers had Martin, a righthanded batter, played heavily to pull. Pepper found a fastball on the outer half from Bridges, however, and smoked a long one into the right–center field gap. Everyone in the park thought that the ball would fall free, except White—who, with the exception of Martin, was the fastest man on the field. White shot like a deer in the direction of the hit, stretched out, and nabbed the ball with the end of his glove as the rest of his body tumbled behind in the worn grass. It ended the inning, and dashed most Cardinal hopes.

By the time the Cardinals batted in the ninth, Dean had been removed in favor of pinch-hitter Pat Crawford the previous inning. Then, with the score same and DeLancey again battling at the plate to keep Cardinal hopes alive, he was almost ejected from the game. He watched three wicked curves from Bridges go by, all called strikes by plate umpire Brick Owens. DeLancey didn't agree, and uttered a few expletives. Owens then mentioned that each new word would cost DeLancey more money in fines, and the young Cardinal was reminded by Tigers catcher Cochrane that he had better keep his mouth shut if he wanted to continue playing in the series. As later noted by Commissioner Landis, Owens did not have the authority to fine DeLancey, but Landis did agree to review the case.

Also in that game, Goslin got into a shouting match with Bill Klem over a play on the bases. Later, in the lobby of the hotel where the Tigers were staying, Goslin offered to shake hands with Klem, but the veteran umpire refused and verbally lambasted the Goose again. "I should have let him have a punch on the chin," Goslin then considered. "But that would have cost me money, so I reported it. If they fine *us* for those things, why not the umpires?"

In finishing the tilt, Bridges had limited the Cardinals to seven scattered hits and no walks while fanning seven. He also worked rapidly, as the game ended in only an hour and 58 minutes.

The box score from Game 5:

Detroit

	AB	R	H	RBI	PO	A	E
White, CF	2	0	0	0	2	0	0
Cochrane, C	4	0	1	0	10	0	0
Gehringer, 2B	4	1	1	1	4	1	0
Goslin, LF	4	0	1	0	1	0	0
Rogell, SS	4	1	2	0	0	2	0
Greenberg, 1B	3	1	0	1	6	0	0
Owen, 3B	4	0	0	0	1	0	0
Fox, RF	4	0	1	1	3	0	0
Bridges, P	4	0	1	0	0	2	0
Totals	33	3	7	3	27	5	0

St. Louis

	AB	R	H	RBI	PO	A	E
Martin, 3B	4	0	2	0	0	1	0
Rothrock, RF	4	0	0	0	2	0	0
Frisch, 2B	4	0	1	0	2	3	0
Medwick, LF	4	0	0	0	3	0	0
Collins, 1B	4	0	1	0	5	1	0
DeLancey, C	4	1	1	1	6	0	0

St. Louis

	AB	R	H	RBI	PO	A	E
Fullis, CF	3	0	0	0	5	0	1
Orsatti, CF	1	0	0	0	0	0	0
Durocher, SS	2	0	1	0	3	2	0
V. Davis, PH	1	0	1	0	0	0	0
Whitehead, SS	1	0	0	0	1	0	0
J. Dean, P	2	0	0	0	0	0	0
Crawford, PH	1	0	0	0	0	0	0
Carleton, P	0	0	0	0	0	0	0
Totals	34	1	7	1	27	7	1

	1	2	3	4	5	6	7	8	9	R	H	E
Detroit	0	1	0	0	0	2	0	0	0	3	7	0
St. Louis	0	0	0	0	0	0	1	0	0	1	7	1

Again with no day for travel, the teams would have to march back to Detroit for Game 6 the next day, October 8. The Cardinals' backs were against the wall, with Detroit only one win away from the title. Most had felt that the momentum had swiftly shifted to the Tigers. "Mickey Cochrane had guessed right on [deciding to pitch] Tennessee Tom," asserted New York writer Kieran upon arriving in Detroit, "and now he is confident that nothing can stop the Tigers except rain."

Frisch, at first, appeared unsure about his starting pitcher for Game 6. He pointed out that Hallahan came through in Game 2 with a good performance, despite the loss. It was Paul Dean's turn, and he had won Game 3. What Frisch was certain of, however, was the accuracy of his choice. "I am sure my decision will send the day's winner to the mound," he stated boldly.

It was Paul, and the hopes of St. Louis rested with the young Dean in Game 6 as he would face the imposing Schoolboy Rowe. Fans in St. Louis were skeptical about their team's chances, as Rowe had ably shut down the Cardinal attack in Game 2. He hadn't pitched since that day (October 4), and thus had the advantage of an extra day's rest on Paul. But the junior Dean had proven himself in big games earlier in the season, and he calmly accepted the challenge. A shoulder-to-shoulder crowd of 44,551 at Navin Field in Detroit, the series' largest, nestled itself in to see if the Tigers could bring the city its first world championship ever. The tall, rangy Schoolboy waltzed out to the mound, after his emergence from the dugout met a chorus of loud cheers.

The Redbirds wasted no time in getting on the scoreboard. In the very first inning, Rothrock doubled to the right field corner, and was subsequently driven home by a Medwick single. The game's next tally came in the bottom of the third, with Detroit already having two out. The speedy Jo-Jo White walked, and everyone in the park knew he was going to try to steal second. He got a good jump as Paul kicked his leg high, and White crashed into Frisch in being safe at second. Frank was dazed, but soon gathered his wits. Meanwhile, the ball scooted loose into the outfield, and White picked himself up and headed into third. "Those Tigers have been hitting the bases and the basemen hard," noticed Kieran, "since Manager Mike spoke to them about their lady-like sauntering in the first three games."

Cochrane was the next hitter, and he tapped a roller down towards first. Paul went to cover the bag as Collins fielded the ball, but was late getting there. Mickey was safe, as White galloped in from third to score the tying run. The play had its price for the Tigers, however, as Paul spiked Cochrane as he went by the bag, and the Detroit manager came up lame. He limped off the field after the third out in terrible pain. Nonetheless, he didn't leave the game, and as he put on his catcher's equipment in the dugout, he winced in agony. The game being too important to sit himself out, he stumbled towards home plate to resume his defensive duty. Later in the game, he would get another blow, as Orsatti would knock him on his back on a play at the plate.

Paul held the Tigers in check into the fifth, when the Cardinals came alive again. The offensive hero this time was Durocher, the normally-harmless shortstop who had just one hit in his first 16 at bats in the series. He led off the inning with a single, and advanced to second on Dean's bunt. Pepper Martin then singled, scoring Leo, and Martin took third as Goslin's throw from left sailed over Cochrane's head. Jack Rothrock drove in Martin, and the Cardinals led 3–1.

In the bottom of the sixth, Cochrane's injury had a direct bearing on a crucial play of the game. He was on second with Gehringer on first, and the Tigers had already scored to close the gap to 3–2. There were no outs, and it looked like Detroit was going to launch a big inning on Paul. Goslin bunted, and the ball deadened in front of the plate. DeLancey popped up quickly, scooped up the ball, and let it fly to Martin at third. Pep was posed in a first baseman's stance in anticipation of the force play. Brick Owens, today the umpire at third after being DeLancey's home-plate nemesis yesterday, said Bill's throw was in time to nail the hobbling Cochrane. The Detroit dugout exploded in disbelief at the call, but Mickey was out. Greenberg later singled home Gehringer to tie the score at three, but that was it; the Tigers had blown their chance to take the lead, and perhaps, the series.

The eager Durocher came back to the plate in the seventh, and put a charge into a Rowe fastball that wound up in the right field gap for a double. Then came Paul, a right-handed hitter who threw his bat at an outside curve ball from the Schoolboy, and the result was a bloop single over Gehringer at second. Durocher skidded across home with the go-ahead run as the Cardinal bench rushed to greet him. Detroit squandered opportunities in the eighth and ninth, and the Cardinals held on for the 4–3 win. It was another big victory for Paul, who by now most people had forgotten was just a 21-year-old rookie. "Paul Dean was at his best in the pinch—the true test of pitching greatness," admired Billy Evans, a former major league manager and umpire who was helping cover the series for the St. Louis papers.

The box score from Game 6:

St. Louis

	AB	*R*	*H*	*RBI*	*PO*	*A*	*E*
Martin, 3B	5	1	1	1	1	2	0
Rothrock, RF	4	1	2	1	1	0	0
Frisch, 2B	4	0	0	0	2	3	1
Medwick, LF	4	0	2	1	0	0	0
Collins, 1B	4	0	0	0	8	0	0
DeLancey, C	4	0	0	0	6	4	0
Orsatti, CF	4	0	1	0	7	0	0
Durocher, SS	4	2	3	0	2	2	0
P. Dean, PH	3	0	1	1	0	0	1
Totals	36	4	10	4	27	11	2

Detroit

	AB	*R*	*H*	*RBI*	*PO*	*A*	*E*
White, CF	2	2	0	0	0	0	0
Cochrane, C	4	0	3	1	7	0	0
Gehringer, 2B	4	1	1	0	0	4	0
Goslin, LF	4	0	1	0	4	0	1
Rogell, SS	4	0	0	0	1	2	0
Greenberg, 1B	4	0	1	1	10	0	0
Owen, 3B	4	0	0	0	3	3	0
Fox, RF	4	0	1	0	2	0	0
Rowe, P	3	0	0	0	0	0	0
Totals	33	3	7	2	27	9	1

	1	2	3	4	5	6	7	8	9	R	H	E
St. Louis	1	0	0	0	2	0	1	0	0	4	10	2
Detroit	0	0	1	0	0	2	0	0	0	3	7	1

Durocher, who before this offensive outburst was not having a good series, crashed open the locker room door in celebration of his 3-for-4 day at the plate. As John Carmichael peeked down the runway, he saw the fervor of the St. Louis men. "Kids out of school, a torrent rushing over a dam, madmen on the loose, that's how the Cardinals stormed into the dressing room." Cochrane mustered three of the Tigers' seven hits in his wounded condition, but it wasn't enough for his club. Rowe would later claim that part of his ineffectiveness was caused by a sore pitching hand, injured the previous day by getting caught in a door jamb. The Cardinals laughed when they heard this, as Medwick asked, "Maybe we can kiss it for him?" As for Cochrane—with the beating laid upon him by the Cardinals—he spent the night in a Detroit hospital for precautionary measures, nursing his spike wound and a strained ligament in his left leg. Paul, with his grand performance, had once again earned the respect of his teammates.

The Tigers had an elaborate camera-and-microphone setup in their locker room, in expectation of a series victory that day.

"HOLD THAT TIGER! HOLD THAT TIGER!" was the cheer in the St. Louis clubhouse. Diz reached over to shake Paul's hand through everyone else's. "You're quite a pitcher, boy," he said to his brother. At the end of the room Rip Collins, the only quiet one in the den, smiled as he opened an anniversary card from his wife. "Married twelve years ago today. I couldn't give my wife a better present." While the acclamation in the room continued, Frisch spoke about the character of his team. "I'm immensely proud of my players. They never give up. They are fighters. They don't know when they are licked." He was already being asked about his starter for the winner-take-all finale tomorrow.

"Dean or Hallahan, I don't know yet," he responded.

But he did know, as did everyone. Dizzy Dean was the only choice. "It will be Dizzy you can bet all the tea in China," predicted Chicago writer John Carmichael. Paul had mentioned that brother Diz had lost 20 pounds in the last month of the season from too much work, but even that didn't matter at this point. Dean would have to face a rabid Detroit crowd, in addition to the powerful Tiger lineup the next day, as the 1934 baseball season had reached its gun lap. Kieran, while in the

Cardinals' locker room after the Game 6 victory, noticed that "Dizzy and Daffy are already trying to talk Manager Frisch into letting them pitch the seventh game, either separately or together.

"As Dizzy remarked, 'This is a family matter.'"

18

Winner Take All

The momentum had shifted again. "En route from St. Louis to Detroit, Mickey Cochrane said the Tigers had the Cardinals in the doghouse," reported Alan Gould of the Associated Press. "The trouble was the doghouse door was open."

The ninth of October, 1934, was a sunny, cool day at Detroit's Navin Field. The fans eagerly lined up at Trumbull and Michigan avenues waiting for the gates to open. Auker, who had been effective against the Cardinals in Game 4 at St. Louis, would be the pitcher trying to guide the Tigers to the title. As expected, Diz was indeed Frisch's choice to start for the Cardinals, and the 24 year old would be trying for his second series win and the Dean family's fourth. Once again, Diz made a pregame visit to the Detroit bullpen, and warmly greeted Eldon. "You don't expect to get anyone out with *that* stuff, do you?" Diz asked.

During the game, other Cardinals chided in with other verbal assaults. In the Detroit paper that morning, Cochrane had been photographed in his hospital bed, covered in bandages. Above his picture on the front page the headline displayed, "OUR STRICKEN LEADER." This invited the Cardinals, Pat Crawford in particular, to ask frequently during the game, "How the hell's our damn stricken leader doing?"

The seventh and final game was an even contest for two innings. Then, as if destiny had lifted the Gas House Gang onto its wings, the Tigers saw their fortress come tumbling down around them. A one-out surge in the Cardinal third was commenced by Dean, when he looped a single to the outfield—or at least that's what left fielder Goose Goslin was thinking. Blitzing through first base coach Buzzy Wares' stop sign, Diz chugged for second as the surprised Goslin hurried to the ball and threw to Gehringer too late. Dean was at second base with a double, and the floodgates were opened. Martin followed with an infield single, and stole second on the following pitch to Rothrock. Much had been made of the baserunning battle between Martin and Cochrane, as if it was a rematch of the 1931 World Series.

Here it was three years later, and Pepper had his first true chance to steal in the series. With Dean watching carefully from third, Martin bolted towards second with Auker's movement towards home. Patentholder of the head-first slide, he lunged for the centerfield corner of second base and scooted under Rogell's late tag. Rothrock then walked to load the bases, as an uneasy groan began to fill the stands. Then Frisch—called "the top clutch hitter of his era" by John McGraw, and who others claimed had his bat emblazoned with a dollar sign for the trademark—laced a double to right field. The liner brought home all the runners and gave the Cardinals a 3–0 lead. Rowe then entered the game and retired Medwick for the second out. The overture of offense, however, soon rang out against the Schoolboy as well. Hits by Collins and DeLancey augmented the lead, and Rowe was pulled in favor of Elon Hogsett, who allowed Orsatti and Durocher to reach on a walk and a hit. The bases were now loaded, as Dean came up again.

He chuckled at Cochrane as he took his warm-up swings. "It's all over, Mick," he told the Detroit catcher, and he dribbled a grounder to Owen at third. Showing great speed down the baseline, he beat it out for his second hit of the inning, scoring DeLancey. By the time Bridges entered as the fourth Detroit pitcher of the inning, the Cardinals had built a 7–0 lead. He was able to get Rothrock to ground out to Greenberg, and the Tigers finally got another turn at bat.

When the Tigers failed to score in the fourth, a rising anger began to boil over in the stands. How could their beloved Tigers let it come to this? Hadn't they coasted so easily through the American League? Weren't they the most talented club in baseball? How could these rag-tag boys from St. Louis beat up on their mighty men? Anger grew to hatred. This hatred spurred the most memorable event of the series, which surfaced in the Cardinals' sixth with Martin on second after his double and two out. Medwick was batting, and he was ironically chasing Martin's record for most hits in a World Series.

Back in the 1931 classic, Martin knocked out a record 12 safeties; and his friend Medwick now stood in the batter's box, currently with ten hits. He peered out wantonly at Bridges as he took his practice swings. He then took hold of a fastball and whistled a liner over White's head in center field, rounded first, rounded second, and charged full-steam for third. Detroit third baseman Owen held up both arms—as if he was anticipating a throw—but no play was made. Medwick got his spikes up as he plowed into him, and Owen brought his foot down with his spikes driving into Ducky's leg. Medwick then kicked back at him, got up, and was ready to fight in his customary stance. Umpire Klem tried to separate them, but the scuffle continued for several seconds. "The Cardinals swarmed from the dugout, a red mob," before Medwick even got up. After tensions between the two had somewhat cooled, Medwick offered his hand for Owen to shake; Owen refused and returned to his third base position. Moments later, Collins drove in Medwick to give the Cardinals a 9–0 lead.

When Joe took his usual place in left field in the bottom of the sixth, an unsightly mob of about 17,000 in the bleachers in that part of the outfield was waiting for him. Yelling and cursing escalated. Finally someone hurled an apple that rolled right up to Medwick's feet. He lazily reached down, picked it up, and flung it in a nonchalant, side-armed manner back towards the fence. The apple opened a barrage. Any debris that could be found—fruit, wadded-up paper, bits of hot dogs, even bottles—were launched at him. When an orange came rolling towards Medwick, he grabbed it and playfully tossed it into Martin at third base. Pepper, amused by the scene, grabbed it and twirled it in the air. The rest of the stands and the other players were watching dumbfounded. From the pressbox, Paul Gallico also witnessed the event.

"I watched the crowd and Medwick and the pelting missiles through my field glasses, and it was a terrifying sight. Every face in the crowd, women and men, was distorted with rage. Mouths were torn wide open, eyes glistened in the sun. All fists were clenched."

Durocher wandered out near Medwick, but didn't get as close to the stands as Joe was. Leo urged him to give it right back to the attackers, but Medwick said amid the debris, "If *you're* so brave, *you* play left field and I'll play shortstop." At one point Cochrane went out to try and subdue the horde with a gesture of his hand, but it "had no more effect than throwing a pebble into the ocean." It was as much as some Detroit police officers were able to do, as they were stationed at the bottom row of the left field bleachers and could do nothing to curb the rioters. "Only the barrier of a steel screen and locked gates prevented them from pouring into the field and mobbing Medwick," Gallico added. By this point, a handful of cameramen had scurried towards left field to get a shot of the crowd, adding further congestion to the war zone. Meanwhile, Pat Crawford brought Diz a jacket from the dugout in the event that further delay would cause his arm to go cold.

Medwick had become a solitary target of the total frustration of the Detroit crowd. After park personnel made a futile attempt to clear all of the garbage, play was about to resume. But after a second barrage from the stands—"with more bottles and less fruit" this time—caused another interruption, Commissioner Landis utilized one of the little-known codicils under his power. Famous for being hired by the owners to "clean up baseball" after the 1919 World Series scandal involving the Chicago White Sox, Landis called Medwick and Owen over to his box seat. Frisch, Cochrane, and Klem also came, standing nearby. Landis then opened the mini-hearing, and the "court transcript" read something like this:

"Mr. Owen," the judge began in his urbane murmur. "Did Mr. Medwick attempt to kick you?"

"Yes sir," replied Owen.

Landis then turned to Medwick. "Is that true? Did you attempt to kick Mr. Owen?" he asked.

"Yes I did, sir," Medwick replied. Durocher would later say that, as his roommate for several years, he never knew Joe Medwick to tell a lie.

"Did you, Mr. Owen," continued Landis, "try to spike Mr. Medwick?"

"No sir," said Owen.

After pausing in thought for a moment, Landis returned to the discussion to issue his verdict. He ordered Frisch to remove Medwick from the game—for the latter's own safety, as well as that of the fans. A police escort then led Jersey Joe from the field "as the boos thundered again," according to one reporter. Offering some final gestures to the Tiger fans yelling at him, Medwick disappeared down the steps of the Cardinals' dugout. Chick Fullis jogged out uneventfully to assume Ducky's position. The outburst had delayed the game for 17 minutes. Perhaps the event was therapeutic for the Detroit faithful; they had made their voices heard and released their anger, but none of this changed the fact that their team was losing by nine runs.

When a few of the Cardinals recalled the event years later, including Whitehead and clubhouse boy Butch Yatkeman, they wondered what Landis would have done if the game was closer in score. Would he still have forced Frisch to remove Medwick, one of his best hitters, from the lineup? It must be remembered that Landis' move also prevented Medwick from further pursuit of Martin's record; his series tally ended at 11 hits after his trouble-stirring triple.

The St. Louis lead increased to 11 runs in the seventh, and Detroit had given up any hope. Diz was still going strong, and with the big lead wanted to experiment with some new pitches. "Hey Frank," he yelled to Frisch at his second base position. "If I'm as good as Hubbell, I should be able to throw a screwball—watch this." He did try a screwball, and the pitch wound up over DeLancey's head at the backstop. "Bear down dammit!!!" Frisch screamed at him. Despite Dean giving Frankie a few more gray hairs, the final score remained 11–0, and Diz had gone the distance for his ninth shutout of the year as he allowed no walks, only six hits, and struck out five.

The box score from Game 7:

St. Louis

	AB	R	H	RBI	PO	A	E
Martin, 3B	5	3	2	1	1	1	0
Rothrock, RF	5	1	2	1	4	0	0
Frisch, 2B	5	1	1	3	3	5	0
Medwick, LF	4	1	1	1	1	0	0
Fullis, LF	1	0	1	0	1	0	0
Collins, 1B	5	1	4	2	7	2	1
DeLancey, C	5	1	1	1	5	0	0
Orsatti, CF	3	1	1	0	2	0	0
Durocher, SS	5	1	2	0	3	4	0
J. Dean, P	5	1	2	1	1	0	0
Totals	43	11	17	10	27	12	1

Detroit

	AB	R	H	RBI	PO	A	E
White, CF	4	0	0	0	3	0	1
Cochrane, C	4	0	0	0	2	2	0
Hayworth, C	0	0	0	0	1	0	0
Gehringer, 2B	4	0	2	0	3	5	1
Goslin, LF	4	0	0	0	4	0	1
Rogell, SS	4	0	1	0	3	2	0
Greenberg, 1B	4	0	1	0	7	0	0
Owen, 3B	4	0	0	0	1	2	0
Fox, RF	3	0	2	0	3	0	0
Auker, P	0	0	0	0	0	0	0
Rowe, P	0	0	0	0	0	0	0
Hogsett, P	0	0	0	0	0	0	0

Detroit

	AB	R	H	RBI	PO	A	E
Bridges, P	2	0	0	0	0	0	0
Marberry, P	0	0	0	0	0	0	0
Walker, PH	1	0	0	0	0	0	0
Crowder, P	0	0	0	0	0	0	0
Totals	34	0	6	0	27	11	3

	1	2	3	4	5	6	7	8	9	R	H	E
St. Louis	0	0	7	0	0	2	2	0	0	11	17	1
Detroit	0	0	1	0	0	2	0	0	0	0	6	3

In the clubhouse, a jubilant Diz embraced Frisch, with Dean appropriately wearing a tiger-hunting safari hat for the photographers. The winners' share (in contrast to Whitehead's recollection) would turn out to be $5,941 for each player. This amount, the largest to date, was made possible in part by the Ford Company pioneering the sponsorship of radio broadcasts for World Series play. The Cardinals received approximately an extra thousand dollars from Ford, while the Tigers earned close to $600 per player. After Cardinal players decided to give $3,000 of their prize to team helpers, the final shares wound up at $5,821 per man. Charley Gelbert (who missed the entire season still recovering from his gunshot wound) was given $1,000, and the team also doled out the following: $500 each to Yatkeman and head groundskeeper William Stockslek, $200 to assistant clubhouse boy Eddie Dale, and $100 each to press gate supervisor Mel Curran, mascot Mike Conlisk, and public address announcer James Kelly.

These bonuses were treasured by everyone involved in the 1934 World Series. In the 1930's, the tough times kept everyone on severely limited budgets, and players needed to help their families as much as they could. That being the case, a fierce battle ensued when different stakes were on the line for the winners and losers during the World Series, and the 1934 series was a prime example. In today's game, the winner's share may amount to pocket change in the minds of the players, and the Series MVP may receive his eighth car to squeeze into his driveway. But for the player of baseball's Golden Age, getting the opportunity to play for the winners' share of the World Series turned into an all-out fight for survival—survival in the real world, not in baseball.

Upon returning to the Cardinals' hotel, Medwick was greeted by two private detectives who were hired by Breadon. Breadon feared reprisals by Detroit fans whose anger had not yet subsided. Joe ate

Paul Dean, Dizzy's wife Pat, and Diz (left to right, sitting in car) celebrate the Cardinals' World Series victory in a St. Louis parade on October 10, 1934. (From the collections of the St. Louis Mercantile Library at the University of Missouri–St. Louis.)

dinner with them in his room, and they tailed him for the remainder of the evening.

Back when the regular season had ended and the World Series began, Dean had already made good on two preseason predictions: (1) It would take 95 wins to get the pennant (the Cardinals' regular season record finished exactly at 95–58); and (2) he and Paul would get 45 wins (they would actually get 49).

Then, for an encore, the Deans got all four wins in the World Series, two by each brother. These victories put the family's season total at 53. Before the series began, Cochrane mentioned that "it will take a great team to beat Dizzy and Daffy in seven tries." He had no idea how right he was.

After a two-year hiatus, the world championship of baseball had returned to St. Louis. "In the wake of Western dust blown up by the two cyclonic Deans," avowed Grantland Rice, "the St. Louis Cardinals take their place today on the top plateau of baseball." Rice also predicted that the Dean legend would ultimately match those of Babe Ruth, Honus Wagner, Christy Mathewson, and Ty Cobb, the most sterling individuals the game had yet seen.

"The twin poisons of sport," Rice called the Dean brothers after their mastery of the Tigers.

A huge celebration awaited the Cardinals as they pulled into Union Station the next morning. Thousands of St. Louisians came out to welcome their heroes, and toilet paper littered the streets in lieu of unavailable ticker tape and streamers. A parade led by mounted police was part of the festivities, and fans lined the streets as the Cardinals passed in open cars. The route took them east on Market Street to Broadway, north on Broadway to Washington, and finally west on Washington to the parade's end at Jefferson. Frisch and Mayor Dickmann rode in the first car, while the Dean brothers traveled in the second automobile surrounded by five police motorcycles (interestingly, Frisch and the mayor were afforded no extra security). "Dizzy and Paul" had become the most famed brother act in the land, and their hands were requested everywhere.

"Hey Diz!" a young fan yelled to him as the parade cars rolled along. "How's it gonna look next year? Is anyone gonna beat us out?"

"No chance," answered Jay. "With great arms like me 'n' Paul's, we could pitch f'rever."

Was baseball dead with Babe Ruth soon to be leaving the game? No way—at least according to Grantland Rice.

"The passing of the eminent Babe was supposed to remove most of the color from the game. But, in his majestic wake, the sky of balldom is still a flare of crimson, green, purple and orange, as the fragrant wayside odor of the sage and the brush fills the autumn air.

"As Babe Ruth fades out, the bounding Deans arrive just in time to fill the gap against the skyline."

New Places, New Faces— 1935–1939

After the World Series came to a close, the Dean boys did not even give themselves a chance to rest. While the remainder of the team headed back to their hometowns to catch a break, Dizzy and Paul immediately began their tour of "barnstorming" dates—exhibitions against notable semi-pro and professional clubs with big paydays for the Deans. Before the Negro leagues were disbanded with baseball integration in the late 1940s, many of these games were against the great black teams of the day, such as the Pittsburgh Crawfords and the Kansas City Monarchs. These games stretched out over much of the nation, as far east as Pennsylvania and west to Nebraska and Kansas. Always grand spectacles, such contests drew several thousand people in some cases; huge masses jamming into second-rate parks not built to hold large gatherings. This was the case in a game at Oxford, Nebraska, where 6,000 people crowded a tiny field to watch the Deans. It was here where Diz met Satchel Paige in one of their legendary battles.

Paige was a longtime Negro League thrower whose best years were behind him when he finally got the call for the major leagues in 1948. He was hailed as "The Black Dizzy Dean," and was using his self-proclaimed "back dodger" (curveball), along with magnificent speed, to baffle hitters everywhere. When questioned about the ethical nature of his pitches, Paige responded, "I never throw an illegal pitch. The problem is, once in a while, I throw one that ain't been seen by this generation." It was certainly a great promotional move to pit Dean and Paige against each other in these types of games. They gained tremendous respect for each other, as they carried similar qualities—both in pitching skill and in self-assuredness. People would come from hundreds of miles around to witness these contests, and sometimes leave pondering for themselves about which man was the better pitcher—especially after a Paige victory.

Meanwhile, a nation across the globe was gearing up for the arrival of another American legend. After the 1934 season was completed, Babe Ruth toured Japan with a collection of major league all-stars, which Grantland Rice said, "should be one of the greatest of all sports expeditionary forces. Jimmy [*sic*] Foxx is also going, and Lou Gehrig hopes to be on hand. Few know that Japan has at least two ball parks with more seating capacity than any baseball plant in the United States of America, outside of the Yankee Stadium." The American team went 17–1 against a collection of Japanese all-stars, as Ruth knocked 13 home runs.

Both Medwick and Diz became holdouts before the 1935 season began. Dean was seeking $25,000, and Medwick a modest $10,000. Breadon had only offered $17,500 to Diz, and threatened to appeal to Judge Landis to support his authority. When news of this reached the wires, sportswriters around the country once again undertook their crusade to promote Dean's worth to the ballclub. "If they don't give him what he asks for," wrote one, "that club in St. Louis will up and fold—how can you argue with a thirty-game winner?" The ultimate amount agreed upon was $18,000, but spring training began without Diz, and he was getting the itch to pitch. Medwick eventually agreed to a lesser amount also; and with contract troubles now behind them, they relaxed and laughed their way through preseason workouts as always.

The only change in the Cardinals' starting lineup for 1935 occurred in center field, where fleet-footed rookie Terry Moore had taken over for Orsatti and Fullis. Moore, who was also blessed with a powerful throwing arm and a competent bat, would patrol the alleys of Sportsman's Park for years to come. Unfortunately, he lost several seasons of his prime to service in World War II. As the newcomer to a championship team, Moore soon learned the personalities of the famous Gas House Gang. Dean, in particular, made quite an impression on Moore in his rookie year. Moore recalled a time during the 1935 season when the Cardinals were playing the Dodgers in Brooklyn. Dean was pitching, and as was customary, he went over the opponent's lineup with

Frisch before the game. Frisch was especially concerned about Sam Leslie, as Moore told the story in the book *Redbirds Revisited*:

"We had the lead in this ballgame, and Dean had pitched Leslie the way *he* wanted to, not the way Frisch had wanted him to when they discussed it before the game. I think Dean may have even struck out Sam three straight times. Late in the game, Dean went back to Frisch and said, 'Now, I'll pitch him the way *you* want me to, Frank.'

"So Dean threw Leslie a high fastball with not too much on it and Leslie hit it nine miles over that outfield fence in Brooklyn, and Dean is out there doubled over with laughter as Leslie's runnin' around the bases. Dean looks at Frisch and yells, 'I told you so!'"

Returning as the defending champions, the Cardinals were optimistic for another great season in 1935. The Boston Braves, on the contrary, had been a franchise that struggled for most of that year. On their way to 116 losses on the season, the inept club relied on an ailing Babe Ruth, in his last major league season, to at least provide some revenue at the turnstiles. The Bambino had nothing left as player, but was nonetheless signed as nothing more than a circus attraction. His body battered from years of abuse, he could hardly walk to the plate and take his swings. On May 7, 1935, the Cardinals played in Boston. In a symbolic transfer of power in the sport, Dizzy Dean pitched against Babe Ruth, ushering in an era of new individual dominance in baseball.

When the all-star team touring Japan had returned home, Ruth learned that the Yankees were not renewing his contract. The club had sold him to Boston, the city where his career began in 1914 with the Red Sox of the American League. The "Red Sox Curse" has been in effect since—the fact that the club has not won a World Series since Red Sox owner and play producer Harry Frazee sold Ruth to the Yankees to pay off losses from several stage flops.

Ruth had always wanted to become manager of the Yankees, but Joe McCarthy—who would lead the New Yorkers to four straight World Series titles from 1936 through 1939, and who many would later consider to be the best manager in history—got the job. The Babe was heartbroken. Colonel Ruppert offered him the manager's job at Newark, the top farm club of the New York team. It was only after Ruth's prodding, however, that Ruppert even suggested the idea of Newark as a possibility. "How can you manage a team when you can't even manage yourself?" he asked the slugger. Ruth was too proud to accept the Newark position. The Braves held the only offer from a major league club, so he took it. The offer included a "handshake" promise for Ruth to become manager in 1936, but the Braves had no real intention of giving him the role. His presence was simply meant to boost attendance.

So as Ruth entered the batter's box against Diz for the first time, Dean tipped his hat out of respect. This was a matchup that all in baseball had dreamed about for a long time, and now it was occurring. The young lion was too much for the old lion as Dean held Ruth hitless in three at bats, and homered himself as the Cardinals won, 7–0. It was a showdown of the two greatest entertainers in baseball history, and the story would quickly end later in the season, with another 0-for-3 day for Ruth against Dean, for an 0-for-6 career total against Diz. He had great respect for the Babe, and said later, "I hated stealin' the show from him like that."

Always the entertainer, Ruth had these words at a 1935 banquet when asked about his uncertain future. "I can't go on forever. Somebody's got to fill my shoes, and take my place. But you can bet your sweet life that I won't play until I drop—but I'll play until I damn near drop."

For the first few months, the 1935 National League race appeared to be another two-team chase between the Giants and the Cardinals. To dispel any rumors that the Gas House pilot light had burned out, Pepper Martin bowled over Cubs catcher Ken O'Dea in the 12th inning for a victory on the Fourth of July. Frisch had gradually transferred most of the second base duties to Whitehead, and focused most of his energy on managing. By Labor Day, the Cardinals held a two game lead over the Giants and a two-and-a-half game margin over the streaking Cubs. The Cardinals stayed hot after the holiday, winning six in a row, while watching the Cubs overtake the Giants into second place. Despite playing two-thirds of the final month at home, however, the Cardinals could not overcome a torrid streak by Chicago in September. Going into a season-ending, five-game series at Sportsman's Park, the Cardinals had beaten the Cubs in 12 out of 15 games during the season. Chicago, however, had won an astounding 18 games in a row heading into the series at St. Louis which began on September 25. In the first contest, Paul Dean became a victim of Warneke, 1–0. The next day, in the opener of a doubleheader, Bill Lee beat Diz, 6–2. The Cubs won the nightcap as well, bringing their amazing streak to 21 in a row. It ended the next day, but Chicago had already clinched the pennant. The press in St. Louis had nicknamed the Cubs the "Grimm Reapers" in honor of their player-manager, first baseman Charlie Grimm, who forecasted a National League championship for Chicago before the season began.

Despite faltering at the end, Diz produced another strong year, in which he had pitched in 324 innings, had 28 wins, and logged 182 strikeouts. The Cards finished in second place with a record of 96–58—one-half game better than their championship season the previous summer—but a full four games behind the Chicago and their 100 victories. The Giants faded once again, finishing eight-and-a-half games behind the Cubs with a final record of 91–62. The financial situation was better for Breadon and the Cardinals, however, as Sportsman's entertained a half-million spectators during the season. Struggling even more, however, were the landlord Browns, who drew an unbelievable audience of 80,000 for the entire 1935 year.

The Tigers returned to the World Series to face the Cubs, and this time the Detroit club was victorious, four games to two. Frank Navin, the owner that was completely devoted to his Tigers, finally enjoyed a world championship by his club. He died a month later on November 13, 1935.

Other notable Cardinal performances for 1935 included Paul reaching 19 wins again, and Medwick and Collins hitting .353 and .313 respectively, each with 23 home runs.

When the next year rolled around, the hot pitcher out of the gate for the Cardinals in 1936 was a Dean, but not the elder. Paul won five straight to start the year, but had not been properly taking care of his arm. Like Diz, he felt that his wing was indestructible, but stiffness in the elbow would make this his last full major league season.

As the 1930s moved along, the breakup of the Gas House Gang occurred in a gradual manner. After the death of Bill DeLancey and the retirement of Spud Davis, a young catcher with a rocket arm took over behind the plate for the Cardinals. Malcolm Owen, better known as "Mickey," became perhaps the first major league catcher to throw out baserunners from his knees. From the Ozarks of southwestern Missouri, Owen is as proud of his stint as Greene County (MO) Sheriff as he is of his professional baseball career. "That job was a lot tougher than being a ballplayer," he admitted.

Other prominent changes took place before the 1936 season. One included Johnny Mize, a big, strong, mountain of a man that took the first base job away from Rip Collins. From the left-handed batter's box, Mize's swing seemed so natural and effortless, yet emitted unbelievable power. Mize had been acquired from the Cincinnati Reds in what was

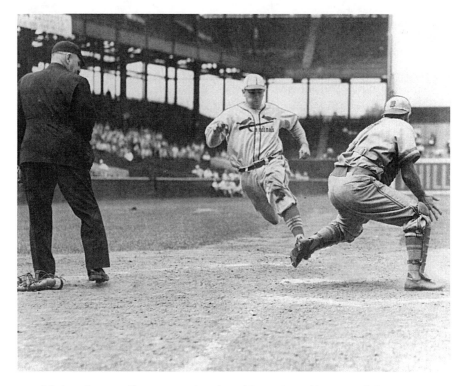

Mickey Owen gallops across the plate. (From the collections of the St. Louis Mercantile Library at the University of Missouri–St. Louis.)

yet another brilliant move by Rickey. The Reds had written off Mize because of a leg injury, but it became fully healed after arriving in St. Louis. Rickey also had dealt Whitehead to the Giants, where the scholar would finally get an everyday job at second base. In return, St. Louis received pitcher Roy Parmalee, a strong number three starter for New York the past couple of seasons behind Hubbell and Schumacher (Parmalee would spend only one year in a Cardinals uniform, being dealt the following winter to Cubs, along with Rip Collins, for Warneke).

Frisch, now 38 and fighting the many aches and pains of the battles behind him, gave the nod for the keystoner job in St. Louis to rookie Stu Martin. Durocher remained at short, and Pepper Martin had moved to right field to replace the retired Rothrock, with Charley Gelbert taking Pepper's spot at third. Gelbert, returning from his hunting accident a full three years before, was not the same player as he once was as he

Not-so-friendly times, 1936: an angry Tex Carleton, now with the Cubs (center, with cap off), is escorted off the field at Sportsman's Park after his fight with Diz. (From the collections of the St. Louis Mercantile Library at the University of Missouri–St. Louis.)

wound up 1936 with a .229 average. Medwick, meanwhile, was establishing himself as the National League's most powerful force. He finished 1936 with 138 RBIs and a record 64 doubles while batting .351 with a league-leading 223 hits. Martin enjoyed another fine year, batting .309 with 36 doubles and 23 stolen bases. Mize chipped in with 19 home runs and a .329 clip, and Moore slammed 39 doubles while playing a sparkling center field. Among all of the position changes remained the constant of Dean, who in 1936 threw over 300 innings for the third consecutive year. It was not enough, however, as the Cardinals could not re-claim the pennant.

It was the pitching that had brought St. Louis down. Besides Dean (3.17) and Jim Winford (3.80), no Cardinal pitcher had an ERA under 4.00. And after Dean's 24 triumphs, the only St. Louis pitchers with double-figure wins were Winford and Parmalee (11 each). Still, with the tremendous offense, they looked forward to 1937 with optimism, and Diz was certain that he had many great years ahead of him.

With Diz shouldering most of the pitching load, the offensive strategy of the team seemed to switch from speed to power with the development of Mize and the ever-dangerous Medwick. Whatever the style of play, the Cardinal spirit remained, and Martin showed that they were still entertainers by his founding of the Musical Mudcats band. With Frenchy Bordagaray (an outfielder), Lon Warneke (newly acquired from the Cubs), Bob Weiland, and Bill McGee (other pitchers), Martin blared away on his harmonica and other homemade instruments to amuse audiences on the road. Bordagaray scratched his tunes on a washboard; Weiland tooted at an empty jug, and Warneke and McGee strummed in with their guitars. When the outback orchestra reached national acclaim, Rickey ordered it disbanded. He thought the boys were more concerned with playing music than winning ballgames.

The 1936 season had also seen the arrival of two prominent rookies, both in the American League. One was a 17-year-old righthanded pitcher from Van Meter, Iowa, whose dad had built him a ball field behind the family barn. His father also had taken him to the 1934 World Series in St. Louis, so that he could see the great Dizzy Dean. His name was Bob Feller, and in his debut on August 23 for the Cleveland Indians, he struck out 15 St. Louis Browns. Three weeks later, he set an American League record by striking out 17 Philadelphia A's. The Indians would not have him for the whole year, however—he had to go back to Van Meter to complete high school.

In New York, the Yankees had a 21-year-old fisherman's son from San Francisco playing for them in centerfield. The owner of a 61-game hitting streak in the Pacific Coast League, Joe DiMaggio was now ready to blast away on major league pitching. The San Francisco Seals of the PCL had tried him at shortstop, but his 11 errors in one game prompted them to move him to the outfield. Along with Gehrig and Bill Dickey, DiMaggio led the Yanks to the American League pennant in '36 by a whopping nineteen-and-a-half games over Mickey Cochrane's Tigers.

After surrendering the NL flag to the Cardinals and Cubs the previous two seasons, the Giants returned to the top. Hubbell took matters into his own hands in August and September, winning his last 16 consecutive decisions and catapulting the Giants into a cross-town World Series showdown with the Yankees. He then won the first game of the series, but was beaten in the fourth contest as the Yankees would eventually win in six.

The baseball equivalent to a shooting star, Dizzy Dean's career virtually ended—for all intents and purposes—at the 1937 All-Star Game in Washington, D.C. A couple of weeks before, he was called for a balk at Sportsman's Park by umpire George Barr, and was thrown out of the game after hollering about the call. When National League president Ford Frick suspended him for his actions, he called Frick and Barr "the two biggest crooks in baseball." As part of his pouting, he threatened not to attend the All-Star Game in protest, but was ultimately convinced to oblige by his wife Pat.

Following a home run off the bat of Gehrig, Cleveland Indians star Earl Averill lined a ball off of Dizzy's left foot and broke the big toe. Trying to pitch the Cardinals to another pennant, he attempted to come back from the injury later in the summer despite still having discomfort in the toe. The pain that remained caused him to alter his delivery, and the result was an unnatural arm motion. His changed style put extreme stress on his elbow, and he had a sore arm for the rest of the year. He wound up with a record of 13–10, part of the Cardinals' 81–73, fourth-place mark. Medwick won the Triple Crown, batting .374 with 31 home runs and 154 runs batted in. Mize, however, wasn't far behind (.364-25-113). In fact, the duo of Medwick and Mize was 1-2 in most league offensive categories (including batting average, slugging average, total bases, doubles, and nearly in hits: Medwick 237, Paul Waner 219, Mize 204).

The following year, the unthinkable happened. With Dean's arm still sore at the beginning of the 1938 season, the Cardinals sold him to the Cubs for $185,000 plus pitchers Clyde Shoun and Curt Davis and outfielder Tuck Stainback. Rickey warned Cubs owner Phillip Wrigley that Dean had a "dead arm," but Wrigley gladly accepted the deal nonetheless. Despite long-standing gripes with the Cardinals' management, Dean was truly sorry to leave St. Louis and his friends behind. Still, he welcomed the chance to prove the Cardinals organization wrong and show that he still had the fire in his arm. Davis would eventually have a good 1938 season for St. Louis (12–8 record, 3.64 ERA). Shoun, however, struggled on the mound, and Stainback would go hitless in only ten at bats.

Regardless of Dean's popularity in St. Louis, the deal was a smart financial move by Breadon and Rickey; the extra money received in the trade would ensure that the club's monetary statement would finish with a profit by season's end. Rickey was in the process of gaining his reputation as a general manager who, notwithstanding the protests of fans, sold or traded off top players. In retrospect, Rickey scored a direct hit with Dean, as Diz would never regain the dominance he once displayed in a Cardinal uniform.

When he went to Chicago, Diz realized that he needed to become a completely different pitcher if he wanted his career to continue. A classic case of a ballplayer's maturation, Diz—who once relied only on his fastball and confidence—now utilized his control and experience. He became a smarter pitcher as a result of the injury; no longer did he try to blow batters away with the "fogger." ("Heck, I don't have enough speed to break a pane of glass," he admitted.) Hitters around the league, who for the last six seasons had seen Dean fastballs zoom by them, couldn't believe how slow he was throwing; it was almost as if there was an entirely different man on the mound. He helped the Cubs win the National League pennant in 1938, and pitched a stellar game in a loss against the New York Yankees as Chicago was swept four games to none. Were the Yankees that good? As Rip Collins stated, who like Dean had come over to the Cubs from the Cardinals, "We came, we saw, and we went home."

Frisch, unable to turn things around for the Cardinals, was fired with 17 games remaining in the 1938 season. After Mike Gonzalez finished out the year, the Cardinals hired Ray Blades as their permanent manager for the 1939 campaign. A reserve outfielder on the 1931 World Series winners, Blades had called the St. Louis area home for many years. He was from nearby Mount Vernon, Illinois, and was expected to lead the Cardinals back to the top. They had finished in sixth place in 1938, with a final record of 71–80. Enos Slaughter had shined as a rookie outfielder, and he was counted on to complement Medwick and Moore in the pastures of Sportsman's Park for the long-term future. Moore and Slaughter would remain; Medwick would not. After a patchwork of leftfielders covered the position for the next two years, a young man from Donora, Pennsylvania, would emerge in September 1941 to firmly entrench himself in the spot. In the season's final 12 games that year, Stanley Frank Musial hit .426, and the job was his for the next twenty years along with numerous major league records.

Also in 1939, Durocher was entering his second year with Brooklyn, and his first as manager. It was during spring training 1937 that he was unknowingly winding down his days with the Cardinals, and never having dreamt of being sent to another team—especially the lowly Dodgers. In his 1948 book *Dodgers and Me*, Durocher gave his side of the ordeal.

"For spring training in the fateful year 1937, Frisch and I drove to Florida together. We roomed together and played golf every day at Daytona Beach. We were pals, I thought, until—one day, after our training chores for the day were finished, Branch Rickey called me over.

"'You and Frisch had a fight?' he asked.

"'No sir!' I replied. 'We hit it off great!'

"'Well, he wants to trade you!' Snapped B.R., belching a cloud of cigar smoke that probably would have floored me, even if his statement had not. Rickey smokes cigars that smell like burning upholstery.

"My jaw dropped. I said no more, but I felt as if I had been hit by a pitched ball.

"After that, Frisch and I slowly drifted apart."

With Leo leading the Dodgers, it would be the starting point for a managerial career that would stretch into five decades. In recalling his first experiences in Ebbets Field, he remembered how he didn't even want to go to work. "How I hated Frankie Frisch—and Branch Rickey— for selling me down the river to Brooklyn, this baseball bughouse! I delayed reporting as long as I could." He actively pursued Medwick as soon as he got the head job, and finally landed him in 1941. It seemed to be the final piece to the puzzle for the pennant-starved borough of Brooklyn, who hadn't seen a National League championship since 1920 and to that point hadn't had a World Series title (during their tenure in Brooklyn, the Dodgers would gain their only Series victory in 1955 before moving to Los Angeles in 1958). Durocher had taken the manager's job from another ex–Cardinal, Burleigh Grimes. Immediately, the Lip had his club playing with enthusiasm, excitement, and Leo's personal hostility, especially when they visited St. Louis.

"Back in 1937, if anyone had told me the time would come when my heart would nearly break at the thought of leaving Brooklyn—for any reason—I would have given out with a horselaugh, king size," Durocher acknowledged.

"Managing a big-league ballclub was the fulfillment of all the baseball dreams I ever had since the day I first talked back to an umpire. But this was when the whole Dodger setup looked like a nightmare— in technicolor."

Durocher's partner on the left side at Sportsman's Park, Pepper Martin, was watching his playing time lessen each year as his accomplished career was reaching its twilight. In 1939, Blades did find enough use for him for 281 at bats, with which he contributed a .306 average, seven triples, and six stolen bases. His statistics were nearly identical the following year, and his playing days finally ended in 1944 at the age of 40—still flying down the base line, and still playing without a cup.

By 1940, Frisch would be back in the big leagues as a manager in Pittsburgh with the Pirates. The clock had finally run out on Pie Traynor, who had spent the previous 19 years with the organization. Like Durocher, Frisch was sought by numerous clubs for the energy and leadership he displayed with the Cardinals. After leaving Pittsburgh in 1946, erstwhile leading the Pirates to a second-place finish in '44 (the Cardinals, under Billy Southworth, took the championship that year), Frisch managed the Cubs from 1949 through 1951. Despite various run-ins with players, umpires, and management over his long career, there almost wasn't a man to be found in baseball that didn't have respect for Frank. "First class all the way," said Johnny Mize of the Flash.

After their World Series victory in 1934, the Cardinals did not win another pennant in the decade. Rickey had made some quick-fix moves to fill in some positions, but he knew it was time to once again tap into the farm system.

No More Fog

With all of his old Gas House teammates going their different directions, Dean found himself back in the minor leagues in 1940, nearly ten years after he left the "bushes." After the Cubs' pennant-winning season of 1938, they dropped to fourth the following year. In 1939, Diz managed a 6–4 record in 13 starts, but still complained of irritation in the arm. "I just can't fog 'em in there like I used to," he complained. It was after a poor beginning to the 1940 campaign that he was sent to Tulsa of the Texas League—a league he had dominated a decade earlier. Both Diz and the Cubs thought it would be a good chance for rehabilitation, but things just simply weren't the same. After a later call-up to the majors, his earned run average for the Cubs on the year ended at 5.17. In 1941, he would throw one inning, getting knocked out by the Pirates after three hits and two runs in an early-season start. He knew enough was enough. He issued a letter of voluntary retirement to the Cubs' front office, which was accepted by Phillip Wrigley. Dizzy thanked them for their confidence in him, and began looking for something else to do with his life.

He soon found that he could put his popularity to work in the broadcast booth as a baseball radio announcer, which he wound up doing for the next three decades. He began with the lowly St. Louis Browns, and received a regular salary for this work from the Falstaff Brewery in St. Louis, the sponsors of the broadcasts. He constantly chided the Browns' inept pitching staff, and this ultimately led to criticism from the players' wives. "Why doesn't he go out there and try it?" they offered. So, he did. On the final day of the 1947 American League season, a crowd of 16,000—extremely large for a Browns game—wandered into Sportsman's Park to watch the 37-year-old Dean throw for the first time in six years. He pitched four scoreless innings against the Chicago White Sox before his wife, Pat, screamed at Browns manager Muddy Ruel to remove Diz from the game before he hurt himself (this coming after Diz smacked a hit when he batted in the bottom of the fourth, and came up lame at second base). When he returned to the booth, he basically did as he pleased. Along with his obliged plugs of Falstaff, others received free publicity over the airwaves via Diz—more often than not, the businesses of his friends. He would excuse himself from the broadcast booth when he got hungry or bored, and would go out for a sandwich.

It is probable that more people remembered Diz as an announcer than as a player. Around the time that he was hitting his peak as a pitcher in the mid–1930s, a young southerner by the name of Red Barber was becoming well-known as the voice of the Cincinnati Reds. Barber would go on to greater fame with the Brooklyn Dodgers, forming a link to contemporary times in partnering with Vin Scully beginning in the 1950s. What was unique about Barber, however, was his rural perspective on calling a baseball game. Phrases such as "Sittin' in the catbird seat" became heard in many homes. When Diz went behind the microphone, he added his own agrarian interpretation of the sport. He would speak of "blue-darters" (line drives) headed into the outfield, the conditions of the pitcher's "soupbone" and "the pasture" (a general term for the baseball field). More prominent than his casual terminology, however, was his butchery of the English language. He would say "slud" instead of "slid," and note that "the runners are returning to their respectable (respective) bases." He received countless letters from English teachers in the St. Louis area, claiming that he was undermining their efforts to keep their students from uttering such improprieties in class.

He moved on to New York to become one of the Yankees' TV announcers in 1950, mainly to do pre- and post-game interviews. The year that he was elected to the Hall of Fame—1953—he began work on the nationally-televised Game of the Week with former major leaguers Buddy Blattner and Pee Wee Reese. He continued to give the nation an informal view of baseball. While doing a game in St. Louis with Reese, Diz spotted a young couple in the grandstand hardly watching the game. "Look-a-there, Pee Wee—those young folks are smooching after every pitch," Diz noted while on the air. "He's kissing her on the strikes, and she's kissing him on the balls." Later, Blattner was unfairly critical of Diz for his casual nature—perhaps because he knew that

Dean was the reason that people tuned in. Despite Dizzy's popularity, he was released from duty when CBS sold Game of the Week rights to NBC in 1966.

In the process of establishing his broadcasting career, Diz had moved to Pat's hometown of Bond, Mississippi, in 1962. A lumber mill town about thirty miles north of Biloxi, Bond provided a comfortable retreat for him. With his broadcasting finished by the late 1960s, and work of any kind presumably done, he was content to live out the rest of his life telling stories and sharing laughs. He dearly loved the peacefulness of southern Mississippi. "The most wonderful folks in the world," he often noted in his broadcasts.

All the years of his young life spent as an emaciated, skinny boy, Dean had gradually put on many pounds after his playing days were over. Those who remember him on the broadcasts saw a full-faced, well-fed man, not the lean, hungry pitcher that stared out from the mound. He was participating in a charity golf tournament in South Lake Tahoe, California, in the summer of 1974 when he felt sharp pains in his chest. His increasing weight had recently become a serious health problem, and now had caused a heart attack. He felt fine after a couple of days, but then a more severe cardiac arrest struck him. Dizzy Dean died on July 17, 1974, bringing down the final curtain on one of baseball's legendary entertainment acts.

His body was returned to Bond for the funeral where he was honored by hundreds of visitors. University of Alabama football coach Paul "Bear" Bryant came to the service, along with political dignitaries and other celebrities. The minister presiding over the services noted that, despite Dizzy's educational shortcomings, he was able to reach all types of people on his radio broadcasts and "was better understood than our best grammarian." He was laid to rest in a humble yard that is still surrounded on three sides by forest and guarded by a chain-link fence. In 1981, Pat passed away and rejoined his side. The locale suggests no grandeur; no signs off of U.S. Route 49 through Bond even note the grave. But that's how Diz wanted to finish his life, "as just a regular folk," he said.

Epilogue

The success in Dizzy Dean's career was much like that of his famed team, the Gas House Gang—short-lived but long-remembered. To date, Dean has the fewest number of career wins (150) than any pitcher in the Hall of Fame. However, the impact he made during his peak (1932–1937) was truly lasting. His talent was coupled with a love of the game that entertained spectators while simultaneously intimidating opponents. Whether he was laughing at a batter, frying eggs on the dugout at Sportsman's Park in 100-degree heat, or taking some swings during the opposing team's batting practice, Dean afforded struggling citizens of the Great Depression what musician Jimmy Buffett currently defines as "escapism"—an excursion from the toils of everyday life into a playful, carefree world of excitement and human triumph.

The farm system that Rickey pioneered in the 1930s made the Cardinals a powerhouse in the 1940s. They were light-years ahead of most other clubs in talent development, and used in-house training in lieu of large signing bonuses to accrue skilled players for their team. With this cultivation, the Cardinals dominated the decade, winning four National League pennants, three World Series championships, and finishing second five other times during the 1940s. In fact, 1940 was the only year in the decade that they didn't finish first or second in the National League. Cardinals great Stan Musial insists that if Moore, Slaughter, and other players from the era had not lost their primes to World War II service, they might have won the pennant every year.

The major leagues as a whole had been weakened by the war. The Browns, forever bridesmaids of the Cardinals, won their first—and only—American League pennant in 1944. The Cardinals beat them in six games for the World Championship, but not before raising some local eyebrows by losing two of the first three games of the series to the Brownies.

The Cardinal teams of the 1940s were not unlike their Gas House predecessors: well-balanced, scrappy, with solid pitching and daring baserunning, plus a reliance on a couple of heavy hitters. In the decade, Musial also established his individual dominance. He won three batting titles ('43, '46, and '48), four slugging titles (aforementioned, plus '44), and led the league in doubles five times. Slaughter embodied the Cardinals' success in the era, generating a dramatic play in the seventh game of the 1946 World Series against the Boston Red Sox. He had broken his arm at the elbow in Game 5 at Boston, but refused to leave the lineup. After having the arm wrapped in Epsom salts on the train all the way back to St. Louis, Slaughter was told by Doc Weaver that he shouldn't play in the sixth game; if he sustained another blow to the arm, it would have to be amputated. Slaughter declined to heed Weaver's advice, and played with the arm heavily bandaged. With the series ending at Sportsman's Park, the final game saw a 3–3 tie enter the bottom of the eighth. With two out, Slaughter was on first after his base hit. Harry Walker came up next and lined a single to left, and Slaughter never stopped running. Boston shortstop Johnny Pesky, perhaps surprised when he glanced at the hard-charging Slaughter barreling around third, bobbled the throw from the outfield. His hesitation gave Enos the split-second he needed to beat the relay throw home. He had scored from first on a *single*. The courageous gallop gave St. Louis a 4–3 lead, and pitcher Harry Brecheen shut down the Red Sox in the ninth to secure the world championship for the Cardinals. Slaughter also noted that, earlier in the game, third base coach Mike Gonzalez had held him up at third on a play in which Slaughter thought he would have scored. After that incident, Cardinals manager Eddie Dyer gave Slaughter the green light to run at his own risk.

Thirty-four seasons after 1934, the Tigers finally got their revenge on the Cardinals. In Denny McLain, Detroit had the first thirty-game winner in the majors in since Dean in '34, so perhaps 1968 was an ominous year from the start. It was definitely a pitcher's year, with the league batting average at .234. Cardinals pitcher Bob Gibson had an ERA of 1.12, topped in National League history only by Three Finger Brown of the Cubs in 1906. Gibson, with his bat as well as his arm, dominated the Red Sox in the 1967 World Series. But although most writers gave St. Louis the edge after winning the '67 championship, the Cardinals lost the 1968 series in seven games.

Interesting comparisons can be made between Dean and Gibson. They were both power pitchers—not only having superior fastballs, but also breaking pitches that were devastating. They both exuded confidence on the mound—Gibson with a cold stare at the hitter, Dean with a defiant laugh. They both pitched their clubs to championships, taking the ball more frequently as their teams needed them down the stretch of pennant races. Both were great athletes, giving extra help to their teams as exceptional hitters and baserunners; and perhaps, most of all, both hated to lose—more than just about anything in life. Durocher knew not to come to the mound and try to tell Dean how to pitch; neither dared Gibson's shortstop Dal Maxvill. They were both in full control, willingly taking their teams' destinies into their own hands. As Dean catapulted Cardinal baseball into excellence in the 1930s, Gibson perpetuated the legacy through the sixties, complemented by Hornsby, Medwick, Musial, Ozzie Smith, Mark McGwire, and the many other great players before, in between, and since.

There are also many other parts of the Cardinals family as enduring as the players. The most brilliant among these are the radio announcers who have graced the airwaves throughout the Midwest. Jack Buck launched his 45th year behind the microphone in 1999, a tenure that dates back to having Harry Caray as his partner. Buck has been the voice of baseball in the Heartland, and multiple generations formed their images of the game through his colorful descriptions. He is now joined by his talented son, Joe, who while bringing his own style and talents to the booth, carries the same Buck enthusiasm and wit as his father.

Over his many years of broadcasting Cardinals baseball, Jack Buck has encountered many interesting personalities along the way. In working with Caray, he often found himself having to take "second fiddle" during the games; Harry often insisted that he, and he alone, would call the important plays of the game. After Harry had a disagreement with Busch, however, he packed up in the late 1960s, and Buck finally was the main man in St. Louis. A third member of their broadcast team in the 1950s and '60s was former Cardinals catcher Joe Garagiola, a St. Louis native who went on to fame with NBC telecasts of the World Series and Game of the Week.

Third baseman and outfielder Mike Shannon joined Buck in the press box after retiring from the Cardinals in the early 1970s. Shannon's style mixed well with Buck's, and the two have formed a great broadcast team for the Redbirds. A native of south St. Louis,

Shannon's voice has become about as synonymous with Cardinal base-ball as his partner's.

Their voices are a bridge between today and yesterday. The good ol' days were really good; it would be wise and educational for a young person today to turn off the TV and tune into KMOX for a ballgame.

Appendix:
1934 Statistics

St. Louis Cardinals Final Batting Statistics

Player	Pos	AB	R	H	2B	3B	HR	RBI	Avg.
Collins	1B	600	116	200	35	12	35	128	.333
Medwick	OF	620	110	198	40	18	18	106	.318
DeLancey	C	253	41	80	18	3	13	40	.316
Healy	C	13	1	4	1	0	0	1	.308
Frisch	2B	550	74	168	30	6	3	75	.305
K. Davis	OF	33	6	10	3	0	1	4	.303
Orsatti	OF	337	39	101	14	4	0	31	.300
V. Davis	C	347	45	104	22	4	9	65	.300
Martin	3B	454	76	131	25	11	5	49	.289
Rothrock	OF	647	106	184	35	3	11	72	.284
G. Moore	OF	18	2	1	0	0	0	1	.278
Whitehead	IF	332	55	92	13	5	1	24	.277
Crawford	IF	70	3	19	2	0	0	16	.271
Durocher	SS	500	62	130	26	5	3	70	.260
Mills	OF	72	7	17	4	1	1	8	.236
Riggs	IF	1	0	0	0	0	0	0	.000
Worthington	IF	1	0	0	0	0	0	0	.000

1934 St. Louis Cardinals Final Pitching Statistics

Pitcher	G	GS	IP	H	BB	SO	W	L	ERA
J. Dean	50	33	312	288	75	199	30	7	2.65
Walker	24	19	153	160	66	76	12	4	3.12
Grimes	4	0	8	5	2	1	0	0	3.38
P. Dean	39	26	233	225	52	150	19	11	3.44
Haines	37	6	90	86	19	17	4	4	3.50
Vance	19	4	59	62	14	33	1	1	3.66
Hallahan	32	26	163	195	66	70	8	12	4.25
Carleton	40	31	241	260	52	103	16	11	4.26
Rhem	5	1	16	26	7	6	1	0	4.50
Heise	1	0	2	3	0	1	0	0	4.50
Martin	1	0	2	1	0	0	0	0	4.50
Mooney	32	7	82	114	49	27	2	4	5.49
Lindsey	11	0	14	21	3	7	0	1	6.43
Winford	5	1	13	17	6	3	0	2	7.61

1934 Final Standings

National League	W	L	Pct	GB
St. Louis	95	58	.621	—
New York	93	60	.608	2
Chicago	86	65	.570	8
Boston	78	73	.517	16
Pittsburgh	74	76	.493	19.5
Brooklyn	71	81	.467	23.5
Philadelphia	55	93	.376	37
Cincinnati	52	99	.344	42

American League	W	L	Pct	GB
Detroit	101	53	.656	—
New York	94	60	.610	7
Cleveland	85	69	.552	16
Boston	76	76	.500	24
Philadelphia	68	82	.453	31
St. Louis	67	85	.441	33
Washington	66	86	.434	34
Chicago	53	99	.349	47

World Series: St. Louis

Player	GP	AB	R	H	2B	3B	HR	RBI	Avg.
Davis	2	2	0	2	0	0	0	1	1.000
Fullis	3	5	0	2	0	0	0	0	.400
Medwick	7	29	4	11	0	1	1	5	.379
Collins	7	30	4	11	1	0	0	4	.367
Martin	7	31	8	11	3	1	0	3	.355
Orsatti	7	22	3	7	0	1	0	2	.318
Durocher	7	27	4	7	1	1	0	0	.259
J. Dean	4	12	3	3	2	0	0	1	.250
Rothrock	7	30	3	7	3	1	0	6	.233
Frisch	7	31	2	6	1	0	0	4	.194
DeLancey	7	29	3	5	3	0	1	4	.172
P. Dean	2	6	0	1	0	0	0	2	.167
Hallahan	1	3	0	0	0	0	0	0	.000
Walker	2	2	0	0	0	0	0	0	.000
Carleton	2	1	0	0	0	0	0	0	.000
Crawford	2	2	0	0	0	0	0	0	.000
Vance	1	0	0	0	0	0	0	0	.000
Haines	1	0	0	0	0	0	0	0	.000
Mooney	1	0	0	0	0	0	0	0	.000
Team	77	262	34	73	14	5	2	32	.279

Pitcher	G	GS	IP	H	BB	SO	ER	W-L	ERA
Haines	1	0	.6	1	0	2	0	0-0	0.00
Mooney	1	0	1	1	0	0	0	0-0	0.00
Vance	1	0	1.3	2	1	3	0	0-0	0.00
P. Dean	2	2	18	15	7	11	2	2-0	1.00
J. Dean	3	3	26	20	5	17	5	2-1	1.73
Hallahan	1	1	8.3	6	4	6	2	0-0	2.16
Walker	2	0	6.3	6	6	2	5	0-2	7.11
Carleton	2	1	3.6	5	2	2	3	0-0	7.36
Team	13	7	65.3	56	25	43	17	4-3	2.34

World Series: Detroit

Player	GP	AB	R	H	2B	3B	HR	RBI	Avg.
Gehringer	7	29	5	11	1	0	1	2	.379
Walker	3	3	0	1	0	0	0	1	.333
Greenberg	7	28	4	9	2	1	1	7	.321
Fox	7	28	1	8	6	0	0	2	.286
Rogell	7	29	3	8	1	0	0	4	.276
Goslin	7	29	2	7	1	0	0	2	.241
Cochrane	7	28	2	6	1	0	0	1	.214
Bridges	3	7	0	1	0	0	0	0	.143
White	7	23	6	3	0	0	0	0	.130
Owen	7	29	0	2	0	0	0	1	.069
Rowe	3	7	0	0	0	0	0	0	.000
Auker	2	4	0	0	0	0	0	0	.000
Hogsett	3	3	0	0	0	0	0	0	.000
Doljack	2	2	0	0	0	0	0	0	.000
Crowder	2	1	0	0	0	0	0	0	.000
Marberry	2	0	0	0	0	0	0	0	.000
Hayworth	1	0	0	0	0	0	0	0	.000
Team	77	250	23	56	12	1	2	20	.224

Pitcher	G	GS	IP	H	BB	SO	ER	W-L	ERA
Hogsett	3	0	7.3	6	3	3	1	0-0	1.23
Crowder	2	1	6	6	1	2	1	0-1	1.50
Rowe	3	2	21.3	19	0	12	7	1-1	2.95
Bridges	3	2	17.3	21	1	12	7	1-1	3.63
Auker	2	2	11.3	16	5	2	7	1-1	5.56
Marberry	2	0	1.6	5	1	0	4	0-0	21.60
Team	15	7	65	73	11	31	27	3-4	3.74

Personal Data on the 1934 St. Louis Cardinals

Player	*Place of Birth*	*Date of Birth*	*Date of Death*
Carleton, Tex	Comanche, TX	8-19-06	1-11-77
Collins, Rip	Altoona, PA	3-30-04	4-16-70
Crawford, Pat	Society Hill, SC	1-28-02	1-25-94
Davis, Virgil	Birmingham, AL	12-20-04	8-14-84
Dean, Dizzy	Lucas, AR	1-16-10	7-17-74
Dean, Paul	Lucas, AR	8-14-13	3-17-81
DeLancey, Bill	Greensboro, NC	11-28-11	11-28-46
Durocher, Leo	W. Springfield, MA	7-27-05	10-7-91
Frisch, Frankie	Bronx, NY	9-9-98	3-12-73
Fullis, Chick	Giardville, PA	2-27-04	3-28-46
Grimes, Burleigh	Clear Lake, WI	8-18-93	12-06-85
Haines, Jesse	Clayton, OH	7-22-93	8-5-78
Hallahan, Bill	Binghamton, NY	8-4-02	7-8-81
Lindsey, Jim	Greensburg, LA	1-24-98	10-25-63
Martin, Pepper	Temple, OK	2-29-04	3-5-65
Medwick, Joe	Carteret, NJ	11-24-11	3-21-75
Mills, Buster	Ranger, TX	9-16-08	12-01-91
Mooney, Jim	Mooresburg, TN	9-4-06	4-27-79
Moore, Gene	Lancaster, TX	8-26-09	3-12-78
Orsatti, Ernie	Los Angeles, CA	9-8-02	9-4-68
Rothrock, Jack	Long Beach, CA	3-14-05	2-2-80
Vance, Dazzy	Orient, IA	3-4-91	2-16-61
Whitehead, Burgess	Tarboro, NC	6-29-10	11-25-93
Winford, Jim	Shelbyville, TN	10-9-09	12-16-70

Index